This _____

1998

POCKET ANNUAL

Bruce Smith

Virgin

World Cup 1998

First published March 1998 by
Virgin Publishing

Virgin Publishing Limited
332 Ladbroke Grove
London
W10 5AH

Typeset by Bruce Smith

Contact Bruce Smith at:

Bruce Smith,
PO Box 382, St. Albans,
Herts, AL2 3JD

email: Bruce-Smith@msn.com

Printed in Great Britain by Caledonian International Books

Disclaimer

In a book of this type it is inevitable that some errors will creep in. While every effort has been made to ensure that the details given in this annual are correct at the time of going to press, neither the editor nor the publishers can accept any responsibility for errors within.

We welcome comments, corrections and additions to this annual. Please send them to Bruce Smith at the address opposite or email them direct to him at: Bruce-Smith@msn.com

CONTENTS

Introduction...

Welcome to your guide to the greatest show on earth. France '98 will be the biggest, most comprehensive World Cup finals ever staged. For the first time 32 teams will play out a total of 64 games across 33 days. Will it simply be the survival of the fittest or will the most talented team come through to secure the biggest prize in international football?

Brazil of course are everyone's favourites but football is football and favourites don't always prevail. If they did then there would be little point in watching the games. And, given the extra games on show, this World Cup will draw the biggest ever world wide TV audience – perhaps even challenging the Olympic games as the biggest TV event ever.

But, whether you are watching on TV or planning to get to some games for yourself, you will find a wide variety of useful and plain anorak-style information packed into these 192 pages. Central to it all is the National Team section with three pages dedicated to each of the 32 finalists. Stats, facts and profiles provide perfect talking points on the terraces or on the sofa.

Elsewhere you will also find details of all 634 qualifying games, details of the venues that will stage the games, and a history of previous World Cup competitions along with results from the finals.

To help you cheer England all the way along there's detailed coverage of Glenn Hoddle's side together with profiles of the players who helped take England there. And beyond that I have given my insight into the players who could just make people take note. Some are already well-known names but there are a few others who may become world-famous, even if only for a day!

In your pocket or on the arm of your favourite chair, the *World Cup Pocket Annual 1998* is a vital companion for any serious football fan.

Naming Conventions

There will be a lot of interesting players with interesting names in France '98. No doubt there will be a variety of spellings and formats for these. Wherever possible in this annual I have used the names and format of names specified by the appropriate country's FA.

List of Acknowledgements

Many thanks to everyone who has contributed to this year's Annual – not least the following: Mark Webb, Hooshar Naraghi of Sportstan Publishing – check out his Iran World Cup web site at www.sportstan.com, Andrew Saunders who runs the Jamaican FA web site, all the other FAs which helped and in particular the Japan FA and South Korean FA, Ron Hocking, and Ben Dunn at Virgin.

More Around

If you like this annual then why not look out for some of the others available, not least the FA Carling Premiership Pocket Annual. Currently in its fifth year, August 1998 will see the 6th Edition published. The bible in your pocket to the FA Premier League.

QUALIFYING FACTS

- The World Cup qualifying competition was divided into six qualifying areas defined by the six FIFA Confederations:

AFC	Asian Football Confederation
CAF	African Football Confederation
CONCACAF	North-Central American and Caribbean Football Confederation
CONMEBOL	South American Football Association
OFC	Oceania Football Confederation
UEFA	Union European Football Association

- In all there were 643 qualifying games played across all Confederations. The number of matches played by Confederation were:

UEFA	228 matches
AFC	131 matches
CONCACAF	98 matches
CAF	91 matches
CONMEBOL	72 matches
OFC	23 matches

- The 643 games produced: 323 home wins, 160 away wins and 129 draws. The remaining 31 games were played at neutral venues.
- 172 nations entered the qualifying competition for the 1998 World Cup.
- There were 1,922 goals scored in the qualifying competition which averaged out at fractionally under three goals per game.
- In the qualifying games 1,134 goals were scored by the home team, 647 were scored by the away team and 141 goals were scored on neutral venues.
- More goals were scored in the second half of games than in the first half of the games in the qualifying round – 1,060 compared to 862.
- Over 15 million spectators attended all the qualifying games with the average match attendance being 23,648.
- The biggest attendance in the qualifying round was the 120,000 who attended the Iran v Saudi Arabia AFC match in Tehran in September 1997. 115,000 people turned out to watch the CONCACAF encounter in Mexico City between Mexico and Jamaica in October 1996.
- Iran were the best-supported team at home in the qualifying rounds – their smallest home crowd being the 50,000 who attended the game against Kuwait in October 1997.
- Iran's Karim Bagheri was the competition's overall top goalscorer with 19 goals from 17 games. His biggest single game haul came against the Maldives when he scored seven – a record.
- Iran's 17-0 win over the Maldives Republic in round one of the AFC region is a record score in the World Cup. The game was played in Damascus in June 1997.

- The goalkeeper that conceded those 17 goals and holds the unfortunate record of being the keeper to concede the most goals was Iqbal Mohamed. Mohamed was, perhaps not surprisingly, not the Maldives' first choice keeper! Their number-one selection, Raheem Aslam Abdul, was back for the return and managed to limit Iran to nine goals but he also picked up a caution eight minutes from time. Perhaps for contesting the legality of a goal?
- Since the qualifying round began with the 1934 World Cup 9,108 goals have been scored by teams looking to qualify for the World Cup finals. The qualifying rounds for the 2002 competition should see one team and one player score the 10,000th goal!
- Only 16 players are able to say that they played in every minute of every game of their country's World Cup qualifying games for France '98. Find out who they are by looking at page 12.
- Liechtenstein conceded the most goals in the qualifying competition – 52 in all.
- Five teams from the UEFA qualified for the World Cup finals without suffering a defeat. They are: Germany, Italy, Norway, Spain and Romania.
- The OFC will be the only FIFA region not represented in the France '98.
- Crazy or what? Australia did not lose a single game throughout their qualifying games and yet failed to qualify for the finals. Having won the OFC group, they were forced to play off with AFC team Iran and lost the tie on the away-goals rule.
- Chelsea players could be representing a number of countries during the World Cup finals. Consider this lot:

England	Graeme Le Saux
France	Franck Leboeuf
Holland	Ed De Goey
Italy	Gianfranco Zola and Roberto Di Matteo
Nigeria	Celestine Babayaro
Norway	Tore Andre Flo and Frode Grodas
Romania	Dan Petrescu

…and who knows – Frank Sinclair may have been accepted to play for Jamaica!
- Holland and Belgium, having found themselves paired in the same qualifying group, find themselves in the same group in the first round of the finals! The two of them will jointly stage Euro 2000 as well.
- The finals will see 64 matches played in just 33 days.

HOW IT WORKS

For the first time ever the World Cup finals will feature 32 teams – a record number. The finalists consist of two automatic qualifiers, the hosts (France) and the previous winners (Brazil), plus 30 teams who have qualified through a variety of tournaments organised by continental governing bodies. A list of all the qualifying results can be found elsewhere in this book.

Group Stage

The first phase of the competition is run on a round-robin basis organised as eight groups of four teams. Each group has a seeded team, the seeded teams being the hosts, the holders and the six top-ranked teams as determined by FIFA. Previous World Cup performances and FIFA rankings were used to determine the top six teams.

The eight seeded teams are: France (hosts), Brazil (holders), Italy, Spain, Holland, Germany, Romania and Argentina. These teams were each assigned a group and the remaining teams were drawn into the other group positions. The draw was arranged in such a way as to prevent teams from like continents being drawn against each other as much as possible.

Each team's position in their group was also allocated by the drawing of lots and this position determined the order of games in the groups.

The draw produced the following eight groups:

Group A	Brazil, Scotland, Morocco, Norway
Group B	Italy, Chile, Cameroon, Austria
Group C	France, South Africa, Saudi Arabia, Denmark
Group D	Spain, Nigeria, Paraguay, Bulgaria
Group E	Holland, Belgium, South Korea, Mexico
Group F	Germany, USA, Yugoslavia, Iran
Group G	Romania, Colombia, England, Tunisia
Group H	Argentina, Japan, Jamaica, Croatia

Each team plays each other team in its group once. Three points are awarded for a win, one point for a draw and no points for a defeat. The two teams that finish at the top of each group (ie, first and second) will progress to the second round. Positions in the groups are decided according to the following criteria in order of application.

1. Number of points
2. Goal difference (ie, goals scored minus goals conceded)
3. Goals scored
4. Score of direct encounter
5. Drawing lots

The last two matches in each group will take place at the same time on the same day to prevent any playing for results. The teams finishing third and fourth in each group are eliminated from the competition.

Second Round

The second round marks the start of sudden death with the winners progressing to the next phase and losers being eliminated. The 16 teams qualifying for the second round play each other in a predetermined order as follows:

Group A Winners v Group B Runners-up = Winner 1
Group B Winners v Group A Runners-up = Winner 2
Group C Winners v Group D Runners-up = Winner 3
Group D Winners v Group C Runners-up = Winner 4
Group E Winners v Group F Runners-up = Winner 5
Group F Winners v Group E Runners-up = Winner 6
Group G Winners v Group H Runners-up = Winner 7
Group H Winners v Group G Runners-up = Winner 8

If any match is level after 90 minutes then 30 minutes of extra time will be played. During this time the golden goal rule applies – simply the first team to score in extra time wins. If no goal is scored during extra time, penalty kicks shall be taken to determine the winner. Each side takes five kicks and the team with the most penalty successes at the end is the winner. If the scores are level then each team takes penalties in turn until one team misses.

Quarter Finals

The quarter finals are played under the same rules as the second round. The order of games is predetermined as follows:

Winner 1 v Winner 4 = Winner A
Winner 2 v Winner 3 = Winner B
Winner 5 v Winner 8 = Winner C
Winner 6 v Winner 7 = Winner D

Semi Finals

The semi finals are played under the same rules as the previous round. The order of games is predetermined as follows:

Winner A v Winner C
Winner B v Winner D

Final Placings

3rd/4th Place Play-Off: The losers of the two semi finals will meet to determine who finishes 3rd and 4th. The game is decided under the same rules as the semi finals.

The Final: The winners of the two semi finals will meet in the final with the game decided under the same rules as the semi finals.

WORLD CUP QUALIFYING NUMBERS

Qualifiers by Finals Percentage

This table lists the 32 finalists for France '98 by their performance in all the World Cup finals they have participated in.

Country	P	W	D	L	F	A	%
1. Brazil … … … … … 73	49	13	11	159	68	84.93
2. Italy … … … … … 60	35	14	11	96	55	81.67
3. Germany … … … … 73	42	16	15	155	98	79.45
4. Denmark … … … … 4	3	0	1	10	6	75.00
5. England … … … … 41	18	12	11	55	38	73.17
6. Holland … … … … 25	12	6	7	45	29	72.00
7. Argentina … … … 52	26	9	17	90	65	67.31
8. Tunisia … … … … 3	1	1	1	3	2	66.67
9. Spain … … … … … 37	15	9	13	53	44	64.86
10. Cameroon … … … 11	3	4	4	11	21	63.64
Paraguay … … … … 11	3	4	4	16	25	63.64
Yugoslavia … … … 33	14	7	12	55	42	63.64
13. France … … … 34	15	5	14	71	56	58.82
Romania… … … … 17	6	4	7	25	29	58.82
15. Austria … … … … 26	12	2	12	40	43	53.85
16. Nigeria … … … … 4	2	0	2	7	4	50.00
Norway … … … … 4	1	1	2	2	3	50.00
Saudi Arabia … … … 4	2	0	2	5	6	50.00
Scotland … … … … 20	4	6	10	23	35	50.00
20. Chile … … … … … 21	7	3	11	26	32	47.62
21. Mexico … … … … 33	8	7	18	32	68	45.45
22. Belgium … … … … 29	9	4	16	37	53	44.83
23. Bulgaria … … … … 23	3	7	13	21	46	43.48
24. Colombia … … … 10	2	2	6	13	20	40.00
Morocco… … … … 10	1	3	6	7	13	40.00
26. USA … … … … … 14	4	1	9	17	33	35.71
27. Iran … … … … … 3	0	1	2	2	8	33.33
28. South Korea … … … 10	0	2	8	9	34	20.00
29. Croatia… … … … … 0	0	0	0	0	0	0.00
Jamaica … … … … 0	0	0	0	0	0	0.00
Japan … … … … … 0	0	0	0	0	0	0.00
South Africa … … … 0	0	0	0	0	0	0.00

Qualifiers by Qualifying Percentage

This table lists the 32 finalists for France '98 by their performance in all qualifying competitions for all World Cups they have participated in.

Country		P	W	D	L	F	A	%
1.	Germany	52	39	12	1	160	37	98.08
2.	Brazil	38	29	8	1	99	15	97.37
3.	Croatia	10	5	4	1	20	13	90.00
4.	Italy	59	41	12	6	130	33	89.83
5.	South Korea	77	48	20	9	158	50	88.31
6.	England	64	40	16	8	159	43	87.50
	Mexico	88	55	22	11	235	66	87.50
8.	Spain	69	44	14	11	152	56	84.06
9.	Argentina	48	28	12	8	87	44	83.33
	Iran	54	33	12	9	121	44	83.33
	South Africa	12	8	2	2	13	7	83.33
	Yugoslavia	79	47	18	14	172	77	83.33
13.	Holland	75	43	18	14	167	61	81.33
14.	Morocco	66	31	21	14	86	45	78.79
15.	Romania	74	42	15	17	148	70	77.03
16.	Cameroon	39	20	10	9	61	36	76.92
17.	Nigeria	56	27	16	13	93	57	76.79
18.	Belgium	83	47	16	20	160	94	75.90
19.	Scotland	79	44	15	20	140	88	74.68
20.	Saudi Arabia	50	24	13	13	77	47	74.00
21.	Tunisia	56	26	15	15	80	47	73.21
22.	Austria	72	37	15	20	134	71	72.22
23.	Japan	61	28	16	17	124	54	72.13
24.	France	68	40	9	19	145	61	72.06
25.	Bulgaria	79	41	12	26	133	104	67.09
26.	Chile	57	25	13	19	95	72	66.67
27.	USA	67	26	18	23	100	108	65.67
28.	Colombia	64	22	20	22	74	78	65.63
29.	Paraguay	66	29	14	23	89	71	65.15
30.	Jamaica	48	19	12	17	51	70	64.58
31.	Denmark	68	29	12	27	108	97	60.29
32.	Norway	76	28	15	33	110	119	56.58

Goals – Players to Score 5+

This list details players who have scored five goals or more in the 1998 qualifying competition.

No.	Player	Team
19	Karim Bagheri	Iran
15	Kazuyoshi Miura	Japan
14	Predrag Mijatovic	Yugoslavia
12	Ivan Zamorano	Chile
10	Carlos Hermosillo	Mexico
9	Raul Diaz Arce	El Salvador
9	Choi Young-su	South Korea
8	Mohamed Salen Al Enazi	Qatar
8	Hakan Sukur	Turkey
7	Toni Polster	Austria
7	Faustino Asprilla	Colombia
7	Dennis Bergkamp	Holland
7	Tony Cascarino	Rep. Ireland
7	Gheorghe Popescu	Romania
7	Khalid Al Mulwallid	Saudi Arabia
7	Noel Berry	Solomon Islands
7	Kenneth Andersson	Sweden
6	John Aloisi	Australia
6	Luis Oliveira	Belgium
6	Emil Kostadinov	Bulgaria
6	Haidong Hao	China
6	Paulo Wanchope	Costa Rica
6	Martinez Dalcourt	Cuba
6	Alex Aguinaga	Ecuador
6	Oliver Bierhoff	Germany
6	Roberto Palaciou	Peru
6	Kevin Gallacher	Scotland
6	Alfonso	Spain
6	Bayazid Al Said	Syria
6	Oleg Shatskikh	Uzbekistan
5	Antonio Alves Paulao Paulo	Angola
5	Mamadou Zongo	Burkina Faso
5	Patrick Mboma	Cameroon
5	Alex Bunbury	Canada
5	Davor Suker	Croatia
5	Alan Shearer	England
5	Antti Sumiala	Finland
5	Juan Carlos Plata	Guatemala
5	Nicolas Suazo	Honduras
5	Walter Boyd	Jamaica
5	Theodore Whitemore	Jamaica
5	Viktor Zubarev	Kazakhstan
5	Jasem Al Huwaidi	Kuwait
5	Jorge Dely Valdes	Panama
5	Eric Wynalda	USA
5	Dean Saunders	Wales
5	Omar Al Ariki	Yemen
5	Vitalis Takawira	Zimbabwe

Qualifying Teams – Top Scores

Listed below are all the qualifying games for France 98 in which one team scored six goals or more.

Match	Result	Stage	Area
Maldives v Iran	0-17	Round 1 Group 2	AFC
Australia v Solomon Islands	13-0	Round 2 Group 1	OCA
Syria v Maldives	12-0	Round 1 Group 2	AFC
Maldives v Syria	0-12	Round 1 Group 2	AFC
Honduras v St. Vincent & G.	11-3	SF Round Group 3	CONCACAF
Liechtenstein v Macedonia	1-11	Group 8	UEFA
Japan v Macau	10-0	Round 1 Group 4	AFC
Macau v Japan	0-10	Round 1 Group 4	AFC
Iran v Maldives	9-0	Round 1 Group 2	AFC

Solomon Islands v Tonga	9-0	Play-off	OCA	
Indonesia v Cambodia	8-0	Round 1 Group 5	AFC	
Trinidad & T. v Dominican R.	8-0	Round 3-Carib. Zone	CONCACAF	
Romania v Liechtenstein	8-0	Group 8	UEFA	
Faroe Islands v Yugoslavia	1-8	Group 6	UEFA	
Liechtenstein v Romania	1-8	Group 8	UEFA	

Players – Most Games Played 16+

The following players have featured in the most games during the qualifying competition – they may not have featured in every one of their country's games though. The list contains players who have featured in 16 qualifying games or more.

Player	Country	Tot	St	Sub	PS
Barrett, Warren	Jamaica	19	19	0	0
Goodison, Ian	Jamaica	19	19	0	0
Whitmore, Theodore	Jamaica	19	19	0	5
Brown, Durrant	Jamaica	18	18	0	3
Dixon, Linval	Jamaica	18	18	0	0
Mahdavi Kia, Mehdi	Iran	17	17	0	0
Daei, Ali	Iran	17	16	1	2
Mansourian, Alireza	Iran	17	16	1	7
Valderrama, Carlos	Colombia	16	16	0	1
Abedzadeh, Ahmadreza	Iran	16	16	0	0
Estili, Hamid	Iran	16	16	0	6
Peyrovani, Ashfin	Iran	16	16	0	0

Players – Ever Present

The following players played in every minute of all their teams' qualifying games.

Player	Country	Games
Mahdavi Kia, Mehdi	Iran	17
Kawagughi, Yoshikatsu	Japan	15
De Wilde, Filip	Belgium	10
Zubizarreta, Andoni	Spain	10
Nielsen, Allan	Denmark	8
Schmeichel, Peter	Denmark	8
de Boer, Frank	Holland	8
Van Der Sar, Edwin	Holland	8
Grodas, Frode	Norway	8
Arendse, Andri	South Africa	8
Radebe, Lucas	South Africa	8
Kalla Kongo, Raymond	Cameroon	6
Mimboe, Bayard	Cameroon	6
Song, Rigobert	Cameroon	6
Songo'o, Jacques	Cameroon	6
Okechukwu	Nigeria	6

The following players appeared in all their teams' qualifying games either as a starter or as a substitute.

Player	Country	Tot	St	Sub	Ps
Herzog, Andreas	Austria	10	10	0	5
Polster, Toni	Austria	10	10	0	1
De Wilde, Filip	Belgium	10	10	0	0
Kalla Kongo, Raymond	Cameroon	6	6	0	0
Mboma, Henri Patrick	Cameroon	6	6	0	1
Mimboe, Bayard	Cameroon	6	6	0	0
Song, Rigobert	Cameroon	6	6	0	0
Songo'o, Jacques	Cameroon	6	6	0	0
Wome, Pierre	Cameroon	6	6	0	1
Boban, Zvonimir	Croatia	10	10	0	1
Valderrama, Carlos	Colombia	16	16	0	1
Helveg, Thomas	Denmark	8	8	0	1
Hogh, Jess	Denmark	8	8	0	1
Nielsen, Allan	Denmark	8	8	0	0
Schmeichel, Peter	Denmark	8	8	0	0
Beckham, David	England	8	8	0	3
de Boer, Frank	Holland	8	8	0	0
Seedorf, Clarence	Holland	8	8	0	4
Van Der Sar, Edwin	Holland	8	8	0	0
Winter, Aron	Holland	8	7	1	3
Daei, Ali	Iran	17	16	1	2
Mahdavi Kia, Mehdi	Iran	17	17	0	0
Mansourian, Alireza	Iran	17	16	1	7
Maldini, Paolo	Italy	10	10	0	1
Kawaguchi, Yoshikatsu	Japan	15	15	0	0
Nakaya, Hiroshi	Japan	15	15	0	3
Soma, Naoki	Japan	15	15	0	2
Yamaguchi, Motohiro	Japan	15	14	1	2
Amokachi, Daniel	Nigeria	6	6	0	1
Okechukwu	Nigeria	6	6	0	0
Okacha, Augustine	Nigeria	6	6	0	2
Grodas, Frode	Norway	8	8	0	0
Rekdal, Kjetil	Norway	8	8	0	2
Strandli, Frank	Norway	8	6	2	3
Petrescu, Dan	Romania	10	10	0	2
Boyd, Tom	Scotland	10	10	0	1
Arendse, Andri	South Africa	8	8	0	0
Radebe, Lucas	South Africa	8	8	0	0
Tinkler, Eric	South Africa	8	8	0	1
Zubizarreta, Andoni	Spain	10	10	0	0
Stojkovic, Dragan	Yugoslavia	12	12	0	2

STAR WATCH

Some of the greatest players in the world today, indeed ever, will be on show in the World Cup finals in France. The likes of Ronaldo, Bergkamp and Sammer are already established greats, but some regular team players will come to the fore and then there will be players who you have never heard of before who will shine out. Perhaps a great goal, perhaps a great save, perhaps a simply scintillating display – something will bring someone to the world's attention. But who will it be?

The greatest player of all time came to the fore in the World Cup finals. In the unlikely setting of Sweden a yellow jersey with a number 10 on the back was worn by a young boy of just 17, already being hailed as the best player this particular South American country had ever produced. Could he live up to it, could his country? Yes. The country was Brazil and the player was Pele – the best player ever!

But World Cups also make stars for the moment. In 1978 it was a Peruvian by the name of Cubillas who helped Peru take their early games by storm. In 1982 it was a goal by Northern Ireland's Gerry Armstrong that beat Spain and made him a national hero and in Italy in 1990 a last minute extra time goal against Belgium heralded the arrival of England's David Platt on the world stage.

Of course there are many more, but who will be the players that will make the biggest impact when France '98 is recalled? Here's my pick of just a few of the players who could produce something out of the ordinary to make them a star or cement their status as truly great players. They are in no particular order. Some are names you will know, several are names you probably will not – now at least.

Marcelo SALAS – Chile
Red Hot Chile – Salas could provide the spice in France with his undoubted goalscoring talents being the envy of the top clubs around the world – including Manchester United.

Goals seem to come easily to Salas, who often looks the coolest player on the pitch when he is in the process of slipping another chance into the back of the opposition's net. Don't expect to see him blasting the ball home. Salas almost looks to pass the ball into the net, no matter where he is in the area. And there is no place in the area where goalkeepers are safe from his ability.

It has been his goals that have helped Argentinean club River Plate to two successive championships – the club that paid just under £2 million to secure his services from Universidad de Chile. His price tag will almost certainly have increased substantially after a summer in France.

Davor SUKER – Croatia
The tide of emotion that swept Croatia into Euro '96 and now into their first ever World Cup finals has helped Davor Suker confirm himself as one of the most talented footballers in the world. Could France '98 be where he establishes himself amongst the all-time greats? His strength belies his close control and he is at home both wide and in the centre. In his first season with Real Madrid (1996-97) his goals, and ability to create them for others, swept his side to the Spanish title.

14

At international level he has one of the best strike rates around with very nearly a goal a game – a record he will be looking to sustain this summer.

DENILSON de Oliveira – Brazil

Being Brazilian, he has a lot to live up to. He lives in the shadow of the World's best footballer – Ronaldo. But Denilson may well be taking over Ronaldo's current tag of world's most expensive footballer when he joins Spanish Club Real Betis from Sao Paulo after the World Cup for what will be a staggering £21.5 million.

The 20-year-old first came to be noticed by Europe when he produced some outstanding performances in Le Tournoi last summer in France. Playing as an attacking wing-back or in midfield, Denilson has given the mighty Brazil a new dimension. He has also added goals from midfield – four goals in his first 14 internationals – something that surprisingly the World Cup holders have lacked in recent years.

Those performances have made Denilson a virtual fixture in the Brazilian starting line-up and he looks set to become an even greater star.

Zinedine ZIDANE – France

The French national teams have known a few gifted midfield players during past World Cups – perhaps the greatest of them all was Michel Platini. Now they have another talent who could be on the verge of emulating the Frenchman who has been responsible for organising this year's event.

'Zuzou', as he is known, has been a dominating force, not just in the French midfield but also in that of his Italian club side, Juventus. His nifty footwork and elegant touch make him an eye catcher when he has the ball at his feet, and his performances in Serie A during the 1997-98 season have shown he has the ability to succeed. If France are to progress in their World Cup then they need their balding play maker to emulate their past master.

Karim BAGHERI – Iran

With 19 goals in his country's World Cup qualifying games, Karim Bagheri was the top scorer in the World Cup qualifying competition. Not bad for a player who operates mainly in midfield! Despite his goalscoring exploits, it is often Ali Daei or Khodadad Azizi, the Asian Player of the Year, whose skills draw the major attention, but it is Bagheri who could shine in France.

His explosive play action has earned him a move from Iranian champions Piruzi to Armenia Bielefeld in Germany's Bundesliga, where the 24-year-old's ability to spray the ball around has earned him rave reviews.

Tap-ins or scorching shots from around the area, Bagheri is a unique talent with his ability to score as many goals from midfield as any strikers up front. Ask the Maldives – he managed to fire seven goals past them in one of their qualifying games. Who knows? Just one strike could earn Iran an upset and Bagheri the World spotlight.

Sami AL JABER – Saudi Arabia

This is Al Jaber's second World Cup and, but for being Saudi, he might already be playing in one of the world's top leagues. But the Saudi Arabian football authorities are trying to establish their own national football league and have put an embargo on any of their top players going abroad.

The 24-year-old plays for Al Hilal where he has been a consistent goal scorer. Extremely fast, he has proved he can compete at the top by being named Man of the Match in the finals of the Asian Cup Winners' Cup and Asian Super Cup last year.

Hidetoshi NAKATA – Japan

Kazu Miura is a national hero in Japan, not least because he became the first Asian player to play in Italy, but it is Hidetoshi Nakata who is Japan's bright hope for the future.

The 21-year-old midfielder plays for Bellmare Hiratsuka and shows the sort of aggression in the middle of the park not normally associated with Asian players. Hard-tackling and with good vision, Nakata will be looking to go further than Miura and not just play in Serie A but establish himself there or in one of the World's top football leagues.

KO JONG Soo – South Korea

Perhaps it's fate that Ko Jong Soo should be heading for France, because in Korea he is very much considered his nation's 'enfant terrible'.

Now 19 years old, he was the youngest player to ever represent Korea at full international level, an honour bestowed on him by the former holder of that honour, the current Korean coach Cha Bum Kun. Operating on the left of midfield, Ko scored in only his second international and plays in the Korean League with the Samsung Bluewings.

Dennis BERGKAMP – Netherlands

The Ice man – they don't come much cooler or more skilful than the Dutchman who, at the start of the 1997-98 season, was in brilliant form with his club Arsenal. His close control and explosive turn of pace make him a danger in and around the area and have had him in the running for honours such as World and European Player of the year already.

Bergkamp was originally a winger and was given his first team debut with Ajax at the age of 17. He subsequently switched to a more central role and invariably operates in the space between midfield and attack.

His performances for the Dutch national side have always been worth watching and by the time of the World Cup he may well have written himself deeper into his country's footballing history by becoming their all-time top scorer.

Gheorghe HAGI – Romania

Time is probably not on Gheorghe Hagi's side. This will almost certainly be the Romanian midfielder's last World Cup and he will do well to emulate some of the performances and some of the brilliant goals he scored in USA 94.

He has carried the nickname 'Maradona of the Carpathians' with him for several years now, not least because of the magic that can be found in his left foot. Since leaving his native Romania – where he had scored 100 goals while still a teenager – he has failed to reach the heights with any of the many big clubs, including Real Madrid and Barcelona, who have sought his signature.

This World Cup would be a fitting stage for Hagi to shine one more time.

Christian VIERI – Italy

Although he only played in half of Italy's World Cup qualifiers, Christian Vieri has been making all the right moves towards a regular place in Italy's World Cup starting line-up. The first of these came a few years back when he travelled west from Atalanta to Juventus. Having to settle in behind more established strikers Vieri got his chance and took it, even managing to oust the much heralded Del Piero from the Juve side.

His performance meant a national call-up was only a matter of time, and when Cesare Minaldi gave it to him he took it perfectly by scoring on his debut – a goal that also happened to be Italy's 1000th!

His powerful build has been on display in Madrid in the colours of Atletico in the past year, but it is in the Azzurri colours where his goals might make the biggest impact before the season is out.

Ole Gunnar SOLSKJAER – Norway

The Norwegian Gunnar hasn't been as prolific for Manchester United this season, but then that's not surprising given his astonishing performance in his first season at Old Trafford. Eighteen goals in 33 appearances (of which 25 were starting appearances) was a phenomenal feat. Solskjaer had been a free scoring striker with Molde but few, even Alex Ferguson, could have expected him to carry that straight on into the Premiership.

Slightly built, Solskjaer looks about eight years younger than his 24-years, but his pace and balance with the ball at his feet make almost anything he does look easy. Not surprisingly Solskjaer scored on his international debut but that hasn't been enough to secure his place in the starting line-up. But with United going so well and Solskjaer still amongst the goals, his biggest impact could still be waiting to happen.

Paul LAMBERT – Scotland

In season 1996-97 a Scottish player won a Champions' Cup medal. Unless you are a follower of the European club game that might come as a surprise to you, but not to the fans of Borussia Dortmund for whom Paul Lambert had an outstanding season.

Lambert had played much of his career in the backwaters of St Mirren, but accepted a trial with Dortmund at the end of his contract in Scotland. Signed, it would seem, as a squad member, Lambert established himself in the Dortmund side and had an extremely memorable season, including a call-up to the national squad.

Not surprisingly, having been ignored by the big two, Celtic were more than happy to take him back to his home land where he scored one of the two goals that helped Celtic secure a 2-0 win over arch rivals Rangers at the start of 1998.

Lambert's power in midfield should be one of the highlights in their opening World Cup game with Brazil.

RAUL Gonzalez – Spain

Known simply as Raul, he played in all but one of Spain's qualifying games that saw them into the World Cup finals and has become an established and important member of the Real Madrid side. Not bad for a 20-year-old who has had to live with the great burden of expectation placed on him by both his country's and club's supporters. But Raul might have been playing for cross-town rivals Atletico had he not been ditched by them as a junior.

Playing just behind the front two for club or country, Raul's individual brilliance is enough in itself to be able to turn a game his way. He has super control and the vision to see passes that most would miss. France '98 could turn Raul into one of world football's hottest properties. If that happens, for once he could also help his nation to realise their undoubted potential.

Predrag MIJATOVIC – Yugoslavia

It is debatable if Yugoslavia have ever had such a prolific goalscorer as Predrag Mijatovic. His performance in the World Cup qualifiers was exceptional and he finished up as the qualifying competition's top scorer – and the UEFA competition's top scorer – with 14 goals. What is more impressive is that those 14 goals came in just 12 games, including hat-tricks in both legs of the play-off games against Hungary.

His partnership up front with Aston Villa's Savo Milosevic (ten goals in nine games – and only six as a starter) should keep defences on the hop and ensure that Real Madrid's main striker becomes a name many will need to get to grips with!

Ariel ORTEGA – Argentina

Not since Maradona broke onto the national scene have Argentina had a player who possesses sublime ball control and great vision. At just 24 years of age, Ariel Ortega is quite possibly the best player to wear the blue and white stripes since Maradona himself.

With well over 50 caps to his name, he missed out on just one of Argentina's 16 qualifying games in the CONMEBOL group and finished as their top scorer with four goals. His performances not surprisingly drew attention and ultimately led him to a move to Valencia for an Argentine record fee of £7 million. A good performance this summer could see him moving on to one of Spain's bigger clubs for an even greater fee and even bigger rewards. The sky's the limit for Ariel.

Carlos GAMARRA – Paraguay

Carlos Gamarra played in every minute of the 15 World Cup qualifying games he was available for. His influence on the Paraguay national team is immense and he plays at the heart of a defence that has been the basis for the current national side, being hailed as the best ever from Paraguay. No team managed to put more than two goals past them in the qualifiers where many of the opposition's chances were simply snuffed out by Gamarra playing in the sweeper's role.

Many have likened him to Daniel Passarella, but there is a great deal more skill in the play of Paraguay's hard man. At 26 years old he is strong and has a fierce desire to win every tackle. But like any sweeper worth his salt he loves to join in the attack. He finished joint top scorer in his team's World Cup games with three goals, including the winner against Bolivia which virtually secured their ticket to France. A good performance could well earn him a return ticket to one of Europe's top clubs.

VENUE DIRECTORY

In all, at least half a million fans are expected to watch the 64 games in the ten stadiums. No two stadiums are over 1,000kms apart and the match schedule is such that stadiums in relatively close proximity will not stage games on the same day. Thus supporters based in the Paris Saint Denis or the Lyon/Saint Etienne areas have the possibility to see games at both venues. A mileage chart showing the distance between stadiums can be found on the next page.

Venue to Venue Distances

	Bordeaux	Lens	Lyon	Marseille	Montpellier	Nantes	Paris	Saint Denis	Saint Etienne	Toulouse
Bordeaux	–	760	538	648	486	323	579	579	507	245
Lens	760	–	644	959	941	566	199	199	702	880
Lyon	538	644	–	313	300	613	462	462	60	537
Marseille	648	954	313	–	166	972	773	773	330	404
Montpellier	486	941	300	166	–	809	760	760	317	241
Nantes	323	566	613	972	809	–	384	384	608	567
Paris	579	199	462	773	760	384	–	–	520	698
Saint Denis	579	199	462	773	760	384	–	–	520	698
Saint Etienne	507	702	60	330	317	608	520	520	–	439
Toulouse	245	880	537	440	241	567	698	698	439	–

All distances in Kms.

BORDEAUX
Parc Lescure

Address:	Rue Juliot-Curie, BP33, 33186 Le Haillan Cedex
Telephone:	0556 161 111
Fax:	0556 575 446
Location:	2km from city centre and 4km from train station
Capacity:	35,200 all-seated, including 15,000 under cover
Improvements:	New press centre which will be converted into a multi-purpose sports centre after World Cup finals. Improved access, players areas and ticketing. New security facilities including new video surveillance system.
Notes:	Capacity before renovation was 45,000 with 21,300 seats. The Lescure Stadium is a fine example of 1930s architecture, it is a national heritage protected monument and is one of Bordeaux's major landmarks. It was first inaugurated on 12 June 1938 with the World Cup quarter final between Brazil and Czechoslovakia.
The Club:	Girondins de Bordeaux
Honours:	League Championship (4) 1950, 1984, 1985, 1987; French Cup (3) 1941, 1986, 1987.
Fixtures:	Jun-11 Group B Italy v Chile
	Jun-16 Group A Scotland v Norway
	Jun-20 Group E Belgium v Mexico

	Jun-24	Group C	South Africa v Saudi Arabia
	Jun-26	Group H	Argentina v Croatia
	Jun-30	2nd Rd	Game 7: 1st Group G v 2nd Group H

LENS
Stade Félix Bollaert

Address:	Rue A.Maes, 62300 Lens
Telephone:	0321 692899
Fax:	0321 692884
Location:	Ten minutes from the city and from the train/TGV station. Motorway exit at stadium.
Capacity:	41,275 seats.
Improvements:	Construction of the Trannin and Delacourt stands. Reconstruction of the Lepagnot, also called the Presidential stand, with new prestige and media seats. New sound system. New lighting. New scoreboards. New surveillance and video monitoring system.
Notes:	The stadium has a very English feel to it and its capacity is greater than the population of the city of Lens itself.
The Club:	Racing Club de Lens
Honours:	No major honours
Fixtures:	Jun-12	Group C	Saudi Arabia v Denmark

	Jun-12	Group C	Saudi Arabia v Denmark
	Jun-14	Group H	Jamaica v Croatia
	Jun-21	Group F	Germany v Yugoslavia
	Jun-24	Group D	Spain v Bulgaria
	Jun-26	Group G	Colombia v England
	Jun-28	2nd Rd	Game 3: 1st Group C v 2nd Group D

LYON
Stade Gerland

Address:	350 Avenue Jean-Jaures, 67007 Lyon
Telephone:	0478 767 604
Fax:	0478 720 399
Location:	Lyon's 7th arrondissement– easily accessible from city centre.
Capacity:	44,000 all seated
Improvements:	Two sides of stadium have been improved with addition of curved sides and a metallo-textile roof to cover them. The Jean-Jaures and Jean Bouin stands have been refurbished with individual seating and new corporate boxes. Lighting, sound and video monitoring have been brought up to

	standard. Externally an esplanade has been built in front of the Jean-Jaures stand with a square added behind the terraces.
Notes:	The Stade Gerland was designed in 1926 and is listed as a historic monument. The stadium is set in a grass embankment that features four symbolic gateways.
The Club:	Olympique Lyonnais
Honours:	French Cup (3) 1964, 1967, 1973.

Fixtures:	Jun-13	Group E	South Korea v Mexico
	Jun-15	Group G	Romania v Colombia
	Jun-21	Group F	USA v Iran
	Jun-24	Group C	France v Denmark
	Jun-26	Group H	Japan v Jamaica
	Jul-04	QF	Game D: Game 6 v Game 7

MARSEILLE
Velodrome

Address:	25 Rue Negresko, BP 124, 13267 Marseille Cedex 08
Telephone:	0291 765 609
Fax:	0291 760 777
Location:	At centre of city.
Capacity:	60,000 seats.
Improvements:	Upgraded totally for World Cup with increase in capacity from 42,000, of which 10,000 has been standing. Modernisation of the changing rooms and boxes. New lighting, sound system, signs, scoreboards, video-surveillance. New media centre and catering area.
Notes:	Will feature as the second stadium of France. Hosted the draw for the finals.
The Club:	Olympique Marseille
Honours:	Championship (8) 1937, 1949, 1971, 1972, 1989, 1990, 1991, 1992; French Cup (10) 1924, 1926, 1927, 1935, 1938, 1943, 1969, 1972, 1976, 1989; Champions' Cup (1) 1993.

Fixtures:	Jun-12	Group C	France v South Africa
	Jun-15	Group G	England v Tunisia
	Jun-20	Group E	Holland v South Korea
	Jun-23	Group A	Brazil v Norway
	Jun-27	2nd Rd	Game 2: 1st Group B v 2nd Group A
	Jul-04	QF	Game C: Game 5 v Game 8
	Jul-07	SF	Game A v Game C

MONTPELLIER
La Masson

Address:	Avenue Albert-Einstein, Domaine de Grammont, 34000 Montpellier
Telephone:	0467 154 600
Fax:	0467 221 273
Location:	In the north west of Montpellier, in the La Paillade quarter, about 4km from the town centre.
Capacity:	35,000 all seated.
Improvements:	The stadium has undergone major renovation including the increase in capacity from 23,500 (of which only 7,500 were seated). A new press centre has been added along with multi-level corporate/VIP stands. Changing rooms and all electrical and security equipment upgraded to World Cup standard.
Notes:	The original stadium was only built as recently as 1988.
The Club:	Montpellier Herault Sports Club
Honours:	French Cup (1) 1990
Fixtures:	Jun-10 Group A Morocco v Norway
	Jun-12 Group D Paraguay v Bulgaria
	Jun-17 Group B Italy v Cameroon
	Jun-22 Group G Colombia v Tunisia
	Jun-25 Group F Germany v Iran
	Jun-29 2nd Rd Game 6: 1st Group F v 2nd Group E

NANTES
Le Beaujoire Louis Fonteneau

Address:	BP 1124, 44311 Nantes Cedex 03
Telephone:	0240 372 929
Fax:	0240 372 921
Location:	Approximately 7km from the town centre.
Capacity:	39,500 all seated.
Improvements:	The rake of the stands has been changed to provide better views and improved to help abate strong Atlantic winds. In addition stands have been re-built. All entrances have been modernised and the playing surface has been upgraded. Lighting and sound systems upgraded. New video and security systems installed.
Notes:	This is the second time the Nantes club have benefited from a major football competition. In 1984 they had a new stadium built for the European Championships.
The Club:	Football Club de Nantes Atlantique

Honours:	League Championship (7) 1965, 1966, 1973, 1977, 1980, 1983, 1995; French Cup (1) 1979.
Fixtures:	Jun-16	Group A	Brazil v Morocco
	Jun-13	Group D	Spain v Nigeria
	Jun-20	Group H	Japan v Croatia
	Jun-23	Group B	Chile v Cameroon
	Jun-25	Group F	USA v Yugoslavia
	Jul-03	QF	Game A: Game 1 v Game 4

PARIS
Parc des Princes

Address:	30 Avenue de Parc des Princes, 75016 Paris
Telephone:	0140 719 191
Fax:	0140 719 397
Location:	In the 16th arrondissement in Paris, to the north of the Peripherique ring road on the Porte Saint Cloud side of the city (west).
Capacity:	49,000 all seated.
Improvements:	Replacement of all seats in stadium. Modernisation of the press areas and changing rooms. Upgrade of all lighting and sound systems.
Notes:	The Parc des Princes is famous for the staging of not just football events but also international rugby.
The Club:	Paris Saint-Germain
Honours:	League Championship (2) 1986, 1994; French Cup (4) 1982, 1983, 1993, 1995; League Cup (1) 1995; Cup-Winners' Cup (1) 1996.
Fixtures:	Jun-15	Group F	Germany v USA
	Jun-19	Group D	Nigeria v Bulgaria
	Jun-21	Group H	Argentina v Jamaica
	Jun-25	Group E	Belgium v South Korea
	Jul-11	3rd Place	Semi final losers

SAINT-DENIS
Stade de France

Address:	93216 Saint Denis, La Plaine, Cedex
Telephone:	00 33 1 55 93 00 50
Fax:	00 33 1 55 93 00 03
Location:	Located on the north side of Paris on the way to Charles de Gaulle Airport.
Capacity:	80,000 all seated for football.

Notes: Built for the World Cup, the Stade de France is the new
           French national stadium and it will play host to the opening
           ceremony and the World Cup final itself. Work began on site
           in May 1995 and was completed in November 1997. The
           stadium has a variable capacity enabling it to be used for a
           wide variety of events ranging from football and rugby
           matches to shows on a grand scale, as well as athletics
           competitions. Capacity variance is achieved by the provision
           of a circle of 25,000 seats in the mobile stands closest to the
           sports area. This stand, when set in a configuration 15 metres
           back from the running track, provides 21,000 seats. The
           middle stand has a capacity of 30,000, and the upper stand
           25,000. In addition, the stadium ground itself can
           accommodate 25,000, bringing the maximum capacity for
           large-scale shows to 105,000.

Fixtures: Jun-10   Group A   Brazil v Scotland
           Jun-13   Group E   Holland v Belgium
           Jun-18   Group C   France v Saudi Arabia
           Jun-23   Group B   Italy v Austria
           Jun-26   Group G   Romania v Tunisia
           Jun-28   2nd Rd   Game 4: 1st Group D v 2nd Group C
           Jul-03   QF   Game B: Game 2 v Game 3
           Jul-08   SF   Game B v Game D
           Jul-12   Final

SAINT-ETIENNE
Geoffroy Guichard

Address: 32 Rue Jean Snella, 42028 Saint Etienne Cedex 01
Telephone: 0377 746 355
Fax: 0377 799 522
Location: About 3km from the city centre.
Capacity: 36,000 all seated.
Improvements: Refurbished to become all-seater with seats installed in the
                standing areas in the north and south stands. Corporate boxes
                installed along with new press areas. All lighting, sound and
                video systems replaced and upgraded. New parking facilities
                along with remodelling of areas surrounding stadium.
Notes: Capacity before renovation was 42,000 of which 19,000 was
                standing. The stadium is known locally as 'chaudron', or
                'cauldron', a nickname acquired in the seventies when Saint
                Etienne were almost unbeatable at home.

	Saint Etienne, one of France's most successful teams, played the 1997-98 season in the French Second Division.	

The Club: AS Saint Etienne

Honours: League Championship (10) 1957, 1964, 1967, 1968, 1969, 1970, 1974, 1975, 1976, 1981; French Cup (6) 1962, 1968, 1970, 1974, 1975, 1977.

Fixtures:

Jun-14	Group F	Yugoslavia v Iran
Jun-17	Group B	Chile v Austria
Jun-19	Group D	Spain v Paraguay
Jun-23	Group A	Scotland v Morocco
Jun-25	Group E	Holland v Mexico
Jun-30	2nd Rd	Game 8: 1st Group H v 2nd Group G

TOULOUSE
The Municipal Stadium

Address: 1 Allee Gabriel-Bienes, 31400 Toulouse

Telephone: 0561 551 111

Fax: 0561 535 567

Location: Ile du Ramier, close to city centre and just 15 minutes from airport and train station.

Capacity: 37,000 all seater and covered.

Improvements: New roof. Construction of 3,500 club-seat dress circle in the north stand. Addition of new corporate boxes. Upgrading of lighting, sound, billboarding and video surveillance systems.

Notes: Built on an island between two branches of the Garonne, it is set on a delightfully green site a stone's throw from the city centre. Perhaps more famous as a rugby venue.

The Club: Toulouse

Honours: French Cup (1) 1957

Fixtures:

Jun-11	Group B	Cameroon v Austria
Jun-14	Group H	Argentina v Japan
Jun-18	Group C	South Africa v Denmark
Jun-22	Group G	Romania v England
Jun-24	Group D	Nigeria v Paraguay
Jun-29	2nd Rd	Game 5: 1st Group E v 2nd Group F

ENGLAND QUALIFIERS

Kishinev, September 1st 1996 – World Cup Qualifying Group Two

MOLDOVA   **ENGLAND**   **0-3**   **8,000**

Barmby (24), Gascoigne (25), Shearer (61)

Moldova: Romanenco, Secu, Nani, Testimitanu, Gaidamasciuc, Belous (Siscin 58), Epureanu, Curtianu, Clescenco, Miterev (Rebeja 61), Popovici.
England: Seaman, Southgate, Pallister, Pearce, G. Neville, Beckham, Ince, Gascoigne (Batty 81), Hinchcliffe, Barmby (Le Tissier 81), Shearer. Subs not used: Walker (gk), Campbell, Stone, Draper, Ferdinand.

Wembley, October 9th 1996 – World Cup Qualifying Group Two

ENGLAND   **POLAND**   **2-1**   **74,663**

Shearer (24, 38)   Citko (7)

England: Seaman, G. Neville, Southgate (Pallister 51), Pearce, Ince, Beckham, McManaman, Gascoigne, Hinchcliffe, Shearer, Ferdinand. Subs not used: Walker (gk), Campbell, Platt, Le Tissier, Sheringham, Barmby.
Poland: Wozniak, Waldoch, Zielinski, Juskowiak, Hajto, Michalski, Baluszynski, Wojtala, Nowak, Citko, Warzycha (Sagamowski 75).

Tiblisi, November 9th 1996 – World Cup Qualifying Group Two

GEORGIA   **ENGLAND**   **0-2**   **48,000**

Sheringham (15), Ferdinand (37)

Georgia: Zoidze, Lobjaindze, Tskhadadze, Sheila, Gogichaishviki (Gudushauri 60), Nemsadze, Kinkladze, Jamarauli, Kobiashvili, Ketsbaia, Aveladze S (Gogrichiani).
England: Seaman, Campbell, Adams, Southgate, Beckham, Ince, Batty, Gascoigne, Hinchcliffe, Sheringham, Ferdinand (I. Wright 81). Subs not used: Walker (gk), G. Neville, Pearce, Platt, McManaman, Le Tissier.

Wembley, February 12th 1997 – World Cup Qualifying Group Two

ENGLAND   **ITALY**   **0-1**   **75,055**

Zola

England: Walker, G. Neville, Pearce, Campbell, Batty (I. Wright 89), McManaman (Merson 77), Beckham, Le Tissier (Ferdinand 61), Le Saux. Subs not used: James (gk), Southgate, Redknapp, Lee.
Italy: Peruzzi, Ferrara, Costacurta, Cannavaro, Di Livio, Dino Baggio, Albertini, Di Matteo, Maldini, Zola (Fuser 90), Casiraghi (Ravanelli 76).

Wembley, April 30th 1997 – World Cup Qualifying Group Two
ENGLAND   GEORGIA   2-0 71,208
Sheringham (43), Shearer (90)

England: Seaman, G. Neville, Campbell, Batty, Adams (Southgate 88), Le
Saux, Beckham, Ince (Redknapp 79), Shearer, Sheringham, Lee.
Subs not used: Flowers (gk), Ferdinand, P. Neville.
Georgia: Zoidze, Chikhradze, Sheqiladze, Tskhadadze, Sheila, Machavariani
(Gogrichiani 30) (Arveladze A 76), Nemsadze, Jamarauli, Ketsbaia,
Kinkladze (Gakhokidze 61), Arveladze S.

Katowice, May 31st 1997 – World Cup Qualifying Group Two
POLAND   ENGLAND   0-2 35,000
                    Shearer (5), Sheringham (90)
Poland: Wozniak, Jozwiak, Zielinski, Kaluzny, Ledwon, Bukalski
(Swierczewski P 46), Nowak (Kucharski 57), Majak, Waldoch, Juskowiak
(Adamczyk 51), Dembinski.
England: Seaman, G. Neville, Southgate, Campbell, Beckham (P. Neville
88), Ince, Gascoigne (Batty 16), Lee, Le Saux, Sheringham, Shearer.
Subs not used: Flowers (gk), Pearce, Keown, Scholes, Wright.

Wembley, September 10th 1997 – World Cup Qualifying Group Two
ENGLAND   MOLDOVA   4-0 74,102
Scholes (28), Wright (46, 90),
Gascoigne (81)
England: Seaman, G. Neville, Campbell, Southgate, Beckham (Ripley 67)
(Butt 75), Batty, Gascoigne, P. Neville, Scholes, Ferdinand (Collymore 82),
Wright. Subs not used: Pallister, Walker (gk), Le Saux, Lee.
Moldova: Roumanenco, Stroenco, Fistican, Tistimitstanu, Spinu, Shishkin
(Popovici 60), Curtean, Culibaba (Suharev 52), Rebetadj, Miterev, Rogaciov
(Cibotari 74).

Rome, October 11th 1997 – World Cup Qualifying Group Two
ITALY   ENGLAND   0-0 81,200
Italy: Peruzzi, Nesta, Costacurta, Cannavaro, Maldini (Benarrivo 31), Di
Livio (sent off), Dino Baggio, Albertini, Zola (Del Piero 64), Inzaghi (Cheisa
ht), Vieri.
England: Seaman, Beckham, Campbell, Adams, Southgate, Le Saux, Ince,
Gascoigne (Butt 88), Batty, Sheringham, Wright. Subs not used: G. Neville,
Walker, P. Neville, Scholes, McManaman, Fowler.

Player Summary

	Player	Club	St	Sub	Tot	SNU	PS
✱ Tony	ADAMS	Arsenal	3	0	3	0	1
Nick	BARMBY	Everton	1	0	1	1	1
✱ David	BATTY	Newcastle United	5	2	7	0	1
✱ David	BECKHAM	Manchester United	8	0	8	0	2
Nicky	~~BUTT~~	Manchester United	0	2	2	0	0
✱ Sol	CAMPBELL	Tottenham Hotspur	6	0	6	2	0
Stan	COLLYMORE	Aston Villa	0	1	1	0	0
Mark	DRAPER	Aston Villa	0	0	0	1	0
✱ Les	FERDINAND	Tottenham Hotspur	3	1	4	2	2
✱ Tim	FLOWERS	Blackburn Rovers	0	0	0	2	0
Robbie	FOWLER	Liverpool	0	0	0	1	0
Paul	GASCOIGNE	Rangers	6	0	6	0	3
Andy	~~HINCHCLIFFE~~	Everton	3	0	3	0	0
Steve	HOWEY	Newcastle United	0	0	0	0	0
✱ Paul	INCE	Liverpool	7	0	7	0	1
David	JAMES	Liverpool	0	0	0	1	0
✱ Martin	KEOWN	Arsenal	0	0	0	1	0
✱ Graeme	LE SAUX	Chelsea	4	0	4	1	0
Matt	LE TISSIER	Southampton	1	1	2	2	1
✱ Robert	LEE	Newcastle United	2	0	2	2	0
Steve	McMANAMAN	Liverpool	2	0	2	1	1
✱ Paul	MERSON	Middlesbrough	0	1	1	0	0
✱ Gary	NEVILLE	Manchester United	6	0	6	2	0
Phil	~~NEVILLE~~	Manchester United	1	1	2	2	0
Gary	PALLISTER	Manchester United	1	1	2	1	0
Stuart	PEARCE	Newcastle United	3	0	3	2	0
David	PLATT	Arsenal	0	0	0	2	0
Jamie	REDKNAPP	Liverpool	0	1	1	1	0
Stuart	RIPLEY	Blackburn Rovers	0	1	1	0	1
✱ Paul	SCHOLES	Manchester United	1	2	3	2	0
✱ David	SEAMAN	Arsenal	7	0	7	0	0
✱ Alan	SHEARER	Newcastle United	5	0	5	0	0
✱ Teddy	SHERINGHAM	Manchester United	4	0	4	1	0
✱ Darren	SOUTHGATE	Aston Villa	6	1	7	1	1
Steve	STONE	Nottingham Forest	0	0	0	1	0
Ian	~~WALKER~~	Tottenham	1	0	1	4	0
Ian	WRIGHT	Arsenal	2	1	3	1	0
Mark	WRIGHT	Liverpool	0	1	1	0	0
✱	OWEN.						
✱	R FERDINAND		29				
✱	ANDERTON						
✱	MARTYN						

APPEARANCE CHART

	Moldova	Poland	Georgia	Italy	Georgia	Poland	Moldova	Italy
ADAMS	-	-	•	-	•(88)	-	-	•
BARMBY	•(81)	*	-	-	-	-	-	-
BATTY	*(81)	-	•	•(89)	•	*(16)	•	•
BECKHAM	•	•	•	•	•	•(88)	•(67)	•
BUTT	-	-	-	-	-	-	*(75)	*(88)
CAMPBELL	*	*	•	•	•	•	•	•
COLLYMORE	-	-	-	-	-	-	*(82)	-
DRAPER	*	-	-	-	-	-	-	-
FERDINAND	*	•	•(81)	*(61)	*	-	•(82)	-
FLOWERS	-	-	-	-	*	*	-	-
FOWLER	-	-	-	-	-	-	-	*
GASCOIGNE	•(81)	•	•	•	-	•(16)	•	•(88)
HINCHCLIFFE	•	•	•	-	-	-	-	-
INCE	•	•	•	•	•(79)	•	-	•
JAMES	-	-	-	*	-	-	-	-
KEOWN	-	-	-	-	-	*	-	-
LE SAUX	-	-	-	•	•	•	*	•
LE TISSIER	*(81)	*	*	•(61)	-	-	-	-
LEE	-	-	-	*	•	•	*	-
McMANAMAN	-	•	*	•(77)	-	-	-	*
MERSON	-	-	-	*(77)	-	-	-	-
NEVILLE G.	•	•	*	•	•	•	•	*
NEVILLE P.	-	-	-	-	*	*(88)	-	*
PALLISTER	•	*(51)	-	-	-	-	*	-
PEARCE	•	•	*	•	-	*	-	-
PLATT	-	*	*	-	-	-	-	-
REDKNAPP	-	-	-	*	*(79)	-	-	-
RIPLEY	-	-	-	-	-	-	*(67)(75)	*
SCHOLES	-	-	•	-	•	*	•	*
SEAMAN	•	•	•	-	•	•	•	•
SHEARER	•	•	•	-	•	•	•	•
SHERINGHAM	-	*	-	-	-	-	-	-
SOUTHGATE	•	•(51)	•	*	*(88)	•	•	•
WALKER	*	*	*	-	-	-	*	-
WRIGHT I.	-	-	-	*(89)	•	*	•	•
WRIGHT M.	-	-	*(81)	-	-	-	-	-

• Started match. * Substitute - No appearance. The number next to an */• gives the minute the substitute entered the match/player left the field.

England's World Cup Finals Record

1950 – Brazil
First Round – Group 2
25.06.50	Chile	Rio de Janeiro	2-0	Mortenson, Mannion
29.06.50	USA	Belo Horizonte	0-1	
02.07.50	Spain	Rio de Janeiro	0-1	

1954 – Switzerland
First Round – Group 4
| 17.06.54 | Belgium | Basle | 4-4† | Broasis (2), Lofthouse (2) |
| 20.06.54 | Switzerland | Berne | 2-0 | Mullen, Wilshaw |

Quarter Final
| 26.06.54 | Uruguay | Basle | 2-4 | Lofthouse, Finney |

1958 – Sweden
First Round – Group 4
08.07.58	USSR	Gothenburg	2-2	Kevan, Finney (pen)
11.06.58	Brazil	Gothenburg	0-0	
15.06.58	Austria	Boras	2-2	Haynes, Kevan

Play-off
| 17.06.58 | USSR | Gothenburg | 0-1 | |

1962 – Chile
First Round – Group 4
31.05.62	Hungary	Rancagua	1-2	Flowers (pen)
02.06.62	Argentina	Rancagua	3-1	Flowers (pen), Charlton, Greaves
07.06.62	Bulgaria	Rancagua	0-0	

Quarter Final
| 10.06.62 | Brazil | Vina del Mar | 1-3 | Hitchens |

1966 – England
First Round – Group 1
11.07.66	Uruguay	Wembley	0-0	
16.07.66	Mexico	Wembley	2-0	Charlton, Hunt
20.07.66	France	Wembley	2-0	Hunt (2)

Quarter Final
| 23.07.66 | Argentina | Wembley | 1-0 | Hurst |

Semi Final
| 26.07.66 | Portugal | Wembley | 2-1 | Charlton R. (2) |

Final
| 30.07.66 | West Germany | Wembley | 4-2† | Hurst (3), Peters |

1970 – Mexico
First Round – Group 3

02.06.70	Romania	Guadalajara	1-0	Hurst
07.06.70	Brazil	Guadalajara	0-1	
11.06.70	Czechoslovakia	Guadalajara	1-0	Clarke (pen)

Quarter Final

14.06.70	West Germany	Leon	2-3 †	Mullery, Peters

1982 – Spain
First Round – Group 4

16.06.82.	France	Bilbao	3-1	Robson (2), Mariner
20.06.82	Czechoslovakia	Bilbao	2-0	Francis, own goal
25.06.82	Kuwait	Bilbao	1-0	Francis

Quarter Finals

29.06.82	West Germany	Madrid	0-0	
05.07.82	Spain	Madrid	0-0	

1986 – Mexico
First Round – Group F

03.06.86	Portugal	Monterrey	0-1	
06.06.86	Morocco	Monterrey	0-0	
11.06.86	Poland	Monterrey	3-0	Lineker

Second Round

18.06.86	Paraguay	Azteca	3-0	Lineker (2), Beardsley

Quarter Final

22.06.86	Argentina	Azteca	1-2	Lineker

1990 – Italy
First Round – Group F

11.06.90	Rep. Ireland	Cagliari	1-1	Lineker
16.06.90	Holland	Cagliari	0-0	
21.06.90	Egypt	Cagliari	1-0	Wright M.

Second Round

26.06.90	Belgium	Bologna	1-0†	Platt

Quarter Final

01.07.90	Cameroon	Naples	3-2†	Platt, Lineker (2 pens)

Semi Final

04.07.90	West Germany	Turin	1-1†	Lineker	4-3 on pens

Third Place

07.07.90	Italy	Bari	1-2	Platt

† after extra time

SQUAD PEN-PICS

Details of the players who might well form the England squad in the World Cup finals in France can be found on the following pages. A brief profile of each player is followed by their England appearance details. A key to the country mnemonics used in the appearance details can be found at the end of the section. An * denotes the fact that the player appeared in the game as a substitute. St=Starting appearances, Sb=Substitute appearances, and Tot=Total appearances. The players listed are those that made appearances for England in the World Cup qualifying competition at some stage and/or are likely to be considered for Glenn Hoddle's final squad.

ADAMS, Tony   Arsenal

Full name: Anthony Alexander Adams
DOB: 10-10-66 Romford, Essex

Nagging injury problems during the past three seasons have limited Adams' time in both the Gunners and England side. His ability to play through the pain however, during vital games for both club and country, has earned him considerable respect in the game.

Regarded as Mr Arsenal, Adams was the England captain throughout Euro 96 and showed a new side to his football last season under manager Arsène Wenger, often joining the attack and scoring three Premiership goals – his best season tally ever. He joined Arsenal on Schoolboy forms in 1984 and led them to the championship in 1989 and '91. Captained the club to a unique FA Cup and Coca Cola Cup double in 1993 as well as successive appearances in the Cup Winners' Cup finals of 1994 and '95. Made his 400th League appearance for Arsenal at the start of the 1997-98 season. At the end of 1997 he had 48 appearances for England and had scored four goals.

Club	Season	Internationals	St	Sb	Tot
Arsenal	1986-87	Sp, Tur, Bra	3	0	3
Arsenal	1987-88	WG, Tur, Yug, Hol, Hun, Sco, Col, Swi, RIr, Hol, USSR	11	0	11
Arsenal	1988-89	Den, Swe, SAr	3	0	3
Arsenal	1990-91	RIr, RIr	2	0	2
Arsenal	1992-93	Nor, Tur, SM, Tur, Hol, Pol, Nor	7	0	7
Arsenal	1993-94	Pol, Hol, Den, Gre, Nor	5	0	5
Arsenal	1994-95	US, Rom, RIr, Uru	4	0	4
Arsenal	1995-96	Col, Nor, Swi, Por, Chn, Swi, Sco, Hol, Sp, Ger	10	0	10
Arsenal	1996-97	Geo, Geo	2	0	2
Arsenal	1997-98	Ita	1	0	1
	Total		48	0	48

BATTY, David   Newcastle United

Full name: David Batty
DOB: 02-12-68 Leeds

When Batty made his way to Newcastle after stints at Leeds United and Blackburn Rovers, he cost the then Magpies manager, Kevin Keegan, £4.5 million and many doubted whether he was worth it. However, it is important to reflect on the fact that Batty has been a linchpin in two championship winning sides at Leeds and Blackburn.

Batty has not only made central midfield his own at St James' Park but he's also forced his way into Glenn Hoddle's England set-up with some energetic and aggressive displays. Although capable of moving forward, he perhaps lacks the final killer pass or shot, preferring to move the ball on. His terrier-like tackling can go wrong against pacier opposition. As a result he picked up a few too many yellow cards last season, yet, surprising to many, his red card at Chelsea in the early part of 1997-98 was the first of his career.

Club	Season	Internationals	St	Sb	Tot
Leeds United	1990-91	USSR*, Arg, Aus, NZ, Mal	4	1	5
Leeds United	1991-92	Ger, Tur, Hun*, Fra, Swe	4	1	5
Leeds United	1992-93	Nor, SM, US, Bra	4	0	4
Blackburn R.	1993-94	Den*	0	1	1
Blackburn R.	1994-95	Jap, Bra	2	0	2
Newcastle U.	1996-97	Mol*, Geo, Ita, Mex, Geo, SAf*, Pol*, Fra	5	3	8
Newcastle U.	1997-98	Mol, Ita	2	0	2
		Total	21	6	27

BECKHAM, David   Manchester United

Full name: David Beckham
DOB: 02-05-75 Leytonstone

David Beckham will have passed his 24th birthday by the time the World Cup finals start and is an established regular in the England side. He will always be remembered for the goal that lifted him to fame around the world – at the start of the 1996-97 season when he lobbed Wimbledon's Neil Sullivan from the halfway line.

As a right-sided midfielder, Beckham is a hardworking and aggressive tackler as well as a precociously talented passer. He can also be dangerous at free kicks around the area and when whipping in corners. He sometimes has to occupy a wide right or wing-back style role for England that many say limits his ability to truly influence a game. Born in the east end of London, Beckham came through the ranks at Old Trafford and won the PFA Young Player of the Year Award for 1996-97. Had yet to score for England at the end of 1997.

Club	Season	Internationals	St	Sb	Tot
Manchester U.	1996-97	Mol, Pol, Geo, Ita, Geo, SAf*, Pol, Ita, Fra	8	1	9
Manchester U.	1997-98	Mol, Ita, Cam	3	0	3
		Total	11	1	12

BUTT, Nicky   **Manchester United**

Full name: Nicholas Butt
DOB: 21-01-75 Manchester

Made his debut for the full England team in the 1996-97 season and had taken his international appearance tally to three – all as a substitute – by the end of 1997.

This Mancunian fulfilled a boyhood dream by making the grade at Old Trafford from trainee, and has seized his chance in the United midfield following a long-term injury to Roy Keane. Butt has learned much from Keane in the Reds' midfield – especially in the tackle where one published statistic suggested he was successful in almost 80% of the tackles he goes into!

He is rarely in the headlines but his committed displays make him a big favourite with the United fans. Butt is a player with stamina and a fierce tackle. His distribution skills are now matched by his dangerous attacking runs which have helped earn him international recognition.

Club	Season	Internationals	St	Sb	Tot
Manchester U.	1996-97	Mex*, S.Af*	0	2	2
	1997-98	Mol•, Ita*	0	2	2
	Total		0	4	4

CAMPBELL, Sol   **Tottenham Hotspur**

Full name: Sulzeer Jeremiah Campbell
DOB: 18-09-74 Newham, London

The 1996-97 campaign may not have been one of the most memorable in the history of Tottenham Hotspur but for Sol Campbell it was a very important season: he established himself in the England set-up and looks set to be the main feature in both defences for many years to come.

Although renowned for his defensive capabilities, he has also revelled in a midfield position when required, for both club and country. An excellent reader of the game with a great tackling ability. Committed himself to Spurs at the end of the 1996-97 season, and if Spurs do maintain their life in the Premiership it will be in no small part due to their skipper.

Club	Season	Internationals	St	Sb	Tot
Tottenham H.	1995-96	Hun*, Sco*	0	2	2
Tottenham H.	1996-97	Geo, Ita, Geo, Pol, Fra, Bra	6	0	6
Tottenham H.	1997-98	Mol, Ita, Cam	3	0	3
	Total		9	2	11

COLE, Andy   **Manchester United**

Full name: Andrew Alexander Cole
DOB: 15-10-71 Nottingham

Prolific striker who caught the public's imagination in the 1993-94 season when he scored 34 league goals for Newcastle United. After a move to United, he at first failed to match his former strike rate until this season. Such has been his rekindled all-round form that he earned a call-up back into the England squad and earned his second cap against Italy in Le Tournoi last summer. Cole's return to form comes at the right time after two seasons in which he has had his fair share of injury and illness problems.

Cole was a trainee at Arsenal before playing for Fulham and Bristol City, transferring to Newcastle for £1.75 million. After firing home 34 Premiership goals in season 1993-94, he was surprisingly transferred to Old Trafford for £7 million. His five goals in the Premier League game against Ipswich Town in March 1995 remains a record.

Club	Season	Internationals		St	Sb	Tot
Manchester U.	1994-95	Uru*		0	1	1
	1996-97	Ita*		0	1	1
	Total			0	2	2

COLLYMORE, Stan   Aston Villa
Full name: Stanley Victor Collymore
DOB: 22-01-71 Stone
Collymore is big and powerful and his goals are often spectacular. However, his career has been blighted by an inability to realise his undoubted potential. He broke into the Premiership as a Nottingham Forest signing from Southend in 1994, and his 23 goals in 37 games in his first season prompted Liverpool to make him the most expensive British footballer at the time.

His time at Anfield was a curious mixture: despite averaging a goal every 2.5 games, he never really settled in to the Liverpool way so as to make a transfer back to his beloved Midlands simply a matter of time. Since then he has been inconsistent and must be considered an outsider for France '98.

Club	Season	Internationals		St	Sb	Tot
Nottingham F.	1994-95	Jap, Bra*		1	1	2
Aston Villa	1997-98	Mol*		0	1	1
	Total			1	2	3

FERDINAND, Les   Tottenham Hotspur
Full name: Leslie Ferdinand
DOB: 18-12-66 Acton
Les Ferdinand only came into the professional game late, playing his first regular season for QPR at the age of 23 following a move from non-league side Hayes. He had a loan spell in Turkey as well, with Besiktas. After 163 league games with Queens Park Rangers, Ferdinand shocked nobody when he moved to Newcastle in a £6 million transfer in the summer of 1995. Ferdinand has ably carried out the task of filling the shoes of Newcastle's prolific Andy Cole. Although Cole's season record has yet to be bettered, Ferdinand was certainly up there in that first season up north as he scored 25 league goals from just 37 appearances.

A change in managership at Tyneside saw Ferdinand move south to Tottenham where he found his season blighted by injury. Big and powerful, Ferdinand had scored five goals for England in his 14 appearances to the end of 1997.

Club	Season	Internationals		St	Sb	Tot
QPR	1992-93	SM, Hol, Nor, US		4	0	4
QPR	1993-94	Pol, SM		2	0	2
QPR	1994-95	US*		0	1	1
Newcastle U.	1995-96	Por, Bul, Hun		3	0	3

Newcastle U.	1996-97	Pol, Geo, Ita*		2	1	3
Tottenham H.	1997-98	Mol		1	0	1
	Total			12	2	14

FERDINAND, Rio — West Ham United

Full name: Rio Gavin Ferdinand
DOB: 07-11-78 London

Second cousin of Spurs striker Les, Rio Ferdinand is regarded as one of the best young talents in England. So much so that, after his early performances, the Hammers tied him to a highly lucrative five-year contract.

A commanding defender who is cool on the ball, he made his first team debut from the bench at the end of the 1995-96 season, and after a couple of early season positions on the subs bench he made his full team debut against Derby County. With Marc Rieper injured, he was regularly in the starting line-up during the latter part of the season, scoring twice in the process. Although normally occupying a central defensive role, Rio Ferdinand always looks comfortable on the ball and has great vision and distribution.

An England Youth and Under-21 international, he won his first international cap in the Wembley friendly against Cameroon in the tail-end of last year and he looks capable of establishing himself at the centre of his nation's defence for many years.

Club	Season	Internationals		St	Sb	Tot
West Ham U.	1997-98	Cam*		0	1	1
	Total			0	1	1

FLOWERS, Tim — Blackburn Rovers

Full name: Timothy David Flowers
DOB: 03-02-67 Kenilworth

Tim Flowers became Britain's most expensive goalkeeper when he moved to Ewood Park for £2.4 million from Southampton in 1993. In the last three seasons he has conceded just over one goal a game on average and has maintained a clean sheet in nearly 30% of his games. A great shot-stopper, like all top keepers he has an almost carefree attitude during games.

Not surprisingly, he has been a regular member of the England squad and briefly had the number-one spot before losing it to David Seaman. Having lost his number-two role for a while, he has shown enough form in the Blackburn goal recently to suggest he will be challenging once again.

Club	Season	Internationals		St	Sb	Tot
Southampton	1992-93	Bra		1	0	1
Blackburn R.	1993-94	Gre		1	0	1
Blackburn R.	1994-95	Ng, Uru, Jap, Swe, Bra		5	0	5
Blackburn R.	1995-96	Chn		1	0	1
Blackburn R.	1996-97	Ita		1	0	1
	Total			9	0	9

FOWLER, Robbie   **Liverpool**

Full name: Robert Bernard Fowler
DOB: 09-04-75 Liverpool

Robbie Fowler is one of the stars of the modern game with a special talent for scoring goals and a big-game temperament. He was top scorer in all competitions in 1996-97 with 31, 18 in the Premiership, including four against Middlesbrough, to take his total to 83, the fourth highest all-time.

A poacher, he is a natural goalscorer the way Liverpool like them. Quick over ten yards and with a powerful shot, Fowler looks certain to add to his England caps and his two England goals to date scored against Mexico and more recently Cameroon.

Club	Season	Internationals	St	Sb	Tot
Liverpool	1995-96	Bul*, Cro, Chn*, Hol*, Sp*	1	4	5
Liverpool	1996-97	Mex	1	0	1
Liverpool	1997-98	Cam	1	0	1
	Total		*3*	*4*	*7*

GASCOIGNE, Paul   **Rangers**

Full name: Paul Gascoigne
DOB: 27-05-67 Gateshead

Arguably England's most talented but also most volatile player, his creative talents in midfield are capable of unhinging even the best teams. He has experienced a chequered career both in club and international football and one that has been plagued by injury. A big-money move to Lazio in Rome was put on hold after he was injured in the early minutes of the 1991 Cup final. Further injuries hampered his career in Italy and it was no real surprise when he returned to the British Isles, where he has now committed his cause to Rangers.

He will be forever remembered for the tears he shed after being booked in the World Cup semi final in Italy against Germany – a booking that would have kept him out of the final had England made it. His goal against Scotland during Euro '96 was arguably the best of the tournament.

Gascoigne made his England debut against Denmark in 1988 and has scored ten goals in his 54 appearances to the end of 1997. He is sure to play a role during the World Cup finals.

Club	Season	Internationals	St	Sb	Tot
Tottenham H.	1988-89	Den*, SAr*, Alb*, Chi, Sco*	1	4	5
Tottenham H.	1989-90	Swe*, Bra*, Cz, Den, Uru, Tun, RIr, Hol, Eg, Bel, Cam, WG	10	2	12
Tottenham H.	1990-91	Hun, Pol, Cam	3	0	3
Lazio	1992-93	Nor, Tur, SM, Tur, Hol, Pol, Nor	7	0	7
Lazio	1993-94	Pol, Den	2	0	2
Lazio	1994-95	Jap*, Swe*, Bra*	0	3	3
Rangers	1995-96	Col, Swi, Por, Bul, Cro, Chn, Swi, Sco, Hol, Sp, Ger	11	0	11
Rangers	1996-97	Mol, Pol, Geo, S.Afr, Pol, Ita*, Fra, Bra	7	1	8
Rangers	1997-98	Mol, Ita, Cam	3	0	3
	Total		*44*	*10*	*54*

HINCHCLIFFE, Andy   Everton

Full name: Andrew George Hinchcliffe
DOB: 05-02-69 Manchester

Defender in his eighth season at Goodison Park, but has really come to the fore in recent seasons for the almost monotonous regularity with which his dead ball kicks hit their intended target. Particularly lethal at corners and contributed greatly to Everton's 1995 FA Cup victory. England Youth and Under-21 international who was first selected for the full international side by Glenn Hoddle against Moldova in the World Cup.

Injury has restricted his chances but there is no doubt that a fully fit Hinchcliffe will be in the frame for a place in the England starting line-up.

Club	Season	Internationals	St	Sb	Tot
Everton	1996-97	Mol, Pol, Geo	3	0	3
	1997-98	Cam	1	0	1
	Total		4	0	4

INCE, Paul   Liverpool

Full name: Paul Ince
DOB: 21-10-67 Ilford

Hard tackler and a fierce competitor, these two attributes often obscure the fact that Paul Ince is also an excellent footballer. Having been given the captaincy for the vital game in Rome against Italy, Ince was selected to represent Europe against the Rest of the World in the exhibition match prior to the draw for the finals.

He started his career at West Ham United, playing nearly 100 games for the Hammers before moving to Manchester United in the summer of 1989. While at Old Trafford he won his first England cap against Spain. After 200 senior games for United he moved to Internazionale, where he remained until last summer, returning to England to play for Liverpool. Has scored twice in his 35 England appearances to the end of 1997.

Club	Season	Internationals	St	Sb	Tot
Manchester U.	1992-93	Sp, Nor, Tur, Tur, Hol, Pol, US, Bra, Ger	9	0	9
Manchester U.	1993-94	Pol, Hol, SM, Den, Nor	5	0	5
Manchester U.	1994-95	Rom, RIr	2	0	2
Internazionale	1995-96	Bul, Cro, Hun, Swi, Sco, Hop, Ger	7	0	7
Internazionale	1996-97	Mol, Pol, Geo, Ita, Mex, Geo, Pol, Ita, Fra*, Bra	9	1	10
Liverpool	1997-98	Ita, Cam	2	0	2
	Total		34	1	35

KEOWN, Martin   Arsenal

Full name: Martin Raymond Keown
DOB: 24-07-66 Oxford

There was a time when Martin Keown was booed by Arsenal supporters when he found the ball at his feet. Now he is openly cheered – such have been his performances. It shouldn't really be a surprise then that he also found himself back in the England squad during 1997, even if it did end with a broken shoulder during the game with Brazil.

Keown is a player who has literally found his feet. A strong man-marker-cum-centre-half, he developed a flair for playing in midfield under Bruce Rioch.

Now in his second spell at Arsenal, having cost the club ten times the £200,000 fee they received for him when they brought him back to Highbury from Everton in 1993. Has scored three goals in his 15 England appearances.

Club	Season	Internationals	St	Sb	Tot
Everton	1991-92	Fra, Cz, CIS, Hun, Bra, Fi, Den, Fe, Swe	9	0	9
Arsenal	1992-93	Hol, Ger*	1	1	2
Arsenal	1996-97	Mex, SAf, Ita, Bra	4	0	4
	Total		14	1	15

LE SAUX, Graeme   Chelsea

Full name: Graeme Pierre Le Saux
DOB: 17-10-68 Jersey

Graeme Le Saux is one of those players that even opposing fans like. A skilful attacking full or wing-back, he suffered a serious injury in December 1995 when he broke his ankle and ruptured tendons when playing against Middlesbrough. The injury kept him out until October 1996, when he made his comeback at West Ham.

He quickly re-established himself not only in the Rovers side but also in the England team. Following rumours of discontent at Ewood Park, he found himself transferred back to Chelsea at the start of the season. A fine crosser of the ball, especially at speed.

Club	Season	Internationals	St	Sb	Tot
Blackburn R.	1993-94	Den, Gre, Nor	3	0	3
Blackburn R.	1994-95	US, Rom, Ng, RIr, Uru, Swe, Bra	7	0	7
Blackburn R.	1995-96	Col, Por*	1	1	2
Blackburn R.	1996-97	Ita, Mex, Geo, SAf, Pol, Ita, Fra, Bra	8	0	8
Chelsea	1997-98	Ita	1	0	1
	Total		20	1	21

LE TISSIER, Matthew   Southampton

Full name: Matthew Paul Le Tissier
DOB: 14-10-68 Guernsey

The first thing manager Dave Jones did on his arrival at the Dell was to ensure 'Le God' (as he is known on the south coast) signed a new four-year contract. He is a Saints player through and through and it looks as though football supporters in general will never know just how good he might have been at a top side. When he plays, there are few better club players in the world and his England recall by Glenn Hoddle just hyped up the Le Tissier – England debate.

Guernsey's most famous export, Le Tissier's goals are spectacular and the majority have probably come from the edge or outside of the area. Tap-ins are simply not his style. Had he been born in South America he would almost certainly have won more than his eight caps to the end of 1997.

Club	Season	Internationals	St	Sb	Tot
Southampton	1993-94	Den*, Gre*, Nor*	0	3	3
Southampton	1994-95	Rom, Ng*, RIr	2	1	3

| Southampton | 1996-97 | Mol*, Ita | 1 | 1 | 2 |
| | Total | | 3 | 5 | 8 |

LEE, Robert   Newcastle United

Full name: Robert Martin Lee
DOB: 01-02-66 West Ham

Signed by Kevin Keegan from Charlton Athletic for £700,000 in September 1992 as a right winger, the London-born player has transformed into an effective attacking midfield player. He joined Charlton on a free transfer from non-league side Hornchurch in the summer of 1983, and played over 300 senior games for the south-London side.

He was an important part of the Division One championship winning side and first captained Newcastle in 1994-95. He scored on his England debut against Romania in 1995 and continues to be one of the key midfield players in the international squad, especially since he links with Shearer and Batty at club level.

Club	Season	Internationals	St	Sb	Tot
Newcastle U.	1994-95	Rom, Ng	2	0	2
Newcastle U.	1995-96	Col*, Nor, Swi, Bul*, Hun	3	2	5
Newcastle U.	1996-97	Mex, Geo, SAf, Pol, Fra*, Bra*	4	2	6
Newcastle U.	1997-98	Cam*	0	1	1
	Total		9	5	14

McMANAMAN, Steve   Liverpool

Full name: Steven McManaman
DOB: 11-02-72 Bootle

Originally a winger, McManaman has more recently played a free role in front of the midfield. Now with 19 caps for England, there's no better sight than international defences retreating in the face of a McManaman marauding run. He hasn't got the killer instinct of a striker but takes his chances while setting up even more.

He picks up his share of bookings but seems to dodge injury in the same way that he dodges defenders. Has yet to establish himself under Glen Hoddle but his recent club form has been exceptional and led to rumours of multi-million bids from Italy and Spain.

Club	Season	Internationals	St	Sb	Tot
Liverpool	1994-95	Ng*, Uru*, Jap*	0	3	3
Liverpool	1995-96	Col, Nor, Swi, Por*, Bul, Cro, Chn, Swi, Sco, Hol, Sp, Ger	11	1	12
Liverpool	1996-97	Pol, Ita, Mex	3	0	3
Liverpool	1997-98	Cam	1	0	1
	Total		15	4	19

MARTYN, Nigel   Leeds United

Full name: Nigel Anthony Martyn
DOB: 11-08-66 St Austell

Enjoyed a personally outstanding first season with Leeds United last season following a £2.25 million move from Crystal Palace to Elland Road in the summer of 1996. Missed just one game for United during 1996-97 and, with 20 clean sheets, including a run of four consecutive games without conceding a goal, he forced his way back into contention for a place in the England squad. His 20 clean sheets represent the second-best record of any keeper since the launch of the Premiership. One-time goalkeeper with non-leaguers St. Blazey, he played 340 games for Bristol Rovers and Palace before signing for Leeds.

Club	Season	Internationals	St	Sb	Tot
Crystal Palace	1991-92	CIS*, Hun	1	1	2
Crystal Palace	1992-93	Ger	1	0	1
Leeds United	1996-97	SAf	1	0	1
Leeds United	1997-98	Cam	1	0	1
	Total		4	1	5

MERSON, Paul   Middlesbrough
Full name: Paul Charles Merson
DOB: 20-03-68 Harlesden

As a player and a person Merson has experienced the highs and lows of life. He won a host of honours with Arsenal under George Graham. *The Merse* then went through a period of drug rehabilitation which saw him not only return to top form with Arsenal, but also re-establish himself in the England squad. It was a shock when Arsenal allowed him to move to Middlesbrough at the start of the 1997-98 season, but his form with the Teeside club has been such that he has been selected for the England squad despite playing in the First Division.

A forward-cum-midfield player, Merson loves to run at defences, cutting in from the left and often firing home great goals. He made his first England appearance as a substitute against Germany in 1991-92.

Club	Season	Internationals	St	Sb	Tot
Arsenal	1991-92	Ger*, Cz, Hun, Bra*, Fi*, Den, Swe*,	3	4	7
Arsenal	1992-93	Sp*, Nor*, Hol*, Bra*, Ger	1	4	5
Arsenal	1993-94	Hol, Gre	2	0	2
Arsenal	1996-97	Ita*	0	1	1
	Total		6	9	15

NEVILLE, Gary   Manchester United
Full name: Gary Alexander Neville
DOB: 18-02-75 Bury

Neville G, a product of the Reds' successful youth policy, established himself as a regular in the United side halfway through the 1994-95 season and has since completed full seasons as a regular.

In the same season he broke into the United side, Neville made his full England debut against Japan in the Umbro Cup. He has made regular appearances for England, at right-back and in central defence when required. His performances in Euro '96 illustrated his skill and assurance. His looping crosses and excellent long throw contribute to the attacking options.

Club	Season	Internationals	St	Sb	Tot
Manchester U.	1994-95	Jap, Bra	2	0	2

Manchester U.	1995-96	Col, Nor, Swi, Por, Bul, Cro, Hun,			
		Chn, Swi, Sco, Hol, Sp	12	0	12
Manchester U.	1996-97	Mol, Pol, Ita, Geo, Pol, Ita*, Fra, Bra*	6	2	8
Manchester U.	1997-98	Mol	1	0	1
	Total		21	2	23

NEVILLE, Phil   Manchester United

Full name: Philip John Neville
DOB: 21-01-77 Bury

The younger brother of Gary, this 20-year-old can play anywhere across the back four at Old Trafford. Philip Neville has made remarkable progress from trainee and a couple of games in 1994-95, to regular in both the United and England set-up.

The youngster suffered a career setback midway through the 1996-97 season when glandular fever struck. He has since recovered and along with big brother he looks sure to make the England squad for the World Cup finals.

Club	Season	Internationals	St	Sb	Tot
Manchester U.	1996-97	SAf, Pol*, Ita, Fra, Bra	4	1	5
Manchester U.	1997-98	Mol, Cam	2	0	2
	Total		6	1	7

PALLISTER, Gary   Manchester United

Full name: Gary Andrew Pallister
DOB: 30-06-65 Ramsgate

Alex Ferguson paid a record £2.3 million for Pallister in 1989, and the ex-Middlesbrough player, after a shaky start, formed a solid partnership with Steve Bruce which amazingly never transferred to the England central defence.

At 6' 4" not too many strikers can cause him problems in the air and he is quick on the turn. When available, Pallister has shown great form this season, but once again has been dogged by injury.

Club	Season	Internationals	St	Sb	Tot
Middlesbrough	1987-88	Hun	1	0	1
Middlesbrough	1988-89	SAr	1	0	1
Manchester U.	1990-91	Cam*, Tur	1	1	2
Manchester U.	1991-92	Ger	1	0	1
Manchester U.	1992-93	Nor, US, Bra, Ger	4	0	4
Manchester U.	1993-94	Pol, Hol, SM, Den	4	0	4
Manchester U.	1994-95	US, Rom, RIr, Uru, Swe	5	0	5
Manchester U.	1995-96	Nor, Swi	2	0	2
Manchester U.	1996-97	Mol, Pol*	1	1	2
	Total		20	2	22

PEARCE Stuart   Newcastle United

Full name: Stuart Pearce
DOB: 24-04-62 Hammersmith

A vastly experienced player, there can be few football supporters who did not come to admire his willingness to step up and fire home a penalty against Germany in the semi finals of Euro '96 – that just six years after missing one against the same team at the same stage of the World Cup finals in Italy.

43

No one player more typifies English football than Stuart Pearce. A ferocious left back who packs a wicked free kick, Pearce started in non-league football with Wealdstone. The bulk of his professional career was spent at Nottingham Forest, to whom he showed great loyalty when they were relegated at the end of 1996-97. However, he earned a surprise move to Newcastle United during last summer and might have been an ever-present in Kenny Dalglish's side but for injury.

Club	Season	Internationals	St	Sb	Tot
Nottingham F.	1987	Bra, Sco	2	0	2
Nottingham F.	1987-88	WG*, Isr, Hun	2	1	3
Nottingham F.	1988-89	Den, Swe, SAr, Gre, Alb, Alb, Chi, Sco, Pol, Den	10	0	10
Nottingham F.	1989-90	Pol, Ita, Yug, Bra, Cz, Den, Uru, Tun, RIr, Hol, Eg, Bel, Cam, WG	14	0	14
Nottingham F.	1990-91	Hun, Pol, RIr, RIr, Cam, Tur, Arg, Aus, NZ, NZ, Mal	11	0	11
Nottingham F.	1991-92	Tur, Pol, Fra, Cz, Bra*, Fi, Den, Fra, Swe	8	1	9
Nottingham F.	1992-93	Sp, Nor, Tur	3	0	3
Nottingham F.	1993-94	Pol, SM, Gre*	2	1	3
Nottingham F.	1994-95	Rom*, Jap, Bra	2	1	3
Nottingham F.	1995-96	Nor, Swi, Por, Bul, Cro, Hun, Swi, Sco, Hol, Sp, Ger	11	0	11
Nottingham F.	1996-97	Mol, Pol, Ita, Mex, SAf, Ita	6	0	6
	Total		72	4	76

REDKNAPP, Jamie   Liverpool

Full name: Jamie Frank Redknapp
DOB: 25-06-73 Barton on Sea

The talented midfielder has established himself as a key figure in the Liverpool set-up. Unfortunately, after putting in an ever-present performance in 1994-95, he suffered injuries to restrict his availability in the seasons since.

Son of West Ham boss Harry, Redknapp was signed by Kenny Dalglish in 1991 from Bournemouth. He was selected for Terry Venables' England squad for Euro '96. Glen Hoddle has him pencilled in as England sweeper if he can get injury free.

Well known for his passing abilities, and skill, teams fear Jamie's ability from set pieces, particularly free kicks within range of the goal.

A fractured ankle kept Redknapp out of contention for the first half of the 1997-98 season following an injury against Scotland in Euro '96, when he virtually turned the game England's way.

Club	Season	Internationals	St	Sb	Tot
Liverpool	1995-96	Col, Nor, Swi, Chn, Sco*	4	1	5
Liverpool	1996-97	Mex*, Geo*, SAf	1	2	3
	Total		5	3	8

RIPLEY, Stuart   Blackburn Rovers

Full name: Stuart Edward Ripley
DOB: 20-11-67 Middlesbrough

A flying winger with tight control and the ability to deliver driven crosses from the right, Ripley's success at Middlesbrough earned him a move to Blackburn. He was another key player in the Rovers' championship side, a fact that earned him his first England cap against San Marino back in 1994.

Having struggled to find his form and get amongst the goals, the arrival of Roy Hodgson at Ewood Park seems to have resparked his career. His form has been such that he earned a recall to the England squad for the penultimate World Cup game against Moldova. It ended disappointingly though: having come on as a sub for Beckham after 67 minutes, he picked up an injury after just nine minutes.

Club	Season	Internationals	St	Sb	Tot
Blackburn R.	1993-94	SM	1	0	1
Blackburn R.	1997-98	Mol*	0	1	1
	Total		1	1	2

SCHOLES, Paul   Manchester United
Full name: Paul Scholes
DOB: 16-11-74 Salford

The 1996-97 season started slowly for Paul Scholes but finished at whirlwind pace. Having been confined to the subs bench for much of the first part of the season, the ginger-haired striker finally got into his club side and enjoyed a run of ten successive games over the Christmas period. At the other end when the dust was settling on another United Premiership title, Scholes found himself playing against Italy in France and scoring a sensational goal for England and making his partner Ian Wright's goal.

Scholes signed for United as a trainee in July 1991 and first broke into their first team during the 1994-95 season. He still hasn't quite managed to secure a regular spot in the Reds' side despite his England call-up. Goals against Moldova and Cameroon increased his tally to three for England – a good return from five games and just four starts for England up to the end of 1997.

Club	Season	Internationals	St	Sb	Tot
Manchester U.	1996-97	SAf*, Ita, Bra	2	1	3
Manchester U.	1997-98	Mol, Cam	2	0	2
	Total		4	1	5

SEAMAN, David   Arsenal
Full name: David Andrew Seaman
DOB: 19-09-63 Rotherham

Now established as England's number one, he missed a significant part of Arsenal's 1996-97 season through injury. An ever-present in 1995-96, his calmness and almost jocular manner instill confidence in the defence in front of him.

During Euro '96 he was arguably England's best player and has built a reputation as an ace penalty saver especially on the big occasions, his stops taking England to a semi final spot in 1996 and Arsenal to a Cup-Winners' Cup Final in 1996.

He is widely regarded as one of the world's best keepers and the debate as to whether he or Peter Schmeichel is best will continue. Played for Peterborough, Birmingham and QPR before joining the Gunners in May 1990. Has played over 600 games and holds the Arsenal record for goalkeeper appearances.

Club	Season	Internationals	St	Sb	Tot
QPR	1988-89	SAr, Den*	1	1	2
QPR	1989-90	Cz*	0	1	1
Arsenal	1990-91	Cam, RIr, Tur, Arg	4	0	4
Arsenal	1991-92	Cz, Hun*	1	1	2
Arsenal	1993-94	Pol, Hol, SM, Den, Nor	5	0	5
Arsenal	1994-95	US, Rom, RIr	3	0	3
Arsenal	1995-96	Col, Nor, Swi, Por, Bul, Cro, Hun, Swi, Sco, Hol, Sp, Ger	12	0	12
Arsenal	1996-97	Mol, Pol, Geo, Geo, Pol, Fra, Bra	7	0	7
Arsenal	1997-98	Mol, Ita	2	0	2
	Total		35	3	38

SHEARER, Alan   Newcastle United

Full name: Alan Shearer
DOB: 13-08-70 Newcastle

Became the world's most expensive player when he signed for Newcastle prior to the start of the 1996-97 season but suffered a long-term injury on the opening day of the 1997-98 season.

Appointed as England captain by Glenn Hoddle, Shearer is a mobile six-foot centre-forward in the classic mould. Just one of his outstanding records is the seven consecutive Premiership games – between September 14th and November 30th 1996 – in which he scored goals. He was the first top-flight player to fire in 30 Premiership goals in three successive seasons, and became the first player to score 100 goals in the Premier League.

He is renowned for an unselfish philosophy that it's not important if he scores so long as the team wins, plus the respect which his utter professionalism earns him amongst other players. He scored in four out of England's five games in Euro '96, taking the Golden Boot award.

Club	Season	Internationals	St	Sb	Tot
Southampton	1991-92	Fra, CIS, Fra	3	0	3
Blackburn R.	1992-93	Sp, Nor, Tur	3	0	3
Blackburn R.	1993-94	Hol, Den, Gre, Nor	4	0	4
Blackburn R.	1994-95	US, Rom, Ng, RIr, Jap, Swe, Bra	7	0	7
Blackburn R.	1995-96	Col, Nor, Swi, Por, Hun*, Chn, Swi, Sco, Hol, Sp, Ger	10	1	11
Newcastle U.	1996-97	Mol, Pol, Ita, Geo, Pol, Fra, Bra	7	0	7
	Total		34	1	35

SHERINGHAM, Teddy   Manchester United

Full name: Edward Paul Sheringham
DOB: 02-04-66 Walthamstow

International class striker whose reputation was wholly enhanced by Euro '96 when he linked to deadly effect with Alan Shearer. He joined Spurs in August 1992 and he was an ever-present in the Tottenham side during the 1994-95 and 1995-96 seasons. He has a distinctive style of play which often involves linking midfield and attack. Often criticised for a lack of pace, Alan Shearer defended him by saying that he had two yards of extra pace in his head. A highly intelligent player and terrific passer of the ball, he ended his association with Spurs at the end of June 1997, joining Manchester United for £3.5 million.

Despite being 32, he looks to have a number of seasons ahead of him at the top flight and his performances will be key to England doing well in the World Cup finals.

Club	Season	Internationals	St	Sb	Tot
Tottenham H.	1992-93	Pol, Nor	2	0	2
Tottenham H.	1994-95	US, Rom*, Ng*, Uru, Jap*, Swe, Bra,	4	3	7
Tottenham H.	1995-96	Col*, Nor*, Swi, Bul, Cro, Hun, Swi,			
		Sco, Hol, Sp, Ger	9	2	11
Tottenham H.	1996-97	Geo, Mex, Geo, SAf, Pol, I, Fra*, Bra	7	1	8
Manchester U.	1997-98	Ita	1	0	1
	Total		23	6	29

SOUTHGATE, Gareth   Aston Villa

Full name: Gareth Southgate
DOB: 03-09-70 Watford

Will always be remembered for that penalty miss against Germany in the semi final of Euro '96. Southgate remains one of the best central defenders in England. Having started his career as a trainee with Crystal Palace, his performances in their 1994-95 relegation side earned him a requested move to Villa Park and the chance to continue to play at the top level. His performances quickly earned him his England call-up and he won his first cap in December 1995 against Portugal.

Since that point he has been plagued by nagging injuries. A knee injury forced him to miss the 1996 Coca Cola win and he has been continually troubled by a recurrent ankle problem.

Club	Season	Internationals	St	Sb	Tot
Aston Villa	1995-96	Por*, Bul, Hun*, Chn, Swi, Sco, Hol, Sp, Ger	7	2	9
Aston Villa	1996-97	Mol, Pol, Geo, Mex, Geo*, SAf, Pol,			
		Ita, Fra, Bra	9	1	10
Aston Villa	1997-98	Mol, Ita, Cam	3	0	3
	Total		19	3	22

SUTTON, Chris   Blackburn Rovers

Full name: Christopher Roy Sutton
DOB: 10-03-73 Nottingham

Sutton was a member of what was regarded as the SAS in the Blackburn Rovers Premiership winning side. Shearer And Sutton – a potent attacking force that could yet feature in France. Yet Sutton started life at Norwich as a defender and, having converted to a free-scoring attacker, moved to Blackburn Rovers for £5 million. He scored 15 goals in the championship-winning campaign but has been troubled by injury since. The 1997-98 season has seen him come back to form and earned him his first cap against Cameroon towards the end of 1997.

Club	Season	Internationals	St	Sb	Tot
Blackburn R.	1997-98	Cam*	0	1	1
	Total		0	1	1

WALKER, Ian   Tottenham Hotspur

Full name: Ian Michael Walker
DOB: 31-10-71 Watford

A dip in confidence and form has seen the Tottenham goalkeeper's place as backup
to David Seaman in the England goal put in doubt. Having established himself as a
contender for the number-one shirt, he suffered a number of set-backs, not least
criticism for Italy's goal at Wembley in the World Cup qualifier. Has missed just a
handful of games for Tottenham in the past few seasons and made his 200th
appearance for Spurs during the 1997-98 season.

Club	Season	Internationals	St	Sb	Tot
Tottenham H.	1995-96	Hun*, Chn*	0	2	2
	1996-97	Ita	1	0	1
	Total		1	2	3

WRIGHT, Ian   Arsenal

Full name: Ian Edward Wright
DOB: 03-11-63 Woolwich

Love him or hate him, there can be no denying Ian Wright's talent as a goalscorer.
He became Arsenal's all-time top scorer when he notched a typical hat-trick against
Bolton Wanderers early in the 1997-98 season. His third goal then was also his
100th in the Premiership.

He started his career at Crystal Palace and came on in their Cup Final defeat to
Manchester United and nearly turned the game in their favour. A real bundle of
speed and skill, he will always try the unexpected that inevitably leads to some
thrilling goals.

At 34 he is one of the oldest attackers in the Premiership and his total
commitment to the cause invariably leads to cautions and subsequent suspensions –
something that hit him hard last season.

Has often struggled to score for England, and four of his nine goals to the end of
1997 came against San Marino in 1994. Was arguably England's best player during
the 0-0 draw in Rome.

Club	Season	Internationals	St	Sb	Tot
Crystal Palace	1990-91	Cam, RIr*, USSR, NZ	3	1	4
Arsenal	1991-92	Hun*	0	1	1
Arsenal	1992-93	Nor, Tur, Tur, Pol*, Nor*, US*, Bra, Ger*	4	4	8
Arsenal	1993-94	Pol*, Hol*, SM, Gre*, Nor*	2	3	5
Arsenal	1994-95	US*, Rom	1	1	2
Arsenal	1996-97	Geo*, Ita*, Mex*, SAf, Ita, F, Bra	4	3	7
Arsenal	1997-98	Ita	1	0	1
	Total		15	13	28

Key to teams:

Arg	Argentina	Ger	Germany	Rom	Romania
Aus	Austria	Gre	Greece	SAf	South Africa
Bra	Brazil	Hol	Holland	SAr	Saudi Arabia
Bul	Bulgaria	Hun	Hungary	Sco	Scotland
Cam	Cameroon	Isr	Israel	SM	San Marino
Chi	Chile	Ita	Italy	Sp	Spain
Chn	China	Jap	Japan	Swe	Sweden
CIS	CIS	Mex	Mexico	Swi	Switzerland
Col	Colombia	Mol	Moldova	Tur	Turkey
Cro	Croatia	Ng	Nigeria	Uru	Uruguay
Cz	Czechoslovakia	Nor	Norway	US	USA
Den	Denmark	NZ	New Zealand	USSR	USSR
Fi	Finland	Pol	Poland	WG	West Germany
Fra	France	Por	Portugal	Yug	Yugoslavia
Geo	Georgia	RIr	Rep.Ireland		

*Substitute appearance.

NATIONAL TEAM DIRECTORY

Introduction

The following pages contain a complete guide to the 32 national teams who qualified for France '98. The countries are listed alphabetically and each entry is arranged as follows:

General: National information including foundation and affiliation dates, address and contact numbers, colours and key personnel.

Review: Outline of the nation's progress to the finals.

Results: Details of all games played by the nation on the road to qualification. Includes date, opponents, venue, result, attendance and scorers with times of goals.

Appearances: Details of players used during each nation's qualifying games. Players are listed alphabetically by surname and forenames and/or nicknames are provided where used. Tot=Total appearances (St+sub); St=Starting appearances (indicates number of times the player started the game); Sub=Substitute appearances (the number of times a player came into the game as a substitute); PS=Player Substituted (the number of times a player was substituted in the games).

Head-to-Head: The heading indicates the first-round group the nation has been drawn. The text lists details of the three first-round games with venue and kick-off time (BST). Note that times are subject to change due to TV requirements. Details of any games played in previous World Cups between the group opponents are then given.

WC Record: Indicates how the nation performed in previous World Cup competitions. This is followed by a PWDLFA analysis of World Cup performance.

Notebook: Where space permits, this gives interesting details relating to previous and current World Cup campaigns.

ARGENTINA

Asociación Del Fútbol Argentino
Founded: 1893   **Affiliations:** Conmebol – 1916. FIFA – 1912
Address: Viamonte 1366/76,1053 Buenos Aires
Phone: +54 1/371 4276   **Fax:** +54 1/375 4410
National Stadium: Antonio Liberti de Nunez (76,000)
Colours: Light Blue and White vertical striped shirts, Black shorts, White socks
Coach: Daniel Passarella   **Key Players:** Gabriel Batistuta, Roberto Ayala

Problems Abound

Although Argentina finished top of the CONMEBOL group, their performances in the first half of the games were far from convincing and, had it not been for a run of good if somewhat narrow victories during the second half of games, they may have struggled to qualify for the finals for the first time since 1970.

Coach Daniel Passarella came under fire from many quarters, not least for his decision to leave the record Argentine goal scorer Gabriel Batistuta out of not only the team but the Argentine squad for nearly ten months. The Argentine coach argued that he was incompatible with Hernan Crespo, but personal differences and in particular Batistuta's refusal to have his hair cut short (!) seemed to be the main factors. Indeed, Passarella's insistence that his players have short hair may yet cause problems for the former World Cup-winning captain.

Having started with a home win over Bolivia, defeat by Ecuador and draws against Peru and Paraguay left the Argentines stuttering. A 5-2 win over Venezuela was followed by two further draws and a defeat by Bolivia that was punctuated only by a win in Colombia. With the vultures flying, a home win over Ecuador in May 1997 saw a turn in fortunes and five successive wins and two draws ensured qualification for the finals.

Many of those early problems were down to Passarella's search for a goalkeeper. With four players taking and failing to capture the position, Carlos Roa showed enough form to earn him the nod as his country's number one. Real Madrid midfielder Fernando Redondo – perhaps Argentina's most gifted player – remains out in the wilderness. He has not played since Passarella took over as coach in 1995 and looks likely to miss out on the finals, having further refused to shed his locks. Redondo, playing alongside the gifted Juan Sebastian Veron and Ariel Ortega, could make the difference for the team. Without him, Argentina may negotiate their group but probably won't get much further. But then Passarella never had respect for skill even as a player.

CONMEBOL Results

Date	Opponents	Ven	Result	Att	Scorers
24.04.96	Bolivia	H	3-1	60,000	Ortega (8, 18); Batistuta (49)
02.06.96	Ecuador	A	0-2	30,000	
07.07.96	Peru	A	0-0	45,000	
09.09.96	Paraguay	H	1-1	40,000	Batistuta
09.10.96	Venezuela	A	5-2	30,000	Ortega (35); Sorin (68), Simeone (77); Morales (86); Albornoz (90)
15.12.96	Chile	H	1-1	60,000	Batistuta (70 pen)
12,01.97	Uruguay	A	0-0	68,000	
12.02.97	Colombia	A	1-0	68,000	C. Lopez (9)
02.04.97	Bolivia	A	1-2	45,000	Garosito (43)
30.04.97	Ecuador	H	2-1	65,000	Ortega (17); Crespo (32)
08.06.97	Peru	H	2-0	70,000	Crespo (45); Simeone (47)
06.07.97	Paraguay	A	2-1	48,000	Gallardo (30); Veron (41)
20.07.97	Venezuela	H	2-0	47,000	Crespo (30); Paz (56)
10.09.97	Chile	A	2-1	80,000	Gallardo (25); C. Lopez (85)
12.10.97	Uruguay	H	0-0	55,000	
16.11.97	Colombia	H	1-1	40,000	Caceres (68)

Scorers: 4– Ortega; 3 – Batistuta, Crespo; 2 – Gallardo, C. Lopez, Simeone; 1– Albornoz, Caceres, Morales, Gorosito, Paz, Sorin, Veron

Sent Off: Berizzo v Colombia (away 66 min); Diaz v Paraguay (away 87 min); Vivas v Bolivia (away 44 min); Zapata v Bolivia (away 81 min)

Group H Opponents Head-to-Head

14 June	Argentina v Japan	Toulouse	1.30 pm
21 June	Argentina v Jamaica	Paris	4.30 pm
26 June	Argentina v Croatia	Bordeaux	3.00 pm

The seeds in Group H, Argentina break new ground, having never played any of their opponents at any stage of the World Cup.

World Cup Notebook

- Argentina have featured in four finals, coming out winners on two occasions and beating finalists on the other two occasions.
- Gabriel Batistuta is Argentina's top international goal scorer. By the end of the qualifying competition he had increased his tally to 39 goals and should add to it during the finals in France.
- Argentina's biggest win in the finals came on home soil in 1978 when they beat Peru 6-0. It was a game they had to win by six goals to ensure qualification for the next stage of the competition!

CONMEBOL Appearances

Name	Tot	St	Sub	PS
Albornoz, Josi	3	2	1	1
Almeyda, Matias	12	12	0	0
Astrada, Leonardo	2	2	0	1
Ayala, Roberto	12	12	0	1
Balbo, Abel	3	1	2	0
Bassedas, Christian	4	2	2	1
Batistuta, Gabriel	7	7	0	2
Berizzo, Eduardo	4	3	1	0
Berti, Sergio	6	2	4	2
Borelli	1	0	1	0
Bossio, Carlos	1	1	0	0
Burgos, German	2	2	0	0
Caceres, Fernando	3	3	0	0
Cagna, Diego	1	1	0	1
Calderon, Josi Luis	2	0	2	0
Camps, Patricio	1	0	1	0
Caniggia, Claudio	3	3	0	2
Cardoso, Rodolfo	1	0	1	0
Cavallero, Pablo	2	2	0	0
Chamot, Jose	9	9	0	0
Crespo, Hernan	10	7	3	5
Cruz, Julio	1	1	0	0
Delgado, Marcelo	1	1	0	1
Diaz, Herman	5	5	0	0

Name	Tot	St	Sub	PS
Esnaider	1	0	1	0
Gallardo	4	4	0	4
Gonzalez, Ignacio Carlo				
	3	3	0	0
Gorosito, Nestor	2	2	0	2
Lopez, Claudio	12	8	4	4
Lopez, Gustavo	2	0	2	0
Molina, Roberto	1	0	1	0
Morales, Hugo	7	6	1	3
Ortega, Ariel	15	13	2	4
Passet, Oscar	1	1	0	0
Paz, Pablo	9	6	3	0
Posse	1	0	1	0
Riquelme	1	0	1	0
Roa, Carlos Angel	7	7	0	0
Schelotto, Guillermo	1	1	0	1
Sensini, Nestor	12	12	0	1
Simeone, Diego	13	13	0	1
Sorin, Juan	4	3	1	0
Veron, Sebastian	9	7	2	1
Vivas, Nelson	4	3	1	1
Zanetti, Javier	9	7	2	2
Zapata, Gustavo	2	2	0	0

World Cup Record

Year	Stage Reached
1930	Runners-up
1934	First Round
1938	Did not enter
1950	Did not enter
1954	Did not enter
1958	First Round
1962	First Round
1966	Quarter Final

Year	Stage Reached
1970	Did not qualify
1974	Second Round
1978	Winners
1982	Second Round
1986	Winners
1990	Runners-up
1994	Second Round

Competition	P	W	D	L	F	A
World Cup Finals	52	26	9	17	90	65
World Cup Qualifiers	48	28	12	8	87	44
World Cup Total	100	54	21	25	177	109

AUSTRIA

Österreichischer Fussball-Bund
Founded: 1904   **Affiliations:** UEFA – 1954. FIFA – 1905
Address: Meiereistr., Ernst Happel-Stadion, Sektor A/F, A-1021, Vienna
Phone: +43 1/727 18   **Fax:** +43 1/728 16 32
National Stadium: Ernst Happel-Stadion (47,500)
Colours: White shirts, Black shorts, Black socks
Coach: Herbert Prohaska
Key Players: Toni Polster, Andrea Herzog

Veteran Performances

Austria surprised many by qualifying automatically for the World Cup finals, especially in a group that contained favourites Sweden and Scotland. But eight wins from ten games proved enough for a team that relied heavily on the form of the veterans Toni Polster and Andrea Herzog, and the goals of the former.

Austrian coach Herbert Prohaska seems to have been in charge of the Austrian reigns for ever and a day – in a career that saw Austria humbled by the Faeroe Islands in 1990 and defeated by Northern Ireland to deny them a place in Euro '96. In fact, Prohaska has kept faith in a side that has changed little in that time, perhaps preferring to rely on the Law of Averages to ensure qualification. In truth, Austria have qualified largely because of their commitment to the cause rather than flair.

A goalless draw at home to Scotland got their qualifying campaign underway and was then lifted by a win in Sweden thanks to a solitary goal by Herzog, who like Polster plies his trade in the Bundesliga in Germany. A win in Latvia was followed by defeat in Scotland. That defeat saw the start of a five-match-winning run, including another one-goal win over Sweden before two wins against Belarus and automatic qualification after the first.

While Polster (Austria's all-time top scorer) and Herzog have been ever presents and will carry the lion's share of Austria's hopes, there is new talent waiting in the wings and not least in goalkeeper Michael Konsel who typifies the spirit in the Austrian camp and will look to build on the seven clean sheets he kept during the qualifying games.

Date	Opponents	Ven	Result	Att	Scorers
31.08.96	Scotland	H	0-0	29,500	
09.10.96	Sweden	A	1-0	36,859	Herzog (12)
09.11.96	Latvia	H	2-1	15,700	Polster (43); Herzog (74)
02.04.97	Scotland	A	0-2	43,295	
30.04.97	Estonia	H	2-0	27,500	Vastic (48); Stöger (87)
08.06.97	Latvia	A	3-1	7,000	Heraf (55); Polster (81); Stöger (85)
20.08.97	Estonia	A	3-0	1,500	Polster (47, 70, 90)
06.09.97	Sweden	H	1-0	48,000	Herzog (76)
10.09.97	Belarus	A	1-0	25,000	Pfeifenberger (50)
11.10.97	Belarus	H	4-0	48,000	Polster (3pen, 16); Stöger (6, 42)

Scorers: 7 – Polster, 4 – Stöger, 3 – Herzog, 1 – Heraf , Pfeifenberger, Vastic

Sent Off: Konsel v Estonia (away 82 mins); Pfeffer v Sweden (home 41 mins)

Name	Tot	St	Sub	PS	Name	Tot	St	Sub	PS
Aigner, Franz	1	1	0	1	Pfeffer, Anton	9	9	0	0
Cerny, Harald	6	6	0	3	Pfeifenberger, Heimo	5	4	1	0
Feiersinger, Wolfg.	8	8	0	0	Polster, Toni	10	10	0	1
Hatz, Michael	1	0	1	0	Prilasnig, Gilbert	4	4	0	1
Heraf, Andreas	6	6	0	0	Ramusch, Dieter	5	1	4	1
Herzog, Andreas	10	10	0	5	Reinmayr, Hannes	1	0	1	0
Hutter, Adolf	3	2	1	1	Sabitzer, Herfried	1	0	1	0
Kartalija, Goran	1	1	0	0	Schopp, Markus	6	4	2	1
Kogler, Walter	5	3	2	0	Schöttel, Peter	8	8	0	2
Konsel, Michael	9	9	0	0	Stöger, Peter	9	4	5	3
Kühbauer, Dietmar	5	4	1	0	Vastic, Ivica	6	5	1	3
Marasek, Stefan	1	1	0	0	Wetl, Arnold	5	5	0	1
Mdhlich, Roman	4	4	0	0	Wohlfahrt, Franz	2	1	1	0
Ogris, Andreas	2	0	2	0					

Group B Opponents Head-to-Head

11 June	Cameroon v Austria	Toulouse	8.00 pm
17 June	Chile v Austria	Saint Etienne	4.30 pm
23 June	Italy v Austria	Saint Denis	3.00 pm

Austria have never played Cameroon or Chile at any stage of the World Cup; they have however encountered Italy in the finals on three occasions with the Italians winning all by a single goal. The most recent encounter came in Rome during the first round of the 1990 finals. The Italians won with a second-half goal from Toto Schillaci and another single goal defeat by Czechoslovakia put paid to any hopes Austria had of progressing to the second stage, although the competition did finish on a small high with a 2-1 win over the USA. The previous two meetings came in 1934 and 1978. That first win denied Austria a place in the 1934 final itself, Guaita's goal being decisive against the much fancied 'Wunderteam' of Hugo Meisl. In 1978 the stage was the quarter finals in a game where the Italians were at their cynical height. Despite dominating the game the Austrians lost to a sensational goal early in the first half from Rossi.

Yr	Round	Opponents	Result	Scorers
1934	Semi Final	Italy	0-1	–
1978	Quarter Final	Italy	0-1	–
1990	First Round	Italy	0-1	–

World Cup Record

Year	Stage Reached	Year	Stage Reached
1930	Did not enter	1970	Did not qualify
1934	Semi Final (4th Place)	1974	Did not qualify
1938	Qualified but withdrew	1978	Quarter Final
1950	Did not enter	1982	Quarter Final
1954	Semi Final (3rd Place)	1986	Did not qualify
1958	First Round	1990	First Round
1962	Withdrew	1994	Did not qualify
1966	Did not qualify		

Competition	P	W	D	L	F	A
World Cup Finals	26	12	2	12	40	43
World Cup Qualifiers	72	37	15	20	134	71
World Cup Total	98	49	17	32	174	114

World Cup Notebook

- For goals Austria rely heavily on the combination of Herzog and Polster – in only two of their Group 4 games did one of these fail to get on the score sheet.
- When Austria take the field with Chile in Saint Etienne on 17 June it will be their 100th game in the World Cup.
- Austria need one more win in World Cup competition to record their 50th victory.
- Austria's two biggest wins in the World Cup finals came in the 1954 finals when they defeated Czechoslovakia 5-0 in the first round and Switzerland 7-5 in the quarter final. Their 6-1 defeat by Germany in the semi-final that year remains their biggest defeat in the finals.
- Only two Austrian players have managed hat-tricks in the World Cup finals and both came in the victories mentioned above. Wagner notched his against Czechoslovakia and Probst's came against hosts Switzerland.
- Austria have played in six previous World Cup finals (see above); they also qualified for one other but then withdrew prior to the finals (1938).

BELGIUM

Union Royal Belge des Sociétés de Football-Association
Founded: 1895   **Affiliations:** UEFA – 1954. FIFA – 1904
Address: Avenue Houba de Strooper 145, B-1020 Bruxelles
Phone: +32 2/477 12 11   **Fax:** +32 2/478 23 91
National Stadium: Roi Baudoin, Brussels (40,000)
Colours: Red shirts, Red shorts, Red socks
Coach: Georges Leekens
Key Players: Luc Nilis, Luis Oliveira

Double Dutch Again

Belgium will point to the record books which show they have qualified for their fifth successive World Cup finals. The manner of their qualification may indicate that it will be a short stay in France. Certainly it was ironic that they should find themselves in the same group as their Benelux neighbours Holland who disposed of them so convincingly when they were paired in the same UEFA qualifying group.

Belgium, though, did achieve something that the Dutch didn't in qualifying – two wins over the Turks. But it was their two three-goal defeats by Holland that killed off any chance they had of automatic qualification. Their patchy form came to the fore in their two play-off games with Ireland in which they were far from convincing. Indeed, only against the minnows of San Marino in the Group 7 games did Belgium look anything other than uninspiring.

The 1998 finals may be a swan-song for what is an ageing team. Francky Van Der Elst is past 36 but is capable of turning in good performances, as is Enzo Scifo, if fit. Whether these players can last the pace in the heat of Marseilles remains to be seen and a lot will depend on the non-stop running of Lorenzo Staelens.

In Luis Oliveira, Belgium's top scorer in qualifying, they do possess a player who has the ability to turn defences at pace and with great balance and he provides a complementary foil for the powerful Luc Nilis, who plays in Holland for PSV Eindhoven.

However, the biggest task facing manager Georges Leekens may be finding a settled side. He used no less than 38 players during their ten qualifying games and only eight of those featured in five or more games. There may lie the problem.

Date	Opponents	Ven	Result	Att	Scorers
31.08.96	Turkey	H	2-1	35,000	Degryse (13); Luis Oliveira (38)
09.10.96	San Marino	A	3-0	1,353	Verheyen (11); Nilis (20, 47)
14.12.96	Holland	H	0-3	36,500	
29.03.97	Wales	A	2-1	15,000	Crasson (24); Staelens (44)
30.04.97	Turkey	A	3-1	29,000	Luis Oliveira (12, 31, 45)
07.06.97	San Marino	H	6-0	22,000	Staelens (16, 85); Van Meir (26); L. Mpenza (27, 45); Luis Oliveira (33)
06.09.97	Holland	A	1-3	45,000	Staelens (67pen)
11.10.97	Wales	H	3-2	34,000	Staelens (4pen); Claessens (32); Wilmots (39)

Play-Off

29.10.97	Rep. Ireland	A	1-1	32,305	Nilis (30)
15.11.97	Rep. Ireland	H	2-1	35,320	Luis Oliveira (25); Nilis (68)

Scorers: 6 – Luis Oliveira; 5 – Staelens; 4 – Nilis; 2 – L. Mpenza;
1 – Verheyen, Crasson, Van Meir, Claessens, Wilmots

Sent Off: Renier v Holland (home 50 min)

Name	Tot	St	Sub	PS	Name	Tot	St	Sub	PS
Albert, Philippe	2	2	0	0	Medved, Dirk	2	2	0	0
Boffin, Danny	3	3	0	0	Mpenza, Lokonda	4	4	0	4
Borkelmans, Vital	2	0	2	0	Mpenza, Mbo	1	0	1	0
Claessens, Gert	2	2	0	2	Nilis, Luc	6	5	1	2
Claeys, Geoffrey	1	1	0	0	Oliveira, Luis	9	9	0	3
Crasson, Bertrand	6	6	0	2	Peiremans, Frederic	1	0	1	0
De Bilde, Gilles	4	0	4	0	Pierre, Frederic	2	0	2	0
De Boeck, Glen	1	1	0	0	Renier, Pascal	3	3	0	0
De Roover, Albert	4	4	0	1	Schepens, Gunther	3	2	1	2
De Wilde, Filip	10	10	0	0	Scifo, Enzo	4	3	1	0
Deflandre, Eric	3	3	0	1	Smidts, Rudy	4	3	1	1
Degryse, Marc	3	3	0	1	Staelens, Lorenzo	7	7	0	0
Doll, Olivier	1	0	1	0	Van Der Elst, Franky	7	7	0	1
Genaux, Regis	2	1	1	0	Van Kerchoven, Nico	9	6	3	1
Goossens, Michael	2	1	1	1	Van Meir, Eric	6	6	0	0
Haagdoren, Filip	1	0	1	0	Verheyen, Gert	4	3	1	2
Jbari, Nordin	1	0	1	0	Verstraeten, Mike	3	2	1	0
Lemoine, Dominique	3	2	1	0	Vidovic, Gordan	4	4	0	1
Leonard, Phillipe	3	2	1	1	Wilmots, Marc	3	3	0	0

Group E Opponents Head-to-Head

13 June	Holland v Belgium	Saint Denis	8.00 pm
20 June	Mexico v Belgium	Bordeaux	4.30 pm
25 June	Belgium v South Korea	Paris	3.00 pm

Belgium have faced all their Group E opponents in the finals before and although they have only met the Dutch once before in the finals they have had some epic battles with them in the qualifying stages of the competition. The most recent of these was in Group 7 of this tournament's preliminaries and details can be found on the previous page. Belgium's record against the Dutch in the qualifiers is poor and they have won just two of their 12 encounters. In the 1994 finals, though, the Belgians got the upper hand in Orlando thanks to a goal from Philippe Albert. With two defeats at the hands of the Mexicans already, Belgium will be looking to make it third time lucky, while the sole encounter with South Korea went with the Belgians.

Yr	Round	Opponents	Result	Scorers
1970	First Round	Mexico	0-1	
1986	First Round	Mexico	1-2	Van Der Bergh
1990	First Round	South Korea	2-0	De Gryse, De Wolf
1994	First Round	Holland	1-0	Albert

World Cup Record

Year	Stage Reached	Year	Stage Reached
1930	First Round	1970	First Round
1934	First Round	1974	Did not qualify
1938	First Round	1978	Did not qualify
1950	Did not enter	1982	Second Round
1954	First Round	1986	Semi Final (4th place)
1958	Did not qualify	1990	Second Round
1962	Did not qualify	1994	Second Round
1966	Did not qualify		

Competition	P	W	D	L	F	A
World Cup Finals	29	9	4	16	37	53
World Cup Qualifiers	83	47	16	20	160	94
World Cup Total	112	56	20	36	197	147

World Cup Notebook

- Belgium's first ever international match was a 3-3 draw against hosts France.
- Their best ever performance came in 1986 when they reached the semi final, only to be knocked out 2-0 by Argentina. Maradona scored twice.
- Belgium need three goals in France to reach the 200 mark in World Cup games.

BRAZIL

Confederação Brasileira De Futebol
Founded: 1914   **Affiliations:** Conmebol – 1916. FIFA – 1923
Address: Rua de Alfandega, 70, P.O. Box 1078, 20.070-001 Rio De Janeiro
Phone: +55 21/509 5937   **Fax:** +55 21/252 9294
National Stadium: Maracana (200,000)
Colours: Yellow with green collar/cuffs shirts, Blue shorts,
         White with green-yellow border socks.
Coach: Mario Zagallo   **Key Players:** Ronaldo, Roberto Carlos

Punter's Choice

Brazil will arrive in France as every punter's choice to retain the World Cup they
won in Pasadena four years ago, not least because their record throughout 1997 was
simply the best. With only two defeats in the previous four years, 1997 came to a
close on the back of 20 games which included 19 wins and a single goalless draw
following what may be a pertinent defeat in Norway at the end of May.

Despite being spared the marathon South American World Cup qualifying
competition, Brazil have been playing at least as often as its rivals with no less than
24 games in venues all around the world. The Brazilians' form has been awesome.

1997 saw Mario Zagallo's team play in the Copa America, the Le Tournoi and
the Confederation Cup in Saudi Arabia. The competitive Copa and Confederation
cups were won with ten wins and one draw in 11 games. The Copa America games
were perhaps the most impressive as the Brazilians won six games in a row, scoring
22 goals, and beating hosts Bolivia at 12,000 feet in the final.

Brazil's only other defeat since the last World Cup was in a 2-0 reverse to
Mexico in the final of the 1996 Gold Cup. However, they refuse to recognise the
Mexico game as a full international, claiming that they fielded an Under-23 team.
FIFA lists the game as a full international because it was the final of a recognised
competition. Interestingly, it was Mexico who gave Brazil the most problems in the
Confederation Cup.

Brazil are contesting their 15th straight World Cup and on paper look to have
the strength to move out of their group without too many problems. However, they
will be wary of Norway – the only team to beat them in 1997 when they produced a
famous performance in Oslo in May 1997.

Despite being the favourites, Brazil have never won the World Cup in Europe
and in Le Tournoi in France last summer could manage only one win (a 1-0 win
over the already crowned tournament winners England) and two draws. Added to
that defeat in Oslo, the Brazilians' record in games in Europe, when taken out of
their overall record for the year, is not so impressive. What they do have in their
favour, though, is the increasing number of players based in Europe – and that
could become a significant factor come France '98.

Results and Appearances 1997

Date	Opponents	Ven	Result	Att	Scorers

Copa America – held in Bolivia

Date	Opponents	Ven	Result	Att	Scorers
13.06.97	Costa Rica	G	5-0	32,000	Djalminha (23); OG (35); Ronaldo (48, 49); Romario (60)
16.06.97	Mexico	G	3-2	35,000	Aldair (48); Romario (62); Leonardo (80)
19.06.97	Colombia	G	2-0	30,000	Dunga (11); Edmundo (67)
22.06.97	Paraguay	QF	2-0	35,000	Ronaldo (17, 34)
26.06.97	Peru	SF	7-0	20,000	Denilson (2); F.Conceciao (28); Romario (36, 48); Leonardo (45, 61); Djalminha (78)
29.06.97	Bolivia	F	3-1	46,000	Edmundo (37); Ronaldo (79); Ze Roberto (90)

Group (G) and QF, SF games in Santa Cruz. Final in La Paz.

Scorers: 5 – Ronaldo ; 4 – Romario; 3 – Leonardo; 2 – Djalminha, Edmundo; 1 – Aldair, Denilson, Dunga, Flavio Conceciao, Ze Roberto, OG

Sent Off: Flavio Conceciao v Mexico (Santa Cruz 89 min)

Name	Tot	St	Sub	PS	Name	Tot	St	Sub	PS
Aldair	6	6	0	0	Goncalves	5	5	0	0
Cafu	5	5	0	2	Leonardo	6	6	0	3
Celio Silva	1	1	0	0	Mauro Silva	3	1	2	0
Cesar Sampaio	1	0	1	0	Paulo Nunes	1	0	1	0
Denilson	5	4	1	0	Roberto Carlos	5	5	0	0
Djalminha	3	2	1	2	Romario	5	5	0	1
Dunga	6	6	0	2	Ronaldo	6	6	0	2
Edmundo	4	1	3	1	Taffarel	6	6	0	0
Flavio Conceicao	5	5	0	1	Ze Maria	3	1	2	0
Giovanni	1	0	1	0	Ze Roberto	3	1	2	0

Above goals and apperances refer to Copa America matches only.

Confederation Cup – held in Riyadd Saudi, Arabia

Date	Opponents	Res	Att	Scorers

Group A

Date	Opponents	Res	Att	Scorers
12.12.97	Saudi Arabia	3-0	50,000	Cesar Sampaio (65); Romario (74, 81)
14.12.97	Australia	0-0	11,000	
16.12.97	Mexico	3-2	20,000	Romario (41pen); Denilson (59); Junior Baiano (66)

Semi Final

Date	Opponents	Res	Att	Scorers
19.12.97	Czech Rep.	2-0	28,000	Romario (54); Ronaldo (83)

Final

Date	Opponents	Res	Att	Scorers
21.12.97	Australia	6-0	65,000	Ronaldo (15, 28, 59); Romario (38, 53, 75pen)

World Cup Record

Year	Stage Reached	Year	Stage Reached
1930	First Round	1970	Winners
1934	First Round	1974	Semi Final (4th Place)
1938	Semi Final	1978	Semi Finals (3rd Place)
1950	Runners-up	1982	Second Round
1954	Quarter Final	1986	Quarter Final
1958	Winners	1990	Second Round
1962	Winners	1994	Winners
1966	First Round		

Competition	P	W	D	L	F	A
World Cup Finals	73	49	13	11	159	68
World Cup Qualifiers	38	29	8	1	99	15
World Cup Total	111	78	21	12	258	83

Group A Opponents Head-to-Head

10 June	Brazil v Scotland	Saint Denis	4.30 pm
16 June	Brazil v Morocco	Nantes	8.00 pm
23 June	Brazil v Norway	Marseilles	8.00 pm

Morocco and Norway will provide new World Cup opponents for Brazil, although both featured in friendly games during 1997. Norway recorded a significant 4-2 win in Oslo while two late goals by Denilson gave Brazil a 2-0 home win. There have been three encounters with the Scots, all in the first-round group stages. The 1974 encounter was goalless largely because the Brazilians for once lacked players capable of converting numerous chances. Goals were easier to come by eight years later, and although the teams were level at 1-1 at the interval, three second-half goals saw the Brazilians comfortably through. In 1990 a goal eight minutes from time by Muller won the day after a blunder by Jim Leighton in the Scots' goal.

Yr	Round	Opponents	Result	Scorers
1974	First Round	Scotland	0-0	
1982	First Round	Scotland	4-1	Zico, Oscar, Eder, Falcao
1990	First Round	Scotland	1-0	Muller

World Cup Notebook

- Brazil have won the World Cup four times – the only country to do so, and they are the only country to have appeared in every World Cup finals.
- Brazil have only ever lost one World Cup qualifying game – that came in the run-up to the 1994 competition when Bolivia beat them 2-0.
- Brazil's 159 goals in the finals is more than any other team and in 1994 they became the only nation to win the trophy via a penalty shoot-out!
- When Brazil win their first game of the 1998 finals, it will be their 50th win in the World Cup finals.

BULGARIA

Bulgarski Futbolen Soius
Founded: 1923   **Affiliations:** UEFA – 1954. FIFA – 1924
Address: Karnigradska 19, Boite postale 559, BG-1000 Sofia
Phone: + 359 2/87 74 90   **Fax:** +359/2 80 32 37
National Stadium: Stadion Vasilij Levski (55,000)
Colours: White shirts, Green shorts, Red socks
Coach: Hristo Bonev
Key Players: Emil Kostadinov, Trifon Ivanov

Ageless Wonders

Bulgaria may be a team of thirtysomethings but they still possess enough skill and guile to make them a threat to their Group D opponents. Their team is still largely the one that delighted neutrals on their way to the semi finals of USA '94, a trip which included a famous quarter-final win over Germany. If that was their high, then the low came in Euro '96 when they flopped and coach Dimitar Penev was sacked. Hristo Bonev was appointed coach but the team that made it to these finals is still largely the one selected by his predecessor.

Success in UEFA Group 5 wasn't guaranteed, with Russia pushing them all the way. The first of two group defeats came in the opening game in Israel despite an early opening lead established by the ever creative Balakov. In their next game in Luxembourg, Bulgaria struggled to victory by getting the best of three goals having been pulled back to 1-1. The performances improved with wins over Cyprus (twice) and in the return legs against Luxembourg and Israel. The calendar then brought on Russia, with the first game ensuring Bulgaria's qualification thanks to Trifon Ivanov's second-half winner. The return game in Moscow, a 4-2 win for Russia, was academic.

Having slid further down the FIFA rankings, the likes of Hristo Stoichkov, Emil Kostadinov, Yordan Lechkov and Trifon Ivanov will need to rediscover their USA form if they are to have a serious chance of progressing to the second stage. If they do it may be as far as they progress and mark the end of an era in Bulgarian football.

UEFA Group 5 Results and Appearances

Date	Opponents	Ven	Result	Att	Scorers
01.09.96	Israel	A	1-2	13,200	Balakov (3)
08.10.96	Luxembourg	A	2-1	3,800	Balakov (14pen); Kostadinov (37)
14.12.96	Cyprus	A	3-1	16,000	Balakov (23, 34); Iliev (70)
02.04.97	Cyprus	H	4-1	33,000	Borimirov (2); Kostadinov (36, 45); Yordanov (66)
08.06.97	Luxembourg	H	4-0	22,000	Stoichkov (42 pen); Kostadinov (47); Balakov (50pen); Lechkov (81)
20.08.97	Israel	H	1-0	25,000	Penev (68)
10.09.97	Russia	H	1-0	60,000	T. Ivanov (55)
11.10.97	Russia	A	2-4	20,000	Gruyev (68); Kostadinov (78)

Scorers: 5 – Balakov, Kostadinov; 1 – Iliev, Yordanov, Stoichkov, Lechkov, Penev, T. Ivanov, Gruyev, Borimirov

Sent Off: Vassilev v Luxembourg (away 59 min)

Name	Tot	St	Sub	PS	Name	Tot	St	Sub	PS
Adonov, Ivaylo	2	1	1	0	Lechkov, Yordan	6	4	2	1
Antonov, Gueorgui	1	1	0	1	Mihaylov, Borislav	3	3	0	1
Balakov, Krassimir	7	7	0	0	Mitov, Dobromir	1	0	1	0
Borimirov, Daniel	6	2	4	2	Nankov, Anatoli	4	3	1	0
Donkov, Georgi	3	3	0	3	Penev, Luboslav	4	3	1	1
Gruyev, Ilia	1	0	1	0	Petkov, Ivaylo	4	4	0	1
Guinchev, Gocho	4	3	1	0	Stoichkov, Hristo	4	4	0	2
Hristov, Marian	1	1	0	1	Trendafilov, Mitko	1	0	1	0
Hubchev, Petar	1	1	0	0	Tzvetanov, Tzanko	3	3	0	0
Iankov, Zlatko	7	7	0	0	Vassilev, Ivan	1	0	1	0
Illiev, Ilian	6	4	2	2	Vidolov, Kostadin	3	0	3	0
Ivanov, Georgi	1	1	0	0	Yordanov, Ivailo	5	5	0	0
Ivanov, Trifon	8	8	0	0	Zafirov, Adalbert	1	1	0	0
Kischuchev, Radostin	7	7	0	1	Zdravkov, Zdravko	6	5	1	0
Kostadinov, Emil	8	7	1	2					

Group D Opponents Head-to-Head

12 June	Paraguay v Bulgaria	Montpellier	1.30 pm
19 June	Nigeria v Bulgaria	Paris	4.30 pm
24 June	Spain v Bulgaria	Lens	8.00 pm

Surprisingly, Bulgaria have never encountered Spain at any stage of the World Cup. Their only previous encounter with any of their group matches came in 1994 when they were defeated 3-0 by Nigeria in the Dallas Cotton Bowl in the first round. Yekeni, Amokachi and Amunike scored the goals. Stoichkov thought he had produced an equaliser, with Nigeria leading 1-0, when he thundered home a 30-yard free kick, but it was disallowed because referee Badilla had clearly signalled for an indirect free kick.

Yr	Round	Opponents	Result	Scorers
1994	First Round	Nigeria	0-3	

World Cup Record

Year	Stage Reached	Year	Stage Reached
1930	Did not enter	1970	First Round
1934	Did not qualify	1974	First Round
1938	Did not qualify	1978	Did not qualify
1950	Did not enter	1982	Did not qualify
1954	Did not qualify	1986	Second Round
1958	Did not qualify	1990	Did not qualify
1962	First Round	1994	Semi Final (4th Place)
1966	First Round		

Competition	P	W	D	L	F	A
World Cup Finals	23	3	7	13	21	46
World Cup Qualifiers	79	41	12	26	133	104
World Cup Total	102	44	19	39	154	150

World Cup Notebook

- Prior to USA '94, Bulgaria had never won a match in the World Cup finals. That record looked set to continue when they lost 3-0 to Nigeria in their opening match but their first ever World Cup finals win came in the next game when they beat Greece 4-0.
- Bulgaria were the only UEFA team to qualify directly for the finals who had lost more than one group match – they lost two, away to Israel and Russia.
- Bulgaria's most capped player is also their top international goal scorer. Hristo Bonev represented his country 96 times and scored 47 goals – that's almost a goal every other game!
- In the 1998 qualifying tournament Ivan Vassilev came on as a half-time substitute in Luxembourg. His game lasted just 14 minutes, though, when he was sent off…

CAMEROON

Fédération Camerounaise De Football
Founded: 1959   **Affiliations:** CAF – 1963. FIFA – 1962
Address: B.P. 1116, Yaoundé
Phone: +237 20 25 38   **Fax:** +237 22 24 30
National Stadium: Omisport (70,000)
Colours: Green shorts, Red shorts, Yellow socks
Coach: Jean Managa Onguene
Key Players: Patrick Mboma, Jacques Songo'o

Lion Hearts

When Cameroon beat Zimbabwe 2-1 in Harare last August they became the
first African team to qualify for three successive World Cup finals and
equalled Morocco's record of a fourth appearance in the finals. It would
appear that Cameroon are here to stay, although it did not look that way after
a poor showing in the 1994 finals and an equally bad display in the 1996
African Nations Cup finals.

The indomitable Lions surprised many of their critics by finishing
unbeaten in their CAF Group 5, culminating in that 2-1 win in Zimbabwe
which was also significant in elevating Patrick Mboma to top scorer for his
team and one to watch in France '98. The 27 year old plays for Japanese first
division side Gamba Osaka and produced two stunning strikes early in the
second half to fire his team to the finals.

But in truth, despite the high-note ending, the early stages showed all the
doubt that had plagued the Cameroons previously. After Togo were
dispatched 4-2 a goalless draw at home to Angola left them in desperate need
to take home field advantage over Zimbabwe in the six-match group. The win
came thanks to the individual skill of Bernard Tchoutang. Two goals in the
final three minutes then secured the points against strugglers Togo before a
draw with nearest rivals Angola all but ensured qualification.

This time around Cameroon do not possess the likes of the charismatic
Roger Milla or Emmanuel Kunde to help them through, although Tchoutang
and Fotso Ndjitap are highly competitive in midfield and 19 year old Joseph-
Desire Job promises to be a talented strike partner for Mboma. A vital
position could be goalkeeper Jacques Songo'o, who plays for Deportivo La
Coruna and kept net for the Rest of the World XI in their win over Europe
prior to the draw for the World Cup finals.

CAF Group 4 Results and Appearances

Date	Opponents	Ven	Result	Att	Scorers
10.11.96	Togo	A	4-2	20,000	Tchami (18, 30, 53); Misse-Misse (68)
12.01.97	Angola	H	0-0	75,000	
06.04.97	Zimbabwe	H	1-0	50,000	Tchoutang (82)
27.04.97	Togo	H	2-0	25,000	Tchoutang (87); Mboma (90)
08.06.97	Angola	A	1-1	60,000	Mboma (54)
17.08.97	Zimbabwe	A	2-1	15,000	Mboma (49, 57)

Scorers: 4 – Mboma; 3 – Tchami; 2 – Tchoutang; 1 – Misse-Misse

Name	Tot	St	Sub	PS	Name	Tot	St	Sub	PS
Bella, Cyrille	1	0	1	0	Moreau, Fabrice	2	2	0	1
Billong, Aimie	2	1	1	0	Moukoko, Simon	1	0	1	0
Embe, David	1	0	1	0	Ndjitap, Geremie Fotso				
Epalle, Joel Dieudonni						5	4	1	0
	2	0	2	0	Ndongo, Mpessa	1	0	1	0
Etchi	1	1	0	0	Oman Biyick, Frangois				
Foe, Marc Vivien	3	3	0	0		1	1	0	1
Kalla Kongo, Raymond					Ousmandou, Sanda	1	1	0	0
	6	6	0	0	Simo, Augustine	1	0	1	0
Mangam, Cyrille	4	3	1	2	Song, Rigobert	6	6	0	0
Mboma, Henri Patrick					Songo'o, Jacques	6	6	0	0
	6	6	0	1	Tchami, Alphonse	5	5	0	5
Mimboe, Bayard	6	6	0	0	Tchango, Joseph	3	1	2	1
Misse-Misse, Jean-Jacques					Tchoutang, Bernard	5	5	0	1
	5	3	2	1	Wome, Pierre	6	6	0	1

Group B Opponents Head-to-Head

11 June	Cameroon v Austria	Toulouse	8.00 pm
17 June	Italy v Cameroon	Montpellier	8.00 pm
23 June	Chile v Cameroon	Nantes	3.00 pm

Cameroon have encountered only one of their opponents before, drawing 1-1 with Italy in the 1982 World Cup finals. The game was the final one in Group 1 of the first round and Italy needed a point from the game to qualify for the second round. Graziani headed them into the lead on the hour only for M'Bida to fire an immediate equaliser. That's the way it stayed and Italy ousted Cameroon from the competition in Spain by virtue of the fact that they had scored one more goal.

Yr	Round	Opponents	Result	Scorers
1982	First Round	Italy	1-1	M'Bida

World Cup Record

Year	Stage Reached		Year	Stage Reached
1930-1966	Did not enter		1982	First Round
1970	Did not qualify		1986	Did not qualify
1974	Did not qualify		1990	Quarter Final
1978	Did not qualify		1994	First Round

Competition	P	W	D	L	F	A
World Cup Finals	11	3	4	4	11	21
World Cup Qualifiers	39	20	10	9	61	36
World Cup Total	50	23	14	13	72	57

World Cup Notebook

- Cameroon have qualified for the finals more often than any other African team – the 1998 World Cup will be their fourth appearance in the finals.
- Roger Milla is perhaps Cameroon's best-known player of all time. He featured in three finals and in 1994 became, at the age of 42, the oldest man to play in the finals. His goal against Russia also makes him the oldest scorer in the World Cup finals!
- Cameroon's first appearance in the World Cup came in Spain in 1982 when they drew 0-0 with Peru.

CHILE

Federación De Fútbol De Chile
Founded: 1895   **Affiliations:** Conmebol – 1916. FIFA – 1912
Address: Avenida Quil'n No. 5635, Casilla Nº 3733, Correo Central, Santiago
Phone: +56 2/284 9000   **Fax:** +56 2/284 3510
National Stadium: Estadiuo Nacional (74,000)
Colours: Red with white collar & cuffs shirts, Blue shorts, White socks
Coach: Nelson Acosta
Key Players: Marcelo Salas, Ivan Zamorano

No Difference

Not since 1982 have Chile qualified for the World Cup finals and in recent
attempts they have been surrounded by controversy. They were banned by
FIFA from the 1994 tournament following an incident during the qualifying
tournament for the 1990 event. Trailing 1-0 to Brazil in Rio, they left the
pitch after claiming that goalkeeper Roberto Rojas, who was carried off on a
stretcher apparently covered in blood, had been hit by a firework that had
been thrown from the crowd. The subsequent FIFA investigation reported that
he had feigned the injury by bursting open a capsule containing blood.

The 1998 finals come as the team look to put their somewhat chequered
past behind them. But the problems were still there this time around, not least
when a players' strike threatened to disrupt preparations for the team's crucial
final two games which also saw 12-goal striker Ivan Zamorano out with a calf
injury. Those last two games came off the back of a 2-1 home defeat by
Argentina. Despite the problems, a total of seven goals were fired past Peru
and Bolivia in Santiago as Chile edged out Peru on goal difference for the
final fourth CONMEBOL qualifying position.

Goals were never a problem for the Chilean team, who thumped 32 past
their round robin opponents, the highlight of which was probably the 4-1
defeat of Colombia. In Zamorano they possess the South American group's
top scorer whose twelve strikes (which included five against Venezuela) was
only one more than the highly talented and highly rated River Plate player
Marcelo Salas. The performance of these two strikers may well hold the key
for how well Chile can perform. Chile also have another potentially great
striker in their midst – the relatively unknown Sebastian Rozental whose knee
problems have limited his chances with Rangers who he signed for over a
year ago for £3.5 million. However, the other key that may unlock their own
door might well be their poor disciplinary record which saw five players sent
off during their qualifying games.

CONMEBOL Results

Date	Opponents	Ven	Result	Att	Scorers
02.06.96	Venezuela	A	1-1	8,074	Margas (89)
07.07.96	Ecuador	H	4-1	69,000	Zamorano (25, 86); Salas (75); Estay (83)
01.09.96	Colombia	A	1-4	34,000	Zamorano (56)
09.10.96	Paraguay	A	1-2	45,000	Margas (22)
12.11.96	Uruguay	H	1-0	66,237	Salas (60)
15.12.96	Argentina	A	1-1	59,970	Cornejo (52)
12.01.97	Peru	A	1-2	35,373	Zamorano (88)
12.02.97	Bolivia	A	1-1	41,908	Gonzalez (44)
29.04.97	Venezuela	H	6-0	42,324	Zamorano (19, 27, 32, 47, 85); Reyes (66)
08.06.97	Ecuador	A	1-1	42,225	Salas (53)
05.07.97	Colombia	H	4-1	75,000	Salas (15, 27, 41); Zamorano (90)
20.07.97	Paraguay	H	2-1	75,143	Zamorano (8pen, 47)
20.08.97	Uruguay	A	0-1	40,000	
10.09.97	Argentina	H	1-2	80,000	Salas (34)
12.10.97	Peru	H	4-0	75,000	Salas (13, 82, 90); Reyes (59)
16.11.97	Bolivia	H	3-0	75,000	Barrera (24); Salas (41); Carreno (85)

Scorers: 12 – Zamorano; 11 – Salas; 2 – Margas, Reyes; 1– Barrera, Carreno, Cornejo, Estay, Gonzalez

Sent Off: C.Castaneda v Ecuador (home 77 min) v Paraguay (home 64 min); Sierra v Colombia (away 89 min); Chavarria v Argentina (away 78 min); Fuentes v Uruguay (away 61 min)

Group B Opponents Head-to-Head

11 June	Italy v Chile	Bordeaux	4.30 pm
17 June	Chile v Austria	Saint Etienne	4.30 pm
23 June	Chile v Cameroon	Nantes	3.00 pm

Chile have met Italy twice in World Cup competition and have won one and lost one. Both games resulted in 2-0 wins. In 1962, Chile won on home soil in a first-round match thanks to late goals from Ramirez and Toto. The match was a violent affair and became known as 'The Battle of Santiago' and Italy played much of the game with ten men and most of the second half with just nine after Ferrini and David were dismissed by English referee Ken Aston. The game finally ended in a brawl. Italy gained revenge at Sunderland's Roker Park in 1966 with Mazzola and Barison scoring.

The only World Cup meeting between Chile and Austria came in Spain in 1982 with a solitary strike from Schachner deciding the game in Oviedo. The game in Nantes on 23 June will be the first encounter between Chile and Cameroon.

Yr	Round	Opponents	Result	Scorers
1962	First Round	Italy	2-0	Ramirez, Toro
1966	First Round	Italy	0-2	
1982	First Round	Austria	0-1	

CONMEBOL Appearances

Name	Tot	St	Sub	PS	Name	Tot	St	Sub	PS
Acuna, Clarence	7	7	0	1	Parraguez, Nelson	2	1	1	0
Barrera, Rodrigo	2	2	0	2	Perez, Luis	1	1	0	1
Basay, Ivo	1	0	1	0	Ponce, Miguel	6	6	0	1
Carreno, Juan	2	0	2	0	Puentes	1	1	0	0
Castaneda, Christian	13	13	0	1	Ramirez, Marcelo	2	2	0	0
Castaneda, Victor	9	7	2	5	Ramirez, Miguel	1	1	0	0
Chavarria, Luis	3	3	0	0	Reyes, Pedro	11	11	0	0
Contreras, Wilson	6	2	4	0	Riveros, Jamie	2	1	1	1
Cornejo, Fernando	8	5	3	0	Rojas, Ricardo	3	3	0	1
Estay, Fabian	4	2	2	1	Romero, Christian	1	1	0	0
Flores, Cristian	1	0	1	0	Rozental, Sebastian	5	3	2	3
Fuentes, Ronald	8	8	0	0	Ruiz, Rodrigo	1	0	1	0
Goldberg, Rodrigo	3	0	3	0	Salas, Marcelo	12	12	0	2
Gonzalez, Juan Carlos	5	2	3	0	Sierra, JoseLuis	7	5	2	3
Gonzalez, Pedro	3	2	1	1	Tapia, Nelson	14	14	0	0
Lee Chong, Oscar	1	0	1	0	Valencia, Esteban	6	2	4	1
Margas, Javier	12	12	0	1	Vega, Marcelo	10	9	1	8
Mendoza, Gabriel	1	1	0	0	Vergara, Fernando	2	2	0	1
Miranda, Marcelo	6	5	1	0	Vilches, Edvardo	1	1	0	0
Mora, Christian	6	4	2	0	Villattoel, Moises	1	0	1	0
Musrri, Luis	11	11	0	3	Zamorano, Ivan	11	10	1	1
Nunez, Claudio	3	1	2	1					

World Cup Record

Year	Stage Reached	Year	Stage Reached
1930	First Round	1970	Did not qualify
1934	Did not enter	1974	First Round
1938	Did not enter	1978	Did not qualify
1950	First Round	1982	First Round
1954	Did not enter	1986	Did not qualify
1958	Did not qualify	1990	Did not qualify
1962	Semi Final (3rd Place)	1994	Did not enter
1966	First Round		

Competition	P	W	D	L	F	A
World Cup Finals	21	7	3	11	26	32
World Cup Qualifiers	57	25	13	19	95	72
World Cup Total	78	32	16	30	121	104

COLOMBIA

Federación Colombiana De Fútbol
Founded: 1924 **Affiliations:** Conmebol – 1940. FIFA – 1936
Address: Avenida 32 No. 16-22, Apdo aéreo 17602, Bogota.
Phone: +57 1/285 3320 **Fax:** +57 1/285 4340
National Stadium: El Campin (52,000)
Colours: Yellow with tricolour border shirts, Blue shorts,
      Red with tricolour border socks
Coach: Herman Dario Gomez Jaramillo
Key Players: Faustino Asprilla, Carlos Valderrama, Antony De Avila

Salsa Same

When you watch Colombia during the 1998 World Cup finals you could be forgiven for thinking you were in a time warp. Having qualified for their third successive finals (but remarkably only their fourth overall) the basic line-up might have been plucked from a team featuring in the 1994 or 1990 events.

Central as always to their game will be captain Carlos Valderrama. The 36 year old still sports the same mass of hair and despite being a homeland hero, his pedestrian style is more often than not the reason Colombia struggle. With over 100 appearances for his country, he has just a handful or so of international goals, which perhaps typifies his reluctance to pass the ball forward too often.

English eyes will be on Tino Asprilla but his appearances in the Premiership will remove the unknown factor from English defenders. His seven goals in the qualifying round were important as were the three added by his partner up front, De Avila.

Prior to the World Cup in 1994, Colombia's hopes were raised a little too sky-high with a 5-0 win in Argentina. Their qualifying performances this time around have been erratic and there will not be the same expectancy of them. Having gone undefeated in the first seven CONMEBOL games, Argentina inflicted a home defeat which marked the start of five games from which just one point was taken. At this stage the chances of qualification looked shaky, but a goal by De Avila at home to Ecuador three minutes from time secured a vital win and follow-up victories over Bolivia and Venezuela finally earned them a place in the finals behind Argentina and Paraguay.

CONMEBOL Results

Date	Opponents	Ven	Result	Att	Scorers
24.04.96	Paraguay	H	1-0	60,000	F. Asprilla (55)
02.06.96	Peru	A	1-1	45,000	Aristizabal (60)
07.07.96	Uruguay	H	3-1	40,000	F. Asprilla (10); Valderrama (23); De Avila (77)
01.09.96	Chile	H	4-1	50,000	F. Asprilla (3, 31, 47); Bermudez (43)
09.10.96	Ecuador	A	1-0	45,000	F. Asprilla (72)
10.11.96	Bolivia	A	2-2	45,000	Serna (40pen); Rincon (54)
15.12.96	Venezuela	A	2-0	25,000	Bermudez (7); Valenciano (50)
12.02.97	Argentina	H	0-1	60,000	
02.04.97	Paraguay	A	1-2	42,000	Serna (37pen)
30.04.97	Peru	H	0-1	30,000	
08.06.97	Uruguay	A	1-1	50,000	Ricard (47)
06.07.97	Chile	A	1-4	75,000	Ricard (50)
20.07.97	Ecuador	H	1-0	30,000	De Avila (87)
20.08.97	Bolivia	H	3-0	35,000	De Avila (1); Valderrama (30pen); F. Asprilla (75)
10.09.97	Venezuela	H	1-0	35,000	Cabrera (67)
16.11.97	Argentina	A	1-1	40,000	Valderrama (8)

Scorers: 7 – F. Asprilla; 3 – De Avila, Valderrama; 2 – Bermudez, Ricard, Serna; 1 – Aristizabal, Cabrera, Rincon, Valenciano

Sent Off: Alvarez v Uruguay (home); F. Asprilla v Paraguay (away 77 min); Palacios v Peru (home 81 min)

Group G Opponents Head-to-Head

15 June	Romania v Colombia	Lyon	4.30 pm
22 June	Colombia v Tunisia	Montpellier	4.30 pm
26 June	Colombia v England	Lens	8.00 pm

Pasadena's Rose Bowl was the venue for the only World Cup meeting between Colombia and Romania. The Californian sun shone on an excellent match that saw outstanding goals and excellent goalkeeping to win it for the Romanians. Adolfo Valencia gave the Colombians some hope by reducing the deficit to 2-1 just before the interval and the result was always in the balance until the Romanians' third goal in the final minute of play. Colombia have not met either England or Tunisia in the World Cup.

Yr	Round	Opponents	Result	Scorers
1994	First Round	Romania	1-3	Valencia

CONMEBOL Appearances

Name	Tot	St	Sub	PS	Name	Tot	St	Sub	PS
Alvarez, Leonel	9	9	0	3	Lozano, Harold	7	5	2	1
Angel, Juan	2	1	1	1	Mafla, Edison	1	0	1	0
Aristizabal, Victor	9	6	3	6	Mendoza, Alexis	8	8	0	0
Asprilla, Carlos	1	1	0	0	Mondragon, Farid	12	12	0	0
Asprilla, Faustino	12	12	0	4	Morantes	1	0	1	0
Bermudez, Jorge	15	15	0	0	Moreno, Antonio	7	7	0	1
Bolando, Jorge	3	1	2	0	Pacheco, Victor	6	0	6	0
Bonilla, Victor	1	0	1	0	Palacios, Eves	1	0	1	0
Cabrera, Wilmer	12	12	0	0	Perez, Wilson	5	4	1	1
Calero	1	1	0	0	Quinones, Luis	2	1	1	1
Cordoba, Ivan Ramiro	4	4	0	0	Ramirez, John	1	0	1	0
Cordoba, O	3	3	0	0	Ricard, Hamilton	6	1	5	0
De Avila, Antony	11	6	5	5	Rincon, Freddy	12	12	0	3
Escobar, Walter	1	1	0	1	Santa, Jose	4	4	0	1
Estrada, Andres	4	1	3	0	Serna, Mauricio	12	12	0	2
Galeano, Hugo	9	8	1	1	Valderrama, Carlos	16	16	0	1
Gaviria, Herman	3	3	0	1	Valencia, Adolfo	4	2	2	1
Herrera, Luis	1	1	0	0	Valenciano, Ivan	3	3	0	2
Lopez, Osman	5	4	1	2					

World Cup Record

Year	Stage Reached	Year	Stage Reached
1930-54	Did not enter	1978	Did not qualify
1958	Did not qualify	1982	Did not qualify
1962	First Round	1986	Did not qualify
1966	Did not qualify	1990	Second Round
1970	Did not qualify	1994	First Round
1974	Did not qualify		

Competition	P	W	D	L	F	A
World Cup Finals	10	2	2	6	13	20
World Cup Qualifiers	64	22	20	22	74	78
World Cup Total	74	24	22	28	87	98

World Cup Notebook

- Following the 1994 World Cup finals, full-back Andreas Escobar was assassinated on his return to Colombia after he had scored an own goal against the USA.
- Remember the scorpion kick? Colombia's former goalkeeper Rene Huguita made the outrageous 'behind the back kick' to clear Jamie Redknapp's goal attempt at Wembley in 1995!
- If Colombia concede two goals in the finals it will be their 99th and 100th against!

CROATIA

Croatian Football Association
Founded: 1912. Refounded: 1991 **Affiliations:** UEFA – 1992. FIFA – 1992
Address: Illica 31, 10000 Zagreb
Phone: +385 1/45 54 100   **Fax:** +385 1/42 46 39
National Stadium: Maksimir (60,000)
Colours: Red and White squared shirts, White shorts, Blue socks
Coach: Miroslav Blazevic
Key Players: Davor Suker, Zvonimir Boban, Robert Prosinecki

Late, Late Show

The national pride that seemed to be sweeping Croatia along looked to be on
the wane as this highly talented side needed to win in their last UEFA group
qualifying game to ensure a place in the play-offs. Suker, Soldo and Boksic
notched the goals in Slovenia that produced the win and a face-off with
Ukraine that was duly won 3-1 on aggregate.

A 4-1 win over arch-rivals Bosnia got the Croats off to a good start in their
group, but three successive home draws against contenders Greece, Denmark
and Slovenia left their qualification chances looking somewhat shaky.
However, a late goal from Davor Suker in Athens was followed up with a late
home win over Bosnia. Having lost to group winners Denmark, Croatia knew
their fate depended on that final game.

Croatian chain-smoking coach Miroslav Blazevic probably came close to
losing his job during the qualifying process but at the end of it he has
produced his nation's biggest footballing achievement to date. Blazevic was
in charge of the team that stuttered through Euro '96 and the squad contains
many names recognisable from that competition.

The pick of the bunch must be the trio of Zvonimir Boban, their hardworking and thoughtful captain and the only Croat to feature in all their
qualifying games, Lazio striker Alen Boksic and Real Madrid's artful striker
Davor Suker, with his lethal left foot.

UEFA Group 1 Results and Appearances

Date	Opponents	Ven	Result	Att	Scorers
08.10.96	Bosnia	A	4-1	1,500	Bilic (14); Vlaovic (32); Boksic (63, 84)
10.11.96	Greece	H	1-1	40,000	Suker (45)
29.03.97	Denmark	H	1-1	34,000	Suker (50)
02.04.97	Slovenia	H	3-3	15,000	Prosinecki (33); Boban (43, 60)
30.04.97	Greece	A	1-0	35,000	Suker (74)
06.09.97	Bosnia	H	3-2	30,000	Bilic (27); Maric (40); Boban (80)
10.09.97	Denmark	A	1-3	41,381	Suker (44)
11.10.97	Slovenia	A	3-1	5,000	Suker (11); Soldo (40); Boksic (53)

Play-Off

29.10.97	Ukraine	H	2-0	20,000	Bilic (11); Vlaovic (49)
15.11.97	Ukraine	A	1-1	77,500	Boksic (27)

Scorers: 5 – Suker; 4 – Boksic; 3 – Bilic, Boban; 2 – Vlaovic; 1 – Maric, Prosinecki, Soldo

Name	Tot	St	Sub	PS	Name	Tot	St	Sub	PS
Asanovic, Aljosa	9	7	2	2	Ladic, Drazen	7	7	0	0
Bilic, Slaven	9	9	0	1	Mamic, Zoran	5	3	2	2
Boban, Zvonimir	10	10	0	1	Maric, Silvio	3	1	2	1
Boksic, Alen	9	9	0	5	Pralija, Nened	2	0	2	0
Cvitanovic, Igor	6	3	3	1	Prosinecki, Robert	6	6	0	2
Erceg, Tomislav	2	0	2	0	Saric, Danijel	3	3	0	1
Gabric, Tonci	2	1	1	1	Simic, Dario	6	5	1	0
Jarni, Robert	8	8	0	0	Soldo, Zvonimir	7	6	1	2
Jerkan, Nikola	4	4	0	0	Stanic, Mario	2	2	0	1
Junic	1	1	0	0	Stimac, Igor	3	3	0	1
Jurcevic, Nicola	1	1	0	1	Suker, Davor	9	9	0	0
Jurcic, Krunoslav	3	1	2	0	Tudor, Igor	1	0	1	0
Juric, Goran	7	6	1	0	Vlaovic, Goran	8	4	4	3
Kovac, Niko	2	1	1	0					

Group H Opponents Head-to-Head

14 June	Jamaica v Croatia	Lens	8.00 pm
20 June	Japan v Croatia	Nantes	1.30 pm
26 June	Argentina v Croatia	Bordeaux	3.00 pm

This is the first World Cup finals that Croatia have taken part in and, as none of the teams in their group come from UEFA member countries, they will be opponents for the very first time.

World Cup Record

Competition	P	W	D	L	F	A
World Cup Finals	0	0	0	0	0	0
World Cup Qualifiers	10	5	4	1	20	13
World Cup Total	10	5	4	1	20	13

World Cup Notebook

- Croatia will be appearing in the World Cup finals for the very first time when they take the field in Lens against the Reggae Boyz of Jamaica on 14 June.
- Croatia have only ever lost one game in World Cup competition. It happened away to Denmark, who won 3-1.
- Zvonimir Boban was the only player to feature in all ten of his team's World Cup matches.

DENMARK

Dansk Boldspil Union
Founded: 1889   **Affiliations:** UEFA – 1954. FIFA – 1904
Address: Idraettens Hus, Bronby Stadion 20, DK-2605 Brondby
Phone: +45 43 26 22 22   **Fax:** +45 43 26 22 45
National Stadium: Parken, Copenhagen (48,000)
Colours: Red shirts, White shorts, Red socks
Coach: Bo Johansson
Key Players: Peter Schmeichel, Brian Laudrup, Michael Laudrup

Defining Moments

A goalless draw in Athens in the final Group 1 game ensured that the Danes went to only their second World Cup finals and not Greece. Indeed, many Danish newspapers made the split much closer than that and pointed to one outstanding save by Peter Schmeichel in the dying stages of that game as the defining moment.

Schmeichel's contribution as one of four ever presents during the qualifying competition was significant, as were the performances of the Laudrup brothers Michael and Brian, for whom this is sure to be their final World Cup. Indeed, Michael has come out of semi-retirement in Japan and moved to Ajax in a bid to help spearhead Denmark's assault.

Both the draw in Greec (although regarded as fortunate) and subsequent progress were only made possible after a stunning 3-1 victory over the highly talented Croats – the brothers being the architects of that particular performance. Indeed, it was Brian Laudrup who scored the goal that earned Denmark a vital point when the teams first met in the group.

A two-goal win in Slovenia saw Denmark off the mark in their first group game and a 2-1 win over Greece set the trend of things to come. After the draw in Croatia, Slovenia were dispatched 4-0 in the return encounter. After a 2-0 win over Bosnia, the Danes stumbled dramatically when they were disposed of by three goals in the Bosnian return to instil some doubt in their abilities, a worry that was revoked admirably by that 3-1 success in Croatia.

With opening games against Saudi Arabia and South Africa, it is quite possible that Denmark may have successfully negotiated the first stage before the pairing with France in Lyon. Their progress even that far may well depend on the inspiration of The Brothers.

Date	Opponents	Ven	Result	Att	Scorers
01.09.96	Slovenia	A	2-0	5,500	A. Nielsen (78); Schjonberg (89)
09.10.96	Greece	H	2-1	40,226	OG (25); B. Laudrup (50)
29.03.97	Croatia	A	1-1	34,000	B. Laudrup (82)
30.04.97	Slovenia	H	4-0	41,278	A. Nielsen (4, 56); Pedersen (27); B. Laudrup (51)
08.06.97	Bosnia H.	H	2-0	41,592	Rieper (67); Molnar (90)
20.08.97	Bosnia H.	A	0-3	35,000	
10.09.97	Croatia	H	3-1	41,381	B. Laudrup (17); M. Laudrup (36); Molnar (41)
11.10.97	Greece	A	0-0	70,000	

Scorers: 4 – B. Laudrup; 3 – A. Nielsen; 2 – Molnar; 1 – M. Laudrup, Pedersen, Rieper, Schjonberg, Own goal.

Name	Tot	St	Sub	PS	Name	Tot	St	Sub	PS
Andersen, Soren	2	0	2	0	Moller, Peter	4	2	2	1
Beck, Mikkel	2	1	1	1	Molnar, Miklos	4	2	2	1
Bisgaard, Morten	1	0	1	0	Nielsen, Allan	8	8	0	0
Bjur, Ole	2	1	1	1	Nielsen, Brian Steen	1	1	0	1
Colding, Soren	1	0	1	0	Nielsen, Peter	1	1	0	1
Frandsen, Per	4	2	2	1	Pedersen, Per	3	2	1	2
Friis-Hansen, Jakob	1	1	0	0	Rieper, Marc	5	5	0	0
Goldbaek, Bjarne	2	0	2	0	Schjonberg, Michael	7	2	5	0
Heintze, Jan	6	6	0	1	Schmeichel, Peter	8	8	0	0
Helveg, Thomas	8	8	0	1	Thomsen, Claus	6	6	0	1
Hogh, Jess	8	8	0	1	Tobiasen	2	2	0	0
Laudrup, Brian	7	7	0	1	Tomasson, Jon Dahl	4	3	1	2
Laudrup, Michael	4	4	0	3	Wieghorst, Marten	1	1	0	1
Laurensen, Jacob	6	6	0	1					

12 June	Saudi Arabia v Denmark	Lens	4.30 pm
18 June	South Africa v Denmark	Toulouse	4.30 pm
24 June	France v Denmark	Lyon	3.00 pm

Denmark have not come up against any of their Group C opponents in previous rounds of the World Cup.

World Cup Record

Year	Stage Reached	Year	Stage Reached
1930-50	Did not enter	1978	Did not qualify
1958	Did not qualify	1982	Did not qualify
1962	Did not enter	1986	Second Round
1966	Did not qualify	1990	Did not qualify
1970	Did not qualify	1994	Did not qualify
1974	Did not qualify		

Competition	P	W	D	L	F	A
World Cup Finals	4	3	0	1	10	6
World Cup Qualifiers	68	29	12	27	108	97
World Cup Total	72	32	12	28	118	103

World Cup Notebook

- Despite being one of the smaller nations, Denmark achieved outstanding success when they won the European Championship in 1992 when they beat Germany 2-0 in the final in Sweden. What made their achievement all the more remarkable was that they failed to qualify for the event and were given a wild-card entry when Yugoslavia dropped out of the competition due to the civil war ensuing in the country.
- Morten Olsen is Denmark's most capped player with 102 appearances.
- Denmark's biggest win in the World Cup came in the 1990 qualifying tournament when they beat Greece 7-1 in a Group 1 game.

ENGLAND

The Football Association
Founded: 1863
Affiliations: UEFA – 1954. FIFA – 1905-20, 1924-28, 1946
Address: 16 Lancaster Gate, London, W2 3LW
Phone: 0171 262 4542   **Fax:** 0171 402 0486
National Stadium: Wembley (79,045)
Colours: White with blue and red trim shirts, Blue shorts,
          White with blue trim socks.
Coach: Glenn Hoddle
Key Players: Alan Shearer, David Beckham

New Age

The end of 1997 saw not only England qualify for the World Cup finals but also move up to fourth place in the FIFA World Rankings. Under coach Glenn Hoddle, England had suffered just two defeats by the end of the qualification process – and both of those to the teams that contested the 1994 World Cup final.

The more significant of the defeats looked to be the one at Wembley where Italy, courtesy of a Giancarlo Zola strike, became the first team to win at Wembley in a World Cup game. The defeat came after three successive wins which included a 2-0 success in Georgia. Another three wins post-Italy, against the same opposition, left England in a strong position, especially given the fact that group rivals Italy had been held scoreless in Georgia.

With England needing to avoid defeat in Rome to qualify, they produced perhaps their best performance under Hoddle to secure a point and were only denied the win by the width of the woodwork.

The last two group games against Moldova and Italy were played without the services of captain and top scorer Alan Shearer, who has sat out much of the season through injury, and it remains to be seen if he will be fit to lead England in the finals.

Elsewhere, one of the most encouraging aspects of England's development is the number of young players in the squad. David Beckham, Paul Scholes and the Neville brothers all look certain starters, while Rio Ferdinand, Robbie Fowler and perhaps Michael Owen will have roles to play. Alongside keeper Seaman, Sol Campbell, Tony Adams and Paul Gascoigne, England have the talent and flair to go a stage further than they did in Euro '96 and the 1990 World Cup.

UEFA Group 2 Results and Appearances

Date	Opponents	Ven	Result	Att	Scorers
01.09.96	Moldova	A	3-0	9,500	Barmby (24); Gascoigne (25); Shearer (61)
09.10.96	Poland	H	2-1	74,663	Shearer (24, 37)
09.11.96	Georgia	A	2-0	75,000	Sheringham (15); Ferdinand (37)
12.02.97	Italy	H	0-1	75,055	
30.04.97	Georgia	H	2-0	71,208	Sheringham (43); Shearer (90)
31.05.97	Poland	A	2-0	35,000	Shearer (5); Sheringham (90)
10.09.97	Moldova	H	4-0	74,102	Scholes (28); Wright (46, 90); Gascoigne (81)
11.10.97	Italy	A	0-0	81,200	

Scorers: 5 – Shearer; 3 – Sheringham; 2 – Gascoigne, Wright; 1– Barmby, Scholes

Name	Tot	St	Sub	PS	Name	Tot	St	Sub	PS
Adams, Tony	3	3	0	1	Merson, Paul	1	0	1	0
Barmby, Nicky	1	1	0	1	Neville, Gary	6	6	0	0
Batty, David	7	5	2	1	Neville, Phil	2	1	1	0
Beckham, David	8	8	0	2	Pallister, Gary	2	1	1	0
Butt, Nicky	2	0	2	0	Pearce, Stuart	3	3	0	0
Campbell, Sol	6	6	0	0	Redknapp, Jamie	1	0	1	0
Collymore, Stan	1	0	1	0	Ripley, Stuart	1	0	1	0
Ferdinand, Les	4	3	1	2	Scholes, Paul	1	1	0	0
Gascoigne, Paul	6	6	0	3	Seaman, David	7	7	0	0
Hinchcliffe, Andy	3	3	0	0	Shearer, Alan	5	5	0	0
Ince, Paul	7	7	0	1	Sheringham, Teddy	4	4	0	0
Le Saux, Graeme	4	4	0	0	Southgate, Gareth	7	6	1	1
Le Tissier, Matt	2	1	1	1	Walker, Ian	1	1	0	0
Lee, Robert	2	2	0	0	Wright, Ian	4	2	2	0
McManaman, Steve	2	2	0	1					

Group G Opponents Head-to-Head

15 June	England v Tunisia	Marseilles	1.30 pm
22 June	Romania v England	Toulouse	8.00 pm
24 June	Colombia v England	Lens	8.00 pm

Tunisia and Colombia will provide new World Cup opponents for England in France. Romania, however, have been encountered in the finals once before, while the teams have also come across one another in two qualifying tournaments. The northern Mexican city of Guadalajara was the setting for the 1970 Group 3 encounter between the teams, which was rather bland and settled by a goal from Geoff Hurst 20 minutes from full-time.

The teams were pitted against each other in the qualifying stages for two successive World Cups, namely the lead-up to the 1982 and 1986 finals. Three of the games ended in draws (twice goalless and once 1-1) with the Romanians winning the very first encounter 2-1 in Bucharest.

Yr	Round	Opponents	Result	Scorers
1970	First Round	Romania	1-0	Hurst

World Cup Record

Year	Stage Reached	Year	Stage Reached
1930	Did not enter	1970	Quarter Final
1934	Did not enter	1974	Did not qualify
1938	Did not enter	1978	Did not qualify
1950	First Round	1982	Second Round
1954	Quarter Final	1986	Quarter Final
1958	First Round	1990	Semi Final (4th Place)
1962	Quarter Final	1994	Did not qualify
1966	Winners		

Competition	P	W	D	L	F	A
World Cup Finals	41	18	12	11	55	38
World Cup Qualifiers	64	40	16	8	159	43
World Cup Total	105	58	28	19	214	81

World Cup Notebook

- England and Scotland are the oldest international teams in the world. The two played each other in the first international match in Glasgow in 1872. The game ended goalless.
- England striker Geoff Hurst scored what is the most disputed goal in World Cup history. It came in extra time of the 1966 final at Wembley when he thundered the ball against the underside of the bar. The argument was whether the ball came down and bounced over the line or on it. After consulting with Russian linesman Bakhramov, Swiss referee Dienst awarded the goal which gave England a 3-2 lead.
- Geoff Hurst became the first player to score a hat-trick in a World Cup final when he notched three goals against West Germany at Wembley Stadium on 30 July 1966.
- Since defeating West Germany in the 1966 final, England have lost twice to them in the competition. They lost 3-2 in the quarter finals in Mexico in 1970, having been 2-0 up, and then suffered a semi-final penalty shoot-out in Italy in 1990.
- When Italy beat England 1-0 at Wembley in February 1997 in a qualifying group game, they became the first team to beat England in the World Cup on home soil.

FRANCE

Federation Française de Football (FFF)
Founded: 1918   **Affiliations:** UEFA – 1954. FIFA – 1904
Address: 60 bis, Avenue d'Iena, F-75783, Paris Cedex 16
Phone: +33 1/44 31 73 00   **Fax:** +33 1/47 20 82 96
National Stadium: Stade de France, Paris (80,000)
Colours: Blue shirts, White shorts, Red with Blue socks
Coach: Aime Jacquet
Key Players: Zinedine Zidane, Youri Djorkaeff, Ibrahim Ba

Attacking the Problem

The luck of the draw seems to have ensured that hosts France reach the
second phase of the competition without too much difficulty. However,
fortunate pairings are not necessarily what the country needs when their
record is scrutinised. In Zinedine Zidane, Marcel Desailly and Youri
Djorkaeff they have players comparable with the best in Europe.

In the fact hard world of results, their record shows that they have only
been defeated twice in 36 games up to the end of 1997, scoring 70 goals and
conceding just 19 in the process. Yet it is in attack that problems seem to be
arising. In their eight games of 1997 they never managed more than two goals
in a game and no player managed two goals in a game, with their 12 goals
being spread around no less than nine players.

But these are the sort of problems hosts often find themselves with. No
competitive matches due to automatic qualification and often the opposition
based on non-UEFA opponents. This cannot be said of France, though, whose
only defeat of the year came at home to England in the successful Le Tournoi
competition which also saw them draw with Brazil and Italy. Wins were
achieved over World Cup finalists Holland, South Africa and Scotland.

Many of these results were missing the Gallic flair one would expect but,
with coach Aime Jacquet searching for the right combination, no less than 33
players were used. The French fans will be looking for a return to the form
that led France to a European Championship win on home soil in 1984, but
alas Michel Platini's role is limited to the World Cup Organising Committee.
Don't write France off yet – especially if the likes of Ibrahim Ba and Patrick
Vieira can learn to make their mark on the national side in the same way they
have for their club sides.

Friendly Results and Appearances 1997

Date	Opponents	Ven	Result	Att	Scorers
22.01.97	Portugal	A	2-0	40,000	Deschamps (10); Ba (60)
26.02.97	Netherlands	H	2-1	35,331	Pires (74); Loko (84)
02.04.97	Sweden	H	1-0	24,000	Djorkaeff (44pen)
03.06.97	Brazil	H	1-1	30,000	Keller (60)
07.06.97	England	H	0-1	28,000	
11.06.97	Italy	H	2-2	30,000	Zidane (12); Djorkaeff (73)
11.10.97	South Africa	H	2-1	29,000	Guivarc'h (53); Ba (83)
12.11.97	Scotland	H	2-1	19,514	Laigle (35); Djorkaeff (78 pen)

Scorers: 3 – Djorkaeff; 2 – Ba; 1 – Deschamps, Pires, Loko, Keller, Zidane, Guivarc'h, Laigle.

Name	Tot	St	Sub	PS	Name	Tot	St	Sub	PS
Ba, Ibrahim	7	6	1	4	Laigle, Pierre	5	4	1	3
Barthez, Fabien	5	5	0	0	Lama, Bernard	1	1	0	0
Blanc, Laurent	7	7	0	0	Laslandes, Lilian	1	1	0	1
Blondeau, Patrick	2	0	2	0	Lebœuf, Franck	1	1	0	0
Boghossian	2	0	2	0	Letizi, Lionel	1	1	0	0
Candela, Vincent	5	3	2	1	Lizarazu, Bixente	4	3	1	1
Charbonnier, Lionel	1	1	0	0	Loko, Patrice	4	0	4	0
Desailly, Marcel	7	7	0	2	Makelele, Claude	1	1	0	0
Deschamps, Didier	6	6	0	1	Maurice, Florian	2	2	0	1
Djetou, Martin	1	0	1	0	N'Gotty, Bruno	4	1	3	0
Djorkaeff, Youri	6	3	3	1	Ouedec	1	1	0	1
Dugarry, Christophe	5	5	0	3	Petit, Emmanuel	2	2	0	2
Gava, Franck	2	0	2	0	Pires, Robert	4	3	1	3
Guivarc'h, Stephane	2	2	0	0	Thuram, Lilian	8	7	1	1
Henry, Thierry	1	1	0	0	Vieira, Patrick	5	3	2	2
Karembeu, Christian	4	4	0	2	Zidane, Zinedine	8	6	2	1
Keller, Marc	3	1	2	0					

Group C Opponents Head-to-Head

12 June	France v South Africa	Marseilles	8.00 pm
18 June	France v Saudi Arabia	Saint Denis	8.00 pm
24 June	France v Denmark	Lyon	3.00 pm

All three Group C opponents provide new World Cup opponents for the hosts. However, South Africa were beaten 2-1 in a friendly match played in October 1997.

World Cup Record

Year	Stage Reached	Year	Stage Reached
1930	First Round	1970	Did not qualify
1934	First Round	1974	First Round
1938	Second Round	1978	First Round
1950	Did not qualify	1982	Semi Final (4th Place)
1954	First Round	1986	Semi Final (3rd Place)
1958	Semi Final (3rd Place)	1990	Did not qualify
1962	Did not qualify	1994	Did not qualify
1966	First Round		

Competition	P	W	D	L	F	A
World Cup Finals	34	15	5	14	71	56
World Cup Qualifiers	68	40	9	19	145	61
World Cup Total	102	55	14	33	216	117

World Cup Notebook

- The World Cup was invented by a Frenchman. The original trophy was named after Jules Rimet and is now owned outright by Brazil, who were awarded the trophy after winning it for the third time.
- France have never won the World Cup but have reached the semi-final stage on three occasions. Their team of 1982 and 1986 is often regarded as one of the best never to win the competition.
- The great French team did succeed in winning the 1984 European Championship, though. Michel Platini inspired his side to a 2-0 win over Spain.
- As hosts, France did not have to play any qualifying games for the 1998 finals. They did play eight friendly games during 1997, though, losing just once – 1-0 to England.

GERMANY

Deutscher Fussball-Bund (DFB)
Founded: 1900
Affiliations: UEFA – 1954. FIFA – 1904-46, 1950
Address: Otto-Fleck-Schneise 6, Postfach 710265, D-60528, Frankfurt am Main
Phone: +49 69/678 80   **Fax:** +49 69/678 82 66
National Stadium: Olympiastadion, Munich (73,000)
Colours: White shirts, Black shorts, White socks
Coach: Berti Vogts
Key Players: Oliver Bierhoff, Matthias Sammer

Last-Gasp Reprieve

On paper, Germany would appear to have a relatively easy passage to the second phase of the competition, but their qualifying games indicate that the reliable machine of recent competitions may be a little rusty here and there. Yugoslavia might yet be the surprise of the finals and both the USA and Iran will give good accounts of themselves.

It was Albania in the qualifying competition that nearly relegated Germany to the play-offs. Needing only a draw at home to book a place in the finals, they found themselves a goal behind early in the second half when Jurgen Kohler headed into his own net. In an increasingly tense game, it needed a last-minute effort by Oliver Bierhoff to secure a fortuitous 4-3 win and automatic qualification.

Bierhoff had been the saviour early on in the competition. With Germany trailing 1-0 to Northern Ireland in Belfast, he came off the bench with 21 minutes to go and secured the match-ball within ten minutes of being on the field, earning himself a place in Germany's record book with the fastest ever hat-trick in his country's international history.

Comebacks were the key for Germany in their Group 9 and it was the former East German striker Ulf Kirsten who came off the bench and almost immediately notched a late equaliser against Portugal in Berlin.

Jurgen Klinsmann, who will have made his 100th international appearance for Germany prior to the finals, used the 4-0 win over Armenia in the penultimate group game to end his international goal drought, scoring after going over nine games without a goal.

Klinsmann is one of several German players the wrong side of 30 and they may need to unearth some new talent prior to France if they are going to make their customary impact.

UEFA Group 9 Results and Appearances

Date	Opponents	Ven	Result	Att	Scorers
09.10.96	Armenia	A	5-1	45,000	Hassler (20, 29); Klinsmann (26); Bobic (69); Kuntz (81)
09.11.96	N.Ireland	H	1-1	40,718	Moller (40)
14.12.96	Portugal	A	0-0	50,000	
02.04.97	Albania	A	3-2	8,000	Kirsten (64, 80, 84)
30.04.97	Ukraine	H	2-0	33,242	Bierhoff (63); Basler (72)
07.06.97	Ukraine	A	0-0	55,000	
20.08.97	N.Ireland	A	3-1	14,500	Bierhoff (72, 77, 78)
06.09.97	Portugal	H	1-1	75800	Kirsten (81)
10.09.97	Armenia	H	4-0	43,000	Klinsmann (70, 84); Hassler (86); Kirsten (90)
11.10.97	Albania	H	4-3	44,522	Helmer (64); Bierhoff (73, 90); Marschall (86)

Scorers: 6 – Bierhoff; 5 – Kirsten; 3 – Hassler, Klinsmann; 1 – Bobic, Kuntz, Helmer, Marschall, Basler, Moller

Name	Tot	St	Sub	PS	Name	Tot	St	Sub	PS
Babbel, Markus	5	3	2	1	Kuntz, Stefan	2	1	1	1
Basler, Mario	5	5	0	2	Marschall, Olaf	1	0	1	1
Bierhoff, Oliver	9	5	4	2	Moller, Andreas	5	5	0	0
Bobic, Freddi	5	4	1	3	Nowotny, Jens	4	3	1	0
Bode, Marco	1	1	0	1	Passlack, Stephan	2	1	1	0
Eilts, Dieter	6	6	0	2	Reuter, Stefan	6	6	0	2
Hassler, Thomas	6	5	1	1	Ricken, Lars	1	0	1	0
Heinrich, Jorg	7	6	1	1	Sammer, Matthias	3	3	0	0
Helmer, Thomas	7	7	0	1	Scholl, Mehmet	2	1	1	0
Khan, Oliver	1	1	0	0	Strunz, Thomas	1	1	0	0
Kirsten, Ulf	6	3	3	1	Tarnat, Michael	6	2	4	1
Klinsmann, Jurgen	9	9	0	0	Thorn, Olaf	2	2	0	0
Kmetsch, Sven	1	1	0	1	Worns, Christian	2	2	0	1
Kohler, Jurgen	9	9	0	0	Wosz, Diriusz	5	4	1	3
Kopke, Andreas	9	9	0	0	Ziege, Christian	6	6	0	0

Group F Opponents Head-to-Head

15 June	Germany v USA	Paris	8.00 pm
21 June	Germany v Yugoslavia	Lens	1.30 pm
25 June	Germany v Iran	Montpellier	8.00 pm

Yugoslavia have proved to be almost regular opponents for Germany, or more correctly West Germany, in the World Cup finals, with the quarter final stage a particularly popular meeting point. Of the five meetings, four have been at this stage of the competition and the Germans have recorded a total of four wins. The most recent encounter, though, came at the first-round stage in Italy as West Germany went on to win the competition.

Iran and the USA provide new World Cup opposition for the Germans.

Yr	Round	Opponents	Result	Scorers
1954	Quarter Final	Yugoslavia	2-0	OG (Horvat), Rahn
1958	Quarter Final	Yugoslavia	1-0	Rahn
1962	Quarter Final	Yugoslavia	0-1	
1974	Quarter Final	Yugoslavia	2-0	Breitner, Muller
1990	First Round	Yugoslavia	4-1	Matthaus (2), Klinsmann, Voeller

World Cup Record

Year	Stage Reached	Year	Stage Reached
1930	Did not enter	1970	Semi Final (3rd Place)
1934	Semi Final (3rd Place)	1974	Winners
1938	First Round	1978	Second Round
1950	Did not enter	1982	Runners-up
1954	Winners	1986	Runners-up
1958	Semi Final (4th Place)	1990	Winners
1962	Quarter Final	1994	Quarter Final
1966	Runners-up		

Competition – West Germany	P	W	D	L	F	A
World Cup Finals	56	31	14	11	107	63
World Cup Qualiers	40	31	8	1	125	28
Total	96	62	22	12	232	91

Germany	P	W	D	L	F	A
World Cup Finals	17	11	2	4	48	35
World Cup Qualifiers	12	8	4	0	35	9
Total	29	19	6	4	83	44

World Cup Notebook

- Germany – which for the sake of this book includes West Germany – have reached the final of the World Cup more times than any other country. They have played in six finals, having won three and lost three.
- Lothar Matthaus and Uwe Seller, both great players with West Germany, have played in 21 matches in the World Cup finals – a record.
- Lothar Matthaus is also Germany's most capped player, with 122 appearances for his country.
- Germany, like Brazil, have played in 73 games in the World Cup finals – another record.
- It needed goals in the 86th and 90th minutes from Marschall and Bierhoff respectively in Germany's last UEFA qualifying group game to secure them a 4-3 win over Albania and thus automatic qualification for the World Cup finals.

HOLLAND

Koininklijke Nederlandsche Voetbalbond (KNV)
Founded: 1889   **Affiliations:** UEFA – 1954. FIFA – 1904
Address: Woudenbergseweg 56, Postbus 515, NL-3700 Am Zeist
Phone: +31 34349 92 11   **Fax:** +31 34349 14 87
National Stadium: Amsterdam Arena (52,000)
Colours: Orange shirts, White shorts, Orange socks
Coach: Guus Hiddink   **Key Players:** Dennis Bergkamp, Clarence Seedorf

There's Oranje

With so much talent in the Oranje squad it seems inconceivable that Holland
will not be among those teams contesting the final itself. Yet they remain an
enigma – a team with no little skill and great vision, but one that can fall
away in dramatic fashion as was illustrated by their performance in Euro '96.
In recent World Cups they have also been plagued by player unrest which has
disrupted and disunited the squad as a whole. However, if their qualifying
performances are any gauge, then the Dutch are on their way back.

Six emphatic wins were the basis of their drive to the finals and only two
disappointing performances against a stubborn Turkish side blighted their
progress. Indeed Turkey inflicted Holland's only defeat in Istanbul midway
through the campaign – a defeat that might have been avoided if Clarence
Seedorf had not missed a penalty he had insisted on taking despite not being
their regular spot kicker.

Four wins from their first four games prior to that reversal had set the
trend. Emphatic demolitions of Wales, in which ten goals were scored, were
cemented by a 3-0 win over arch Benelux rivals Belgium in Brussels, a team
which was regarded as main threat to Holland's automatic qualification.
Another ten goals trounced San Marino across two matches either side of the
defeat in Turkey. A 3-1 home win over Belgium guaranteed qualification in
their penultimate group game before Turkey held on to a goalless draw in
Amsterdam to complete the round robin games.

Dennis Bergkamp contributed seven of the 26 Dutch goals and by the end
of their qualifying campaign had moved to within three goals of becoming the
all-time top scorer for Holland. How well he performs in France may well
determine the extent of Holland's ambition. Having started the season in
blinding form with Arsenal and been in the running for most player honours,
his contributions faded into 1998.

Consistency is not something that will worry the de Boer twins, Frank and
Ronald, who provide the powerhouse for the Dutch team. Frank was one of

only four players to be ever present in the side in qualifying and his goal contribution is also important. The form of Patrick Kluivert remains the imponderable factor. His career was blighted by a car accident in which a by-stander was killed and a move to Milan has not yet seen him find the form that once caused him to be hailed the greatest Dutch find ever.

UEFA Group 7 Results and Appearances

Date	Opponents	Ven	Result	Att	Scorers
05.10.96	Wales	A	3-1	25,000	Van Hooijdonk (72, 75); R. de Boer (79)
09.11.96	Wales	H	7-1	27,000	Bergkamp (22, 73, 79); R. de Boer (33); Jonk (34); F. de Boer (45); Cocu (62)
14.12.96	Belgium	A	3-0	36,5000	Bergkamp (25); Seedorf (29); Jonk (90pen)
29.03.97	San Marino	H	4-0	48,000	Kluivert (44); F. de Boer (58, 90); Van Hooijdonk (82)
02.04.97	Turkey	A	0-1	30,000	
30.04.97	San Marino	A	6-0	2,8000	Bergkamp (40, 90); A.Winter (63); Van Hooijdonk (70); F. de Boer (74); J. Bosman (85)
06.09.97	Belgium	H	3-1	45,000	Stam (32); Kluivert (53); Bergkamp (84)
11.10.97	Turkey	H	0-0	50,000	

Scorers: 7 – Bergkamp; 4 – F. de Boer, Van Hooijdonk; 2 – R. de Boer, Jonk, Kluivert; 1 – Cocu, Seedorf, Winter, Stam, Bosman

Name	Tot	St	Sub	PS	Name	Tot	St	Sub	PS
Bergkamp, Dennis	6	6	0	1	Reiziger, Michael	7	6	1	2
Bogarde, Winston	3	1	2	0	Seedorf, Clarence	8	8	0	4
Bosman, John	1	0	1	0	Stam, Joap	7	7	0	0
Cocu, Philip	7	7	0	0	Valckx, Stan	1	1	0	0
Cruyff, Jordi	1	1	0	1	Van Bronchorst, Giovanni				
de Boer, Frank	8	8	0	0		4	1	3	1
de Boer, Ronald	6	6	0	5	Van Der Sar, Edwin	8	8	0	0
Jonk, Wim	7	7	0	2	Van Hooijdonk, Pierre	6	1	5	0
Kluivert, Patrick	5	4	1	0	Vierklau, Ferdy	1	1	0	1
Makaay, Roy	1	0	1	0	Winter, Aron	8	7	1	3
Numan, Arthur	7	7	0	1	Witschge, Richard	1	0	1	0
Overmars, Marc	5	0	5	0	Zenden, Boudewijn	1	1	0	0

Group E Opponents Head-to-Head

13 June	Holland v Belgium	Saint Denis	8.00 pm
20 June	Holland v South Korea	Marseilles	8.00 pm
25 June	Holland v Mexico	Saint Etienne	3.00 pm

Although Holland have never faced either South Korea or Mexico in the World Cup before, they have had some epic encounters with their Benelux neighbours Belgium. The most recent of these was in Group 7 of this tournament's preliminaries and details can be found on the previous page. The Dutch record against the Belgians in the qualifiers is excellent and they have won seven of their 12 encounters. In the 1994 finals, though, the Belgians got the upper hand in Orlando thanks to a goal from Newcastle United's Philippe Albert.

Yr	Round	Opponents	Result	Scorers
1994	First Round	Belgium	0-1	

World Cup Record

Year	Stage Reached	Year	Stage Reached
1930	Did not enter	1970	Did not qualify
1934	First Round	1974	Runners-up
1938	First Round	1978	Runners-up
1950	Did not enter	1982	Did not qualify
1954	Did not enter	1986	Did not qualify
1958	Did not qualify	1990	Second Round
1962	Did not qualify	1994	Quarter Final
1966	Did not qualify		

Competition	P	W	D	L	F	A
World Cup Finals	25	12	6	7	45	29
World Cup Qualifiers	75	43	18	14	167	61
Total	100	55	24	21	212	90

World Cup Notebook

- Holland have never won the World Cup, but they have come close. In 1974 and 1978, they reached the final playing a brand of open and highly attractive football that coined the term 'Total Football'. Unfortunately it wasn't enough and the Dutch lost to the host nations, West Germany and Argentina, in both finals.
- By the time Holland kick off their first match in the 1998 finals against Belgium, Dennis Bergkamp may have already become the all-time top scorer for the Oranje. By the end of the qualifying tournament he was in equal second place with 33 goals – just two behind Fraas Wilkes.
- When Holland lost 4-1 to England in Euro '96, it was their heaviest defeat for 20 years.

IRAN

Iran Football Federation
Founded: 1920   **Affiliations:** AFC – 1958. FIFA – 1945
Address: Shahaid Keshvari Sports Complex, Mirdamad Ave, Raazan Jonoobi St, Tehran 15875
Phone: +98 21/225 8151   **Fax:** +98 21/225 8123
National Stadium: Azadi, Tehran (120,000)
Colours: White shirts, White shorts, White socks
Coach: Tomislav Ivic   **Key Players:** Khodadad Azizi, Kahim Bagheri

Mother of all Comebacks

Come back kings is a term that might best describe Iran. Having missed automatic qualification out of their AFC group, they missed out again in a play-off against Japan, who won with a golden goal in extra time. If that wasn't bad enough, in the last chance saloon of a play-off with the OFC winner Australia, they were held 1-1 at home and trailed 2-0 in Melbourne with 14 minutes remaining. Down? Possibly. Out? No. Within three minutes goals from Karim Bagheri and Asia's Player of the Year Khodadad Azizi had changed all that. Their strikes levelled the score at 2-2, and with the aggregate scores at 3-3, Iran qualified for the finals on the away-goals rule.

It perhaps makes a mockery of qualification that Australia missed out without losing a game and Iran qualified having lost three. No one, though, could doubt the Iranians' resolve.

Iran made headlines in the very first of their 17 games to France. On 2 June in Damascus they crushed the Maldives 17-0 to record the highest ever score in the World Cup's 67-year history. They hit them for nine in the return match-up.

Despite the goals and the string of good early results, there was turmoil reported from within the camp, with then coach Mayeli Kohan at logger-heads with several of his key players that came to a head following a decisive defeat by Saudi Arabia. Mayeli Kohan was sacked and replaced by Brazilian Valdeir Vieira who himself was replaced by Tomislav Ivic in January.

Iran found their problems compounded when Karim Bagheri was dismissed in their final game against Qatar. Bagheri, who was top overall scorer with 19 goals in the qualifying stages, was forced to sit out the games against Japan and Australia. Had he been available for the first game, matters might have turned out differently. With Bagheri back for the second leg against Australia, he and Cologne striker Azizi fired Iran to France '98 in sensational fashion.

AFC Results and Appearances

Date	Opponents	Ven	Result	Att	Scorers

Round 1 – Group 2

Date	Opponents	Ven	Result	Att	Scorers
02.06.97	Maldives	*	17-0	10,000	Bagheri (9, 13, 16, 60, 66, 67, 83); Azizi (35, 36); Estili (29,47, 55); Shahroudi (56); A. Daei (75, 77); Mahdavi Kia (63); Minavand (87).
04.06.97	Kyrgystan	*	7-0	5,000	Bagheri (35, 51); F. Majedi (76, 88); A. Daei (58); Minavand (76); Hasan Zadeh (82)
06.06.97	Syria	*	1-0	50,000	A. Daei (65)
09.06.97	Kyrgystan	†	3-1	15,000	Azizi (3, 79); Bagheri (52)
11.06.97	Maldives	†	9-0	50,000	Mansourian (15, 45); Bagheri (22, 39); A. Daei (33, 43); Mahdavi Kia (35); Shahroudi (68); Azizi (88)
13.06.97	Syria	†	2-2	100,000	Shahroudi (9); Mansourian (27)

*Played in Damascus. †Played in Tehran.

Round 2 – Group A

Date	Opponents	Ven	Result	Att	Scorers
13.09.97	China PR	A	4-2	40,000	Bagheri (60pen); Mahdavi Kia (68, 84); Modir-Roosta (86)
19.09.97	Saudi Arabia	H	1-1	110,000	Bagheri (63)
26.09.97	Kuwait	A	1-1	20,000	Bagheri (90)
03.10.97	Qatar	H	3-0	80,000	A. Daei (34); Bagheri (45, 58)
17.10.97	China PR	H	4-1	100,000	Mansourian (3); Modir-Roosta (44); Bagheri (64); A. Daei (68)
24.10.97	Saudi Arabia	A	0-1		
31.10.97	Kuwait	H	0-0	50,000	
07.11.97	Qatar	A	0-2		

AFC Third Place Play-Off

Date	Opponents	Ven	Result	Att	Scorers
16.11.97	Japan	N	2-3		Azizi, A. Daei

AFC-OFC Play-Off

Date	Opponents	Ven	Result	Att	Scorers
22.11.97	Australia	H	1-1	110,000	Azizi (42)
29.11.97	Australia	A	2-2	100,000	Bagheri (77); Azizi (80)

3-3 on aggregate. Iran qualified on away goals rule.

Scorers: 19 – Bagheri; 9 – A. Daei; 8 – Azizi; 4 – Mahdavi Kia, Mansourian; 3 – Estili, Shahroudi; 2 – F. Majedi, Minavand, Modir-Roosta; 1 – Hasan Zadeh

Sent Off: Aliakbar Ostad Asadi v Saudi Arabia (away 75 min), Karim Bagheri v Qatar (away)

Name	Tot	St	Sub	PS
Abedzadeh, Ahmadreza	16	16	0	0
Azizi, Khodadad	14	13	1	5
Bagheri, Karim	14	14	0	1
Bakhtiarizadeh	1	0	1	0
Daei, Ali	17	16	1	2
Estili, Hamid	16	16	0	6
Garoossi, Mohsen	5	1	4	1
Golmohammadi, Yahya	8	7	1	0
Hadi Tabatabaei, Seyed	1	1	0	0
Hasan Zadeh, Ali Mosani	2	0	2	0
Heidari, Hashem	1	0	1	0
Helali, Esmail	1	0	1	0
Khakpour, Mohammad	15	15	0	0
Mahdavi Kia, Mehdi	17	17	0	0
Majedi, Farhad	7	1	6	0
Mansourian, Alireza	17	16	1	7
Minavand, Mehrdad	12	3	9	2
Modir-Roosta, Aliasghar	9	4	5	4
Namjou Motlagh, Majid	1	1	0	1
Ostad Asadi, Ali Akbar	12	10	2	2
Pashazadeh, Mehdi	3	2	1	0
Petrossyan, Samsoon	1	0	1	0
Peyrovani, Ashfin	16	16	0	0
Sadavi, Naim	2	2	0	1
Shahroudi, Reza	13	13	0	5
Shoukri, Javid	1	0	1	0
Tahami, Ebrahim	1	0	1	1
Yazdani, Dariush	2	1	1	0
Zarinche, Reza	1	1	0	1

Group F Opponents Head-to-Head

13 June	Yugoslavia v Iran	Saint Etienne	4.30 pm
21 June	USA v Iran	Lyon	8.00 pm
25 June	Germany v Iran	Montpellier	8.00 pm

Yugoslavia, USA and Germany will all provide new World Cup opponents for Iran.

World Cup Record

Year	Stage Reached	Year	Stage Reached
1930-70	Did not enter	1986	Did not enter
1974	Did not qualify	1990	Did not qualify
1978	First Round	1994	Did not qualify
1982	Did not enter		

Competition	P	W	D	L	F	A
World Cup Finals	3	0	1	2	2	8
World Cup Qualifying	54	33	12	9	121	44
Total	57	33	13	11	123	52

World Cup Notebook

- Iran are the top scorers in the World Cup qualifying competition with 57 goals.
- Bagheri was the qualifying tournament's top scorer with 19 goals from 17 games.

ITALY

Federazione Italiana Giuoco Calcio
Founded: 1898   **Affiliations:** UEFA – 1954. FIFA – 1905
Address: Via Gregorio Allegri 14, CP2450, 1-00198 Rome
Phone: +39 6/849 11 11   **Fax:** +39 6/849 91 22 39
National Stadium: Stadio Olimpico, Rome (80,000)
Colours: Blue shirts, White shorts, Blue socks
Coach: Cesare Maldini
Key Players: Gianfranco Zola, Paolo Maldini

Unbeaten Runners-up

Italy may have qualified for the World Cup finals via the back door but they remained unbeaten in Group 2 and conceded just one goal in their eight qualifying games. World Cup history shows that the Italians are written off at peril but coach Cesare Maldini knows that he will need to add greater invention to an all-too-often dour midfield.

With a lack of invention, goals were often difficult to come by. Their total of 11 is the lowest of any of the UEFA qualifiers and nine of these came in 3-0 wins over lowly Moldova (twice) and Poland. With three goalless draws, their two other goals ensured 1-0 wins, the most significant of which was the 1-0 win over England at Wembley in the early part of 1997. The waning and wandering Fabrizio Ravanelli's three goals (one a penalty) made him top scorer in Italy's campaign.

Under the guidance of Arrigo Sacchi, Italy started their qualifying campaign with four straight wins but a disappointing draw in Poland was followed by a devastating draw in Georgia, by which time Cesare Maldini was in charge of matters. Needing a win over England in Rome to secure automatic qualification, Italy's lack of creativity was further exposed and the ensuing draw (goalless, of course) meant a two-legged play-off against Russia. In two games best forgotten, Italy foraged through and now find themselves in a finals group that should not pose too many problems. However, if Italy are to progress much further than the second stage, they will not only need to harness the creative form that Zola and Del Piero can provide but also plug the undoubted weakness down their right flank.

Ronaldo (Brazil)

Zinedine Zidane (France)

Gabriel Batistuta (Argentina)

Peter Schmeichel (Denmark)

David Beckham (England)

Gianfranco Zola (Italy)

Karim Bagheri (Iran)

Deon Burton (Jamaica)

Marcello Salas (Chile)

Davor Suker (Croatia)

Gheorghe Hagi (Romania)

Predrag Mitjatovic (Yugoslavia)

Mark Fish (South Africa)

Kazu Miura (Japan)

Matthias Sammer (Germany)

Dennis Bergkamp (Holland)

Date	Opponents	Ven	Result	Att	Scorers
05.10.96	Moldova	A	3-1	15,000	Ravanelli (8, 87pen); Casiraghi (69)
09.10.96	Georgia	H	1-0	16,146	Ravanelli (42)
12.02.97	England	A	1-0	75,055	Zola (19)
29.03.97	Moldova	H	3-0	25,000	Maldini (24); Zola (44); Vieri (49)
02.04.97	Poland	A	0-0	32,000	
30.04.97	Poland	H	3-0	37,5000	Di Matteo (23); Maldini (37); R. Baggio (66)
10.09.97	Georgia	A	0-0	60,000	
11.10.97	England	H	0-0	81,200	
Play-Off					
29.10.97	Russia	A	1-1	20,000	Vieri (49)
15.11.97	Russia	H	1-0	76,500	Casiraghi (53)

Italy win 2-1 on aggregate.

Scorers: 3 – Ravanelli; 2 – Casiraghi, Maldini, Vieri, Zola; 1 – R. Baggio, Di Matteo

Name	Tot	St	Sub	PS	Name	Tot	St	Sub	PS
Albertini, Demetrio	6	6	0	0	Ferrara, Ciro	8	8	0	1
Baggio, Dino	9	8	1	1	Fuser, Diego	3	1	2	1
Baggio, Roberto	2	0	2	0	Inzaghi, Filippo	2	1	1	1
Benarrivo, Antonio	2	0	2	0	Lombardo, Attilio	1	1	0	1
Buffon, Gian Luigi	1	0	1	0	Maldini, Paolo	10	10	0	1
Cannavaro, Fabio	8	7	1	0	Nesta, Alessandro	7	6	1	1
Carboni, Amedeo	3	2	1	2	Padovano, Michele	1	0	1	0
Casiraghi, Pierluigi	5	4	1	1	Pagliuca, Gianluca	1	1	0	1
Chiesa, Enrico	2	1	1	1	Panucci, Christian	2	0	2	0
Conte, Antonio	2	2	0	1	Peruzzi, Angelo	7	7	0	0
Costacurta, Alessandro	8	8	0	0	Pessotto, Gianluca	3	3	0	2
Del Piero, Alessandro	3	0	3	0	Ravanelli, Fabrizio	6	5	1	2
Di Livio, Angelo	8	7	1	2	Toldo, Franceso	2	2	0	0
Di Matteo, Roberto	9	9	0	0	Vieri, Christian	5	5	0	2
Eranio, Stefano	1	0	1	0	Zola, Gianfranco	8	6	2	4

Group B Opponents Head-to-Head

11 June	Italy v Chile	Bordeaux	4.30 pm
17 June	Italy v Cameroon	Montpellier	8.00 pm
23 June	Italy v Austria	Saint Denis	3.00 pm

Italy have played both Chile and Austria in the World Cup finals. The two encounters with Chile both came in the 1960s when honours were even. In 1962

Chile won 2-0 in what became known as 'The Battle of Santiago', with Italy playing much of the game with nine men. They gained some revenge at Sunderland's Roker Park in 1966 with Mazzola and Barison scoring.

Italy have played and beaten Austria three times – each by a single goal. The most recent encounter came in Rome during the first round of the 1990 finals. The Italians won with a second-half goal from Toto Schillaci. The previous two meetings were in 1934 and 1978. That first win came in the semi-finals with Guaita's goal being decisive against the much fancied 'Wunderteam' of Hugo Meisl. In 1978, the stage was the quarter finals and was settled by a sensational goal early in the first half from Rossi.

Yr	Round	Opponents	Result	Scorers
1934	Semi Final	Austria	1-0	Guaita
1962	First Round	Chile	0-2	
1966	First Round	Chile	2-0	Mazzola, Barison
1978	Quarter Final	Austria	1-0	Rossi
1990	First Round	Austria	1-0	Schillaci

World Cup Record

Year	Stage Reached	Year	Stage Reached
1930	Did not enter	1970	Runners-up
1934	Winners	1974	First Round
1938	Winners	1978	Semi Final (4th Place)
1950	First Round	1982	Winners
1954	First Round	1986	Second Round
1958	Did not qualify	1990	Semi Final (3rd Place)
1962	First Round	1994	Runners-up
1966	First Round		

Competition	P	W	D	L	F	A
World Cup Finals	60	35	14	11	96	55
World Cup Qualifiers	59	41	12	6	130	33
Total	119	76	26	17	226	88

World Cup Notebook

- When Zola scored the winning goal against England at Wembley in February 1997, it meant that Italy became the first team to beat England on their home soil in a World Cup match.
- Italy have known World Cup shocks. In 1966 they were beaten by North Korea in one of the greatest upsets in World Cup history.
- Italy have appeared in five World Cup final matches, having won the trophy on three occasions.
- Italy are affectionately know as the 'Azzurri' by their fans – the Italian for 'Blues'.

JAMAICA

Jamaica Football Federation
Founded: 1910   **Affiliations:** Concacaf – 1963. FIFA – 1962
Address: Room 8, Nat. Arena, Institute Sports, Independence Park, Kingston 6
Phone: +1 809/929 0484   **Fax:** +1 809/929 0484
National Stadium: National Stadium, Kingston (33,000)
Colours: Green shirts, Black shorts, Gold socks
Coach: Rene Simoes
Key Players: Deon Burton, Robbie Earle, Ian Goodison

Boyz Own

That a country which has the population of a small-sized English town has
qualified for the World Cup finals is nothing short of miraculous. Indeed,
they are the first Caribbean team to qualify since Haiti in 1974, and the first
ever to make it from the English-speaking Caribbean. What has been equally
as sensational is the ever increasing number of Jamaican footballers who
seem to have come out of the woodwork.

Having negotiated two-legged knock-out games with Surinam and
Barbados, the 'Reggae Boyz' found themselves, along with group rivals
Mexico, in the final CONCACAF round and showing the sort of form that
had their tiny island going football crazy.

Their Brazilian coach Rene Simoes then found himself under pressure as
he looked to strengthen his side for the final phase of games. To much dismay
and following a number of confrontations, out went top scorer Walter Boyd
and striking partner Onandi Lowe and in came four England-based players:
Derby's Deon Burton, Portsmouth's Paul Hall and Fitzroy Simpson, and
Wimbledon's Robbie Earle.

Two goalless draws with the USA and Canada were punctuated with a six
goal thrashing in front of 120,000 people in Mexico. Defeat in Costa Rica
made the skies look less than blue but Williams made his mark with a goal
and scored a turning point winner against El Salvador. At that point it was
Burton who started to prove his worth and four goals from the Derby striker
in successive games provided three wins and a draw that all but
mathematically earned Jamaica's trip to Europe.

Since then, Messrs Boyd and Lowe have expressed a desire to rejoin their
national side and players the world over are checking their birth certificates.
Well done, the Reggae Boyz, but don't get crushed under the bandwagon.

CONCACAF Results

Date	Opponents	Ven	Result	Att	Scorers
Caribbean Zone – Second Round					
31.03.96	Surinam	A	1-0	5,000	Whitmore (56)
21.04.96	Surinam	H	1-0	10,000	Davis (72)
Caribbean Zone – Third Round					
23.06.96	Barbados	A	1-0	6,000	Boyd (89)
30.06.96	Barbados	H	2-0	6,000	Whitmore (23); Boyd (71)
Group 3					
15.09.96	Honduras	H	3-0	15,000	Boyd (14, 51); Whitmore (42)
23.09.96	St Vincent	A	2-1	4,000	Young (21, 40)
16.10.96	Mexico	A	1-2	100,000	Boyd (79)
27.10.96	Honduras	A	0-0		
10.11.96	St Vincent	H	5-0	20,000	Whitmore (10, 13); Young (64); Cargill (66); Lowe (85).
17.11.96	Mexico	H	1-0	12,000	Goodison (82)
Final Round					
02.03.97	USA	H	0-0	35, 246	
13.04.97	Mexico	A	0-6	120,000	
27.04.97	Canada	A	0-0		
11.05.97	Costa Rica	A	1-3	15,000	Williams (60)
18.05.97	El Salvador	H	1-0	15,000	Williams (23)
07.09.97	Canada	H	1-0	32,000	Burton (53)
14.09.97	Costa Rica	H	1-0	30,000	Burton (56)
03.10.97	USA	A	1-1	51,000	Burton (51)
09.11.97	El Salvador	A	2-2	40,000	Burton (51); Stewart (78)
16.11.97	Mexico	H	0-0	33,000	

Scorers: 5 – Boyd, Whitmore; 4 – Burton; 3 – Young; 2 – Williams; 1 – Davis, Cargill, Lowe, Goodison, Stewart

Sent Off: Boyd v Honduras (away 67 min)

Group H Opponents Head-to-Head

14 June	Jamaica v Croatia	Lens	8.00 pm
21 June	Argentina v Jamica	Paris	4.30 pm
26 June	Japan v Jamaica	Lyon	3.00 pm

Jamaica have never played Argentina, Croatia or Japan in the World Cup.

CONCACAF Appearances

Name	Tot	St	Sub	PS	Name	Tot	St	Sub	PS
Barrett, Warren	19	19	0	0	Humberto	1	0	1	0
Boyd, Walter	11	8	3	2	Lawrence, Aaron	1	1	0	0
Brown, Dexter	1	1	0	0	Lowe, Onandi	9	8	1	4
Brown, Durrant	18	18	0	3	Malcolm, Steve	14	14	0	4
Burton, Deon	5	5	0	3	McCreath, Tony	6	2	4	2
Butler, Altimont	12	2	10	2	Messam, Gregory	15	14	0	0
Cargill, Peter	15	15	0	3	Palmer, Wayne	2	0	2	0
David, Paul	5	2	3	0	Peterkin, Garth	4	2	2	1
Davis, Fabian	9	7	2	1	Reid, Roderick	1	0	1	0
Dawes, Chris	5	4	1	2	Sewell, Dean	7	4	3	0
Dixon, Linval	18	18	0	0	Simpson, Fitzroy	5	5	0	0
Earle, Robbie	2	0	2	0	Stewart, Donald	3	3	0	0
Gardener, Ricardo	7	6	1	1	Watkins, Fabian	1	1	0	0
Goodison, Ian	19	19	0	0	Whitmore, Theodore	19	19	0	5
Graham, Michael	2	2	0	1	Williams, Andrew	4	4	0	1
Hall, Paul	5	5	0	1	Wright, Hector	7	6	1	5
Harris, Wolde	6	2	4	1	Young, Paul	11	4	7	4

World Cup Record

Year	Stage Reached		Year	Stage Reached
1930-62	Did not enter		1982	Did not enter
1966	Did not qualify		1986	Did not enter
1970	Did not qualify		1990	Did not qualify
1974	Did not enter		1994	Did not qualify
1978	Did not qualify			

Competition	P	W	D	L	F	A
World Cup Finals	0	0	0	0	0	0
World Cup Qualifiers	48	19	12	17	51	70
Total	48	19	12	17	51	70

World Cup Notebook

- Jamaica are appearing in the World Cup finals for the first time ever. Their record was: P20 W11 D6 L3 F24 A15
- Jamaica played no less than 20 games to qualify for the World Cup finals. Ian Goodison and Theodore Whitmore both played in 19 of the games.
- The players who earned the Reggae Boyz, trip to France were each awarded a luxury villa on the coast in Jamaica.
- The team's success saw a lot of new-found Jamaican footballers coming to the fore given a chance to play in the World Cup finals.

JAPAN

Japan Football Association
Founded: 1921   **Affiliations:** AFC – 1954. FIFA – 1929-45, 1950
Address: 2nd Floor, Gotoh Ikueikai Bldg, 1-10-7 Dogenzaka, Shibuya-Ku, Tokyo
Phone: +81 3/3476 2011   **Fax:** +81 3/3476 2291
Colours: Blue shirt, White shorts, Blue socks
Coach: Takeshi Okanda
Key Players: Hidetoshi Nakata, Kazu Miura, Masami Ihara

Dream Team

Japan's first ever appearance in the World Cup finals, after 44 years of trying,
finally came good – and the manner in which it materialised was the stuff of
dreams. Masayuki Okano had sat patiently on the subs bench throughout his
country's games in the final qualifying round. Such was his position again for
the sudden-death play-off with Iran to decide who would go to the finals or
who would face another play-off. With just five minutes of extra time
remaining, Okano, who had finally got his chance, blasted the sudden-death
goal that had his name splashed across his nation's newspapers the next
morning and for many weeks after.

If fact, Okano was one of two inspired substitutions made by coach
Takeshi Okanda. The other was the introduction of Shoji Jo, who produced
the equaliser that sent the game to extra time.

Their progress to that play-off game came after first slicing through the
first-round stage in a group containing Oman, Macao and Nepal. The second
round got off to a good start with a 6-3 win over Uzbekistan but four draws
and a defeat left group rivals South Korea in the driving seat and eventually
led to the elevation of Okano from unknown to cult figure. Takeshi Okanda
was the second coach the Japanese had used during qualifying. The original
incumbent, Shu Kamo, was dismissed during the run of disappointing draws.

Kazu Miura shouldered the goal-scoring burden in those group games,
contributing 15 but failing to find the net again after the initial success over
Uzbekistan. Wagner Lopes, a Brazilian-born forward who became a Japanese
citizen in September, immediately made an impact with important goals, and
his flair may well be one of the highlights in France.

AFC Results

Date	Opponents	Ven	Result	Att	Scorers
Round 1 – Group 4					
23.03.97	Oman	†	1-0	10,000	Omura (10)
25.03.97	Macao	†	10-0	10,000	Takagi (14, 33, 60); Ihara (43); Miura (53, 87pen, 90); Nanami (65); Morishima (78, 80)
27.03.97	Nepal	†	6-0	10,000	Nanami (24); Takagi (50, 54, 60); Omura (72); Honda (89)
22.06.97	Macao	*	10-0	10,000	Nakata (17, 61); Nishizawa (20); Nanami (41); Miura (23, 29, 44, 53, 62, 79)
25.06.97	Nepal	*	3-0	5,000	Nishizawa (45); Miura (73, 87)
28.06.97	Oman	*	1-1	11,000	Nakata (5)

† Played in Muscat. * Played in Tokyo.

Date	Opponents	Ven	Result	Att	Scorers
Round 2 – Group B					
07.09.97	Uzbekistan	H	6-3	54,000	Miura (5, 24, 68, 81); Nakata (40); Jo (45)
19.09.97	UAE	A	0-0	40,000	
28.09.97	South Korea	H	1-2	60,000	Yamaguchi (65)
04.10.97	Kazakhstan	A	1-1	12,000	Akita (23)
11.10.97	Uzbekistan	A	1-1	10,000	Lopes (88)
26.10.97	UAE	H	1-1	56,089	Lopes (3)
01.11.97	South Korea	A	2-0	80,000	Nanami (2); Lopes (37)
08.11.97	Kazakhstan	H	5-1	56,032	Akita (12); Nakata (16); Nakayama (44); Ihara (67); Takagi (79)

Play-Off

Date	Opponents	Ven	Result	Att	Scorers
15.11.97	Iran	†	3-2 aet	22,000	Nakayama (40); Jo (45); Okano (115 – golden goal)

† Johor Bahro, Malaysia.

Scorers: 15 – Miura; 7 – Takagi; 5 – Nakata; 4 – Nanami; 3 – Lopes;
2 – Omura, Ihara, Morishima, Nishizawa, Akita, Jo, Nakayama;
1 – Honda, Yamaguchi, Okano

Group H Opponents Head-to-Head

14 June	Argentina v Japan	Toulouse	1.30 pm
20 June	Japan v Croatia	Nantes	1.30 pm
26 June	Japan v Jamaica	Lyon	3.00 pm

Japan have never played Argentina, Croatia or Jamaica in the World Cup.

AFC Appearances

Name	Tot	St	Sub	PS
Akita, Yutaka	12	10	2	0
Hirano, Takashi	3	1	2	1
Honda, Yasuto	9	7	2	4
Ihara, Masami	14	14	0	1
Jo, Shoji	8	6	2	2
Kawaguchi, Yoshikatsu	15	15	0	0
Kitazawa, Tsuyoshi	7	4	3	3
Lopes, Wagner	6	4	2	1
Miura, Kazuyoshi	13	13	0	1
Mochizuki, Shigeyoshi	1	0	1	0
Morishima, Hiroaki	7	4	3	1
Nakamura, Tadashi	4	3	1	1
Nakanishi, Eisuke	4	1	3	1

Name	Tot	St	Sub	PS
Nakata, Hidetoshi	12	11	1	1
Nakayama, Masashi	1	1	0	1
Nanami, Hiroshi	15	15	0	3
Narahashi, Akira	11	9	2	2
Nishizawa, Akinori	4	2	2	2
Okano, Masayuki	4	0	4	0
Omura, Norio	7	7	0	0
Saito, Toshihide	3	3	0	1
Soma, Naoki	15	15	0	2
Suzuki, Hideto	1	1	0	0
Takagi, Takuya	3	2	1	1
Yamaguchi, Motohiro	15	14	1	2
Yanagimoto, Hiroshige	3	3	0	1

World Cup Record

Year	Stage Reached
1930-50	Did not enter
1954	Did not qualify
1958	Did not enter
1962	Did not qualify
1966	Did not enter
1970	Did not qualify

Year	Stage Reached
1974	Did not qualify
1978	Did not qualify
1982	Did not qualify
1986	Did not qualify
1990	Did not qualify
1994	Did not qualify

Competition	P	W	D	L	F	A
World Cup Finals	0	0	0	0	0	0
World Cup Qualifying	61	28	16	17	124	54
Total	61	28	16	17	124	54

World Cup Notebook

- Takeshi Okanda is Japan's second manager during the 1998 World Cup campaign. The first, Shu Kamo, was sacked after the draw in Uzbekistan.
- Japan reached the World Cup finals after beating Iran in a play-off. Having been 2-1 down, they won the tie with a golden goal scored five minutes from the end of extra time by Masayuki Okano.
- Japan scored an incredible 53 goals in their 15 qualifying games. Twenty of these came in double 10-0 thrashings of Macao. Their full qualifying record was: P15 W9 D5 L1 F53 A12.

MEXICO

Federación Mexicana De Fútbol
Founded: 1927   **Affiliations:** Concacaf – 1961. FIFA – 1929
Address: Abraham Gonzalez 74, C.P. 06600 Mexico DF
Phone: +52 5/566 2155   **Fax:** +52 5/566 7580
National Stadium: Azteca, Mexico City (110,000)
Colours: Green with white collar shirts, White shorts, Red socks
Coach: Manuel Lapuente
Key Players: Luis Alves ('Zague'), Jorge Campos

Colourful Progress

Given their population and the talent that so many of their footballers possess,
Mexico should be annual contenders in the final stages of the competition.
That they are not, they put down to their lack of competition at the highest
standard, and there lies the rub. By staying in CONCACAF they are virtually
guaranteed a place in the finals every four years. A move to the stronger
CONMEBOL with its South American teams would provide the stronger
competition but at what might be the cost of non-qualification.

Despite the quandary, Mexico's qualification for this year's event was far
from convincing. Whilst they topped the CONCACAF group and were
unbeaten, they failed to win any of their last four matches. These included
two successive 0-0 draws with USA and, having led 3-1 in their penultimate
game, a 3-3 draw with Costa Rica. The result was that they were booed off
the pitch in the final match in which they made sure of their finals place! Bora
Milutinovic, the coach, paid the penalty in December when he was replaced
by Manuel Lapuente.

Nevertheless, Mexico look to have a real chance of progressing to the
second phase of the competition and have a squad that is composed of players
who gained experience in USA '94, in which they beat Ireland and only went
out of the competition on penalties to Bulgaria.

In France, Mexico will have the colourful Jorge Campos back in goal for
them. Highly agile, he has also played in attack for his country and for
USA '94 he had special dispensation from FIFA to be registered as both a
goalkeeper and outfield player. Other names that stood out in America and
are likely to figure again are Garcia Aspe, Luis Alves – also known as Zague
or Zaguinho – and top scorer Carlos Hermosillo.

CONCACAF Results

Date	Opponents	Ven	Result	Att	Scorers
Central America – Semi Final Round					
15.06.96	St Vincent	A	3-0	1,600	Pelaez (51, 89); Alvarez (89)
21.09.96	Honduras	A	1-2	19,120	R. Ramirez (63)
16.10.96	Jamaica	H	2-1	110,000	Zague (44); Hermosillo (55)
30.10.96	St Vincent	H	5-1	27,000	Galindo (20, 29); Dos Santos (48); Hermosillo (70); OG (80)
06.11.96	Honduras	H	3-1	105,000	Galindo (32); Hermosillo (35); Zague (45)
17.11.96	Jamaica	A	0-1	32,000	
Final Round					
02.03.97	Canada	H	4-0	100,000	Hermosillo (50, 80); Galindo (59pen); Zague (87)
16.03.97	Costa Rica	A	0-0	28,000	
13.04.97	Jamaica	H	6-0	120,000	Galindo (10pen); Hermosillo (17, 39, 46); Del Olmo (51); Hernandez (85)
20.04.97	USA	A	2-2	54,407	Hermosillo (1); Hernandez (54)
08.06.97	El Salvador	A	1-0	40,000	Luis Garcia (66)
05.10.97	El Salvador	H	5-0	120,000	Galindo (30, 38); Garcia Aspe (35); Zague (47); Luis Garcia (82)
12.10.97	Canada	A	2-2	11,800	Alfaro (8); R. Ramirez (85)
02.11.97	USA	H	0-0	105,000	
09.11.97	Costa Rica	H	3-3	60,000	Chavez (1); Galindo (41); Hermosillo (68)
16.11.97	Jamaica	A	0-0	33,000	

Scorers: 10 – Hermosillo; 8 – Galindo; 4 – Zague; 2 – Pelaez, Hernandez, Luis Garcia; 1 – Alvarez, Dos Santos, Del Olmo, Chavez, Garcia Aspe, Alfaro, OG

Group E Opponents Head-to-Head

13 June	South Korea v Mexico	Lyon	4.30 pm
20 June	Belgium v Mexico	Bordeaux	4.30 pm
25 June	Holland v Mexico	Saint Etienne	3.00 pm

Mexico have encountered Belgium twice at the first-round stage of the World Cup finals and won on both occasions. Curiously, both meetings came in World Cups staged in Mexico. The first was in Mexico City in 1970 when a penalty from Pena was enough to decide the contest after Vadivia took a dive early in the game. The second pairing was settled with headers by Quirarte and Sanchez and marked the first win by Mexico in the finals since their 1970 win over Belgium.

Yr	Round	Opponents	Result	Scorers
1970	First Round	Mexico	1-0	Pena (pen)
1986	First Round	Mexico	2-1	Quirarte, Sanchez

CONCACAF Appearances

Name	Tot	St	Sub	PS	Name	Tot	St	Sub	PS
Abundis, Josi	1	0	1	0	Hermosillo, Carlos	14	14	0	4
Alfaro Rojas, Enrique	5	5	0	5	Hernandez, Luis	6	4	2	1
Alvarado	1	0	1	0	Lara	1	1	0	0
Alvarez, Damian	4	0	4	0	Lozano	1	1	0	1
Bernal, Marcelino	7	6	1	1	Palaez, Ricardo	1	0	1	0
Blanco, Cuauhtemoc	8	1	7	1	Palencia, Francisco	1	1	0	1
Campos, Jorge	8	8	0	0	Pardo, Pavel	14	14	0	0
Chavez	2	2	0	0	Patino	1	1	0	1
Coyote, Alberto	13	12	1	3	Pelaez, Ricardo	7	2	5	1
Davino, Duilio	12	12	0	0	Ramirez, E. Nicolas	5	1	4	0
De Anda, Francisco	2	1	1	0	Ramirez, J. Ramon	14	13	1	2
Del Olmo, Joaquin	7	3	4	1	Rios Gacia	5	5	0	0
Dos Santos, Luis	3	3	0	1	Rodriguez, Jorge	2	2	0	1
Fernandez	1	1	0	0	Romero	4	4	0	0
Galindo, Benjamin	13	13	0	8	Sanchez, Joel	5	5	0	0
Garcia Aspe, Alberto	13	13	0	6	Sol	1	0	1	0
Garcia Postigo, Luis	1	0	1	0	Suarez, Claudio	13	13	0	1
Garcia, Luis	8	1	7	1	Turrubiates	1	1	0	0
Guiterrez, Raul	2	2	0	0	Villa, German	4	3	1	0
Guzman	1	0	1	0	'Zague' (Luis Alves)	8	8	0	4

World Cup Record

Year	Stage Reached	Year	Stage Reached
1930	First Round	1934	Did not qualify
1938	Did not enter	1950	First Round
1954	First Round	1958	First Round
1962	First Round	1966	First Round
1970	Quarter Final	1974	Second Round
1978	First Round	1982	Did not qualify
1986	Quarter Final	1990	Did not enter
1994	Second Round		

Competition	P	W	D	L	F	A
World Cup Finals	33	8	7	18	32	68
World Cup Qualifiers	88	55	22	11	235	66
Total	121	63	29	29	267	134

MOROCCO

Fédération Royale Marocaine De Football
Founded: 1955   **Affiliations:** CAF – 1966. FIFA – 1956
Address: Av. Ibn Sina, C.N.S. Bellevue, BP 51, Rabat
Phone: +212 7/67 27 06/08   **Fax:** +:212 7/67 10 70
National Stadium: Mohamed V, Casablanca (80,000)
Colours: Red shirts, Red shorts, Red socks
Coach: Henri Michel   **Key Players:** Saladdine Bassir, Noureddine Naybet

Review

Moroccan football has gone through a transformation since the national side's disappointing performance in the 1994 World Cup finals. The game has become professional and the national side will have also competed in the African Nations Cup finals which will have been held in Burkina Faso in the early part of 1998. The Lions are appearing in their fourth finals, a record for an African nation, and consider that they have a good chance of competing with Scotland and Norway for the second Group A qualifying spot.

Qualification for Morocco was relatively straightforward with five wins and a draw from their six group games and came in their penultimate game at home in front of 90,000 supporters when a header by Khalid Raghib secured a 1-0 win. It was one of 14 goals scored by the team which conceded just two in a draw in Ghana. Their game in Gabon in April 1997 was won with just 55 minutes of play when the home supporters invaded the pitch, causing the game to be abandoned. Morocco's 4-0 lead at the time was allowed to stand.

On the bench, Morocco have great talent in coach Henri Michel, who took charge in October 1995 and has been to the finals twice before, with France in 1986 and Cameroon in 1994. The French connection does not stop there because another former French national team coach, Michel Hidalgo, is employed as a consultant to their national federation.

The talent of the Moroccan side has not gone unnoticed and left back Abdelkrim Hadrioui now plays in Portugal with Benfica while Saladdine Bassir (ten goals in 16 internationals) and Noureddine Naybet have pursued promising careers in Spain with La Coruna. Many of the Moroccans will see France '98 as an opportunity to follow them.

The progress of the national team may well continue in France and they will be buoyed by the fact that it needed goals in the final ten minutes by Denilson to earn Brazil a victory over them when the countries met in South America for a friendly last October. One other factor that will weigh in their favour is the anticipated arrival of some 20,000 plus Moroccans at the finals.

CAF Group 5 Results and Appearances

Date	Opponents	Ven	Result	Att	Scorers
09.11.96	Sierra Leone	H	4-0	30,000	Hababi (18); Khalid Raghib (50, 55); Fertout (57)
12.01.97	Ghana	A	2-2	45,000	Bassir (30); Hadjiel
06.04.97	Gabon *	A	4-0	40,000	Ahmed Bahja (2, 5); Bassir (38, 42)
26.04.97	Sierra Leone	A	1-0		Bassir (40)
08.06.97	Ghana	H	1-0	90,000	Khalid Raghib (77)
17.08.97	Gabon	H	2-0		Naybet (25); Amhed Bahja (45)

* Match abandoned after 55 minutes when home supporters invaded pitch.

Scorers: 4 – Bassir; 2 – Ahmed Bahja, Khalid Raghib; 1 – Hababi, Hadjiel, Naybet, Fertout

Name	Tot	St	Sub	PS	Name	Tot	St	Sub	PS
Abrami, Lahcene	2	2	0	0	Hadjiel, Mustapha	4	4	0	0
Arraki, Abdellatif	1	0	1	0	Hadrioui, Abdelkrim	2	2	0	0
Azzouzi, Rachid	3	3	0	1	Jrindou, Abdellatif	1	0	1	0
Bahja, Ahmed	1	1	0	1	Khalif, Mustapha	2	0	2	0
Bassir, Saladdine	3	3	0	1	Nader, Hassan	1	0	1	0
Bouyboud, Abdelmajid	2	2	0	1	Naybet, Nourredine	4	4	0	0
Chiba, Said	1	1	0	1	Nazir, Abdelkrim	0	0	1	0
Chippo, Youssef	3	3	0	0	Raghib, Khalid	3	1	2	1
El Brazi, Abdelkader	4	4	0	1	Rossi, Youssef	2	2	0	0
El Khalej, Tahar	2	1	1	0	Saber, Abdelilah	4	4	0	0
Fertout, Youssef	3	3	0	0	Sellami, Jamal	2	2	0	2
Hababi, El Arbit	1	1	0	1	Triki, Smahi	2	1	1	0

Does not include games v Gabon.

Group A Opponents Head-to-Head

10 June	Morocco v Norway	Montpellier	8.00 pm
16 June	Brazil v Morocco	Nantes	8.00 pm
23 June	Scotland v Morocco	Saint Etienne	8.00 pm

Brazil, Norway and Scotland will provide new World Cup opponents for Morocco.

World Cup Record

Year	Stage Reached		Year	Stage Reached
1930-58	Did not enter		1978	Did not qualify
1962	Did not qualify		1982	Did not qualify
1966	Did not enter		1986	Second Round
1970	First Round		1990	Did not qualify
1974	Did not qualify		1994	First Round

Competition	P	W	D	L	F	A
World Cup Finals	10	1	3	6	7	13
World Cup Qualifiers	66	31	21	14	86	45
Total	76	32	24	20	93	58

World Cup Notebook

- Morocco's qualifying game in Gabon was abandoned after 55 minutes of play when the home fans invaded the pitch. Morocco were leading 4-0 and the result was allowed to stand.
- Morocco conceded just two goals in their qualifying campaign, both of which came in a 2-2 draw in Ghana.
- The 1998 World Cup finals mark Morocco's fourth appearance in the finals.

NIGERIA

Nigeria Football Association
Founded: 1945   **Affiliations:** CAF – 1959. FIFA – 1959
Address: National Stadium, PO Box 466, Lagos
Phone: +234 9-523 7322/4/5/6   **Fax:** +234 9-523 7323/7
National Stadium: National Stadium, Lagos (50,000)
Colours: Green shirts, White shorts, Green socks
Coach: Bora Mitutinovic (Philippe Troussier – sacked at end November 1997)
Key Players: Nwanku Kanu, Daniel Amokachi

Eagle Eyed

Few who saw Nigeria's first ever game in the World Cup finals in 1994 will
ever forget it, as the Eagles stunned eventual quarter finalists Bulgaria 3-0 in
Dallas. The sheer power, pace and even naivety of the Nigerians was
bewildering to watch and elevated Yekini, Amokachi and Amunike to
household names. How ironic that they find themselves paired with the
Bulgarians once again.

Their route to the finals has not just been about winning their CAF
Group 1 but dealing with the politics that had human rights campaigners
demanding their exclusion for the undoubted atrocities that have prevailed
under the military junta of General Sani Abacha.

It would seem that an African country is still a long way off from
contesting the ultimate game – that of the final itself. However, Nigeria won
the 1996 Olympic title, beating strong Brazilian and Argentine sides in the
process and will upset any who do not take them seriously enough.

Nigeria were the first nation to qualify for the finals, having done so in
June last year with a 3-0 win over Kenya. This rendered their final game in
Guinea meaningless, and not surprisingly saw their only defeat in a group that
also saw victories over Burkina Faso (twice) and Guinea.

How well Nigeria progress could well depend on the availability of
Nwanko Kanu, their skipper in that Olympic victory, who is now back
playing following heart surgery that had threatened his career. Victor Ikpeba,
part of Monaco's Champions League side, was voted CAF African Footballer
of the Year for 1997 – the fourth Nigerian in five years to win the award. He
will also have an important role to play on the wing with teammates looking
to him to supply the ammunition for the likes of Daniel Amokachi.

CAF Group 1 Results and Appearances

Date	Opponents	Ven	Result	Att	Scorers
09.11.96	Burkina Faso	H	2-0	55,000	Amokachi (46, 75)
12.01.97	Kenya	A	1-1	60,000	Akpoborie (48)
05.04.97	Guinea	H	2-1	50,000	Amokachi (65, 76)
27.04.97	Burkina Faso	A	2-1		Adepoju (42); Amunike (58)
07.06.97	Kenya	H	3-0	50,000	Oliseh (12); Amunike (43); Oruma (81)
17.08.97	Guinea	A	0-1	12,000	

Scorers: 4 – Amokachi; 2 – Amunike; 1 – Akpoborie , Adepoju, Oliseh, Oruma

Sent Off: Eguavon v Guinea (home 77 min)

Name	Tot	St	Sub	PS	Name	Tot	St	Sub	PS
Adepoju, Mutiu	4	4	0	0	Nwanu, Chidi	1	1	0	0
Akpoborie, Jon	5	4	1	4	Ohenhen, Christopher	1	0	1	0
Amokachi, Daniel	6	6	0	1	Ojigwe	1	0	1	0
Amunike, Emmanuel	5	3	2	1	Okafor, Vchenna	1	1	0	0
Babangida, Tijani	2	0	2	0	Okechukwu, Uche	6	6	0	0
Babayaro, Celestine	5	4	1	0	Okocha, Augustine	6	6	0	2
Baruwa, Abiodun	2	2	0	0	Okpara, Goodwin	2	1	1	0
Dosu, Joseph	2	2	0	0	Oliseh, Sunday	5	5	0	0
Eguavon, Augustine Owen	1	1	0	0	Oparaku, Mobi Patrick	3	3	0	1
Ekdku, Efangwu	1	0	1	0	Oruma, Wilson	1	0	1	0
Findi, George	4	4	0	3	Rufai	1	1	0	0
Ikpeba Nosa, Victor	4	1	3	1	Shorunmu, Ike	1	1	0	0
Iroha, Benedict	1	1	0	0	West, Taribo	5	5	0	0
Kanu	1	0	1	0	Yekini, Rasheed	1	1	0	1
Lawal, Garba	3	3	0	1					

Group D Opponents Head-to-Head

13 June	Spain v Nigeria	Nantes	1.30 pm
19 June	Nigeria v Bulgaria	Saint Etienne	4.30 pm
24 June	Nigeria v Paraguay	Toulouse	9.00 pm

Nigeria marked their first ever match in the World Cup finals with a sensational 3-0 win over Bulgaria in the Dallas Cotton Bowl. Yekini, Amokachi and Amunike scored the goals.

Yr	Round	Opponents	Result	Scorers
1994	First Round	Bulgaria	3-0	Yekini, Amokachi, Amunike

World Cup Record

Year	Stage Reached		Year	Stage Reached
1930-58	Did not enter		1978	Did not qualify
1962	Did not qualify		1982	Did not qualify
1966	Did not enter		1986	Did not qualify
1970	Did not qualify		1990	Did not qualify
1974	Did not qualify		1994	Second Round

Competition	P	W	D	L	F	A
World Cup Finals	4	2	0	2	7	4
World Cup Qualifiers	56	27	16	13	93	57
Total	60	29	16	15	100	61

World Cup Notebook

- Nigeria became the first team to qualify for the 1998 World Cup finals when they beat Kenya 3-0 in June 1997.
- In 1994 it took a last-minute solo effort from Roberto Baggio to give Italy a narrow win over the Eagles in the quarter finals of the competition.
- Nigeria had a sensational start to their first ever World Cup finals when they beat Bulgaria 3-0 in 1994. The scorer of their first goal was Yekini after 21 minutes.
- Nigeria sacked manager Philippe Troussier after he had guided them to the finals for only the second time in their history!

NORWAY

Norges Fotballforbund
Founded: 1902   **Affiliations:** UEFA – 1954. FIFA – 1908
Address: Ullevål Hageby, Boks 3823, N-0805 Oslo
Phone: +47 22 02 45 00   **Fax:** +47 22 95 10 10
National Stadium: Ullevaal Stadion, Oslo (28,000)
Colours: Red shirts, White shorts, Blue socks
Coach: Egil Olsen
Key Players: Henning Berg, Petter Rudi, Tore Andre Flo

Defensive Mood

Norway were only one of four UEFA teams to go undefeated in qualifying games, winning six of their eight Group 3 games, scoring 21 goals and conceding just two goals – with England the best defensive record in the UEFA groups. Their performance was such that they finished eight points clear of second-placed Hungary. Indeed, both Finland and Hungary, who managed to score against the Norwegians, were the only teams who managed to take points off them. The form of goalkeeping captain Frode Grodas was a key factor in this and he was just one of four players who were ever present in the qualifying games.

In among all this was a sensational 4-2 win over France '98 group rivals Brazil in a friendly match in Oslo. The Norwegians were outstanding on that night and produced a significant passing game that has not been the cornerstone of Egil Olsen's career as coach.

The 1998 finals will mark the end of Olsen's reign and, despite the criticism of his style, he more than any has been responsible for pulling Norway out of the world soccer doldrums – USA '94 was the first time they had ever qualified for the finals.

The foundation of the Norwegian team is based around players who ply their trade in the FA Premier League. Petter Rudi, Tore Andre Flo, Egil Ostenstad, Henning Berg, Lars Bohinen – the list goes on and their performances against group rivals Scotland may decide who progresses to the second phase.

In qualifying, Norway started and ended their round robin games with three straight wins but the calibre of teams in what was arguably the weakest UEFA group may not have helped Norway's cause. However, there is simply too much talent in the side to be ignored, especially if Ole Gunnar Solskjaer can reproduce his Manchester United form.

UEFA Group 3 Results and Appearances

Date	Opponents	Ven	Result	Att	Scorers
02.06.96	Azerbaijan	H	5-0	14,012	Solbakken (8, 46); Solskjaer (37, 89); Strandli (60)
09.10.96	Hungary	H	3-0	22,480	Rekdal (83, 89, 90)
10.11.96	Switzerland	A	1-0	22,000	Leonhardsen (32)
30.04.97	Finland	H	1-1	22,287	Solksjaer (83)
08.06.97	Hungary	A	1-1	20,000	Rudi (8)
20.08.97	Finland	A	4-0	15,000	Solbakken (8); Rudi (12); J. Flo (48); TA. Flo (84)
06.09.97	Azerbaijan	A	1-0	12,000	TA. Flo (43)
10.09.97	Switzerland	H	5-0	22,603	Jakobsen (46); Solbakken (50); Eggen (65); Ostenstad (74); TA. Flo (85)

Scorers: 4 – Solbakken; 3 – TA. Flo, Rekdal, Solskjaer; 2 – Rudi; 1 – Eggen, J. Flo, Jakobsen, Leonhardsen, Ostenstad, Strandli

Name	Tot	St	Sub	PS	Name	Tot	St	Sub	PS
Berg, Henning	8	8	0	0	Leonhardsen, Oyvind	4	4	0	2
Bjornebye, Stig Inge	7	7	0	0	Mykland, Erik	6	6	0	3
Bohinen, Lars	1	1	0	0	Nielsen, Roger	1	1	0	0
Eggen, Dan	4	4	0	0	Olsen, Odd Inge	1	0	1	0
Flo, Havard	2	0	2	0	Ostenstad, Egil	4	1	3	0
Flo, Jostine	5	3	2	3	Rekdal, Kjetil	8	8	0	2
Flo, Tore Andre	7	6	1	2	Rudi, Petter	5	5	0	0
Grodas, Frode	8	8	0	0	Skammelsrud, Bent	2	0	2	0
Haaland, Alf-Inge	6	4	2	0	Solbakken, Staale	7	5	2	1
Halle, Gunnar	4	2	2	1	Solskjaer, Ole Gunnar	4	3	1	1
Jakobsen, John Ivar	1	1	0	1	Strandli, Frank	8	6	2	3
Johnsen, Ronnie	5	5	0	1	Svindal Larsen	1	0	1	0

Group A Opponents Head-to-Head

10 June	Morocco v Norway	Montpellier	8.00 pm
16 June	Scotland v Norway	Bordeaux	4.30 pm
23 June	Brazil v Norway	Marseilles	8.00 pm

Norway have met only Scotland before in the World Cup. In the qualifying competition for the 1990 tournament they were paired together in Group 5. The first game in the group saw Scotland win 2-1 in Oslo. By the time the two played out a 1-1 draw in Glasgow, the Norwegians were already out of the tournament.

World Cup Record

Year	Stage Reached		Year	Stage Reached
1930-34	Did not enter		1970	Did not qualify
1938	First Round		1974	Did not qualify
1950	Did not enter		1978	Did not qualify
1954	Did not qualify		1982	Did not qualify
1958	Did not qualify		1986	Did not qualify
1962	Did not qualify		1990	Did not qualify
1966	Did not qualify		1994	First Round

Competition	P	W	D	L	F	A
Wrld Cup Finals	4	1	1	2	2	3
World Cup Qualifiers	76	28	15	33	110	119
Total	80	29	16	35	112	122

World Cup Notebook

- Norway's qualification for the 1994 World Cup finals surprised everyone, not least Holland, England and Poland who they beat for top spot in their qualifying group.
- Manager Egil Olsen will retire after the finals in France.
- Norway were unbeaten in their qualifying group, scoring 20 goals and conceding just two goals in the process.

PARAGUAY

Liga Paraguaya De Fútbol
Founded: 1906   **Affiliations:** Conmebol – 1921. FIFA – 1921
Address: Estadio Defensores del Chaco, Calles Mayor Martinez y Alejo Garcia,
    Asuncion
Phone: +595 21/48 01 20   **Fax:** +595 21/48 01 24
National Stadium: Defensores del Chaco (60,000)
Colours: Red and White vertical striped shirt, Blue shorts, Blue socks
Coach: Paulo Cesar Carpeggiani
Key Players: Jose Luis Chilavert, Roberto Acuna

Paraguay's Best

You will find few people to argue against the fact that the Paraguay team that
goes to only their fourth ever finals is the best in the nation's history. Under
coach and former Brazilian international Paulo Cesar Carpeggiani, they have
played a wing-back formation that has provided a tight five-man defence
when required but capable of joining in with the attack. Something that has
helped secured nine wins from their 16 group games.

Paraguay finished as runner-up to Argentina in the CONMEBOL group
and Argentina remained the only team they failed to take at least one point
from. A 1-0 defeat in Colombia in the first qualifying game was the catalyst
for a run of nine games without defeat, which included a 2-1 revenge win
over Colombia in Asuncion. The match degenerated into a brawl and ended in
their goalkeeper and captain Jose Luis Chilavert being dismissed with
Faustino Asprilla in the 77th minute. In his ensuing four-match ban, Paraguay
lost three successive games and only on his return did they steady the ship to
record the wins over Peru and Venezuela they needed to secure qualification.

Chilavert is Paraguay's all-action hero. He keeps goal, takes penalties and
has been known to join in with the attack when the situation requires. His
temper is his failing and so expect him to contest every adverse decision
during France '98.

Paraguay used 38 players in their campaign and although no one player
featured in all games, Carlos Gamarra, Roberto Acuna and Julio Enciso
featured in all but one and will be certain starters in France. Gamarra in
particular is central to the team's defence and is an accomplished sweeper in
his own right as well as being a regular on the team's score sheet.

CONMEBOL Group Results and Appearances

Date	Opponents	Ven	Result	Att	Scorers
24.04.96	Colombia	A	0-1	60,000	
02.06.96	Uruguay	A	2-0	60,000	Arce (10); Rojas (89)
01.09.96	Argentina	A	1-1	40,000	Chilavert (42)
09.10.96	Chile	H	2-1	40,000	Gamarra (24); Rivarola (63)
10.11.96	Ecuador	H	1-0	37,000	Benitez (23)
15.12.96	Bolivia	A	0-0	25,000	
12.01.97	Venezuela	A	2-0	16,000	Benitez (6); Enciso (61)
12.02.97	Peru	H	2-1	35,000	Rivarola (12); Rojas (40)
02.04.97	Colombia	H	2-1	42,000	Gamarra (24); Soto (85)
30.04.97	Uruguay	H	3-1	45,000	Rojas (37); Cardozo (73pen); Soto (83)
06.07.97	Argentina	H	1-2	48,000	Acuna (58pen)
20.07.97	Chile	A	1-2	75,143	Brizuela (62)
20.08.97	Ecuador	A	1-2	12,000	R. Baez (5)
10.09.97	Bolivia	H	2-1	45,000	Benitez (27); Gamarra (36)
12.10.97	Venezuela	H	1-0	30,000	Torres (69)
16.11.97	Peru	A	0-1	25,000	

Scorers: 3 – Benitez, Gamarra, Rojas; 2 – Soto; 1 – Arce, Chilavert, Rivarola, Enciso, Cardozo, Acona, R. Baez, Torres, Brizola, Rivarola

Sent Off: Chilavert v Colombia (home 77 min); Rivarola v Uruguay (home 90 min); Brizuela v Chile (away 64 min)

Name	Tot	St	Sub	PS	Name	Tot	St	Sub	PS
Aceval, Danilo	2	2	0	0	Ferreira, Virgilo	5	1	4	1
Acuna, Roberto	15	15	0	4	Gamarra, Carlos	15	15	0	0
Alcaraz, Jorge	6	3	3	0	Gonzalez, Gabriel	4	0	4	0
Arce, Francisco	10	10	0	0	Jara, Juan	2	2	0	1
Ayala, Celso	14	14	0	0	Meza, Justo	2	0	2	0
Baez, Edgar	1	1	0	1	Ovelar	2	2	0	1
Baez, Richart	7	7	0	4	Ramirez	2	1	1	1
Benitez, Miguel	10	9	1	3	Rivarola, Catalino	11	11	0	0
Bourdier, Harles	7	5	2	0	Rojas, Aristides	14	11	3	6
Brizuela, Hugo	3	1	2	0	Rojas, R.	4	0	4	0
Caballero, Mauro	1	1	0	1	Romad, B.	1	0	1	0
Campos, Jorge	2	1	1	1	Santos, M.	1	0	1	0
Caniza, Denis	3	3	0	2	Sarabia, Pedro	6	4	2	1
Cardozo, Josi	5	3	2	1	Sotelo, Angel	1	1	0	0
Chilavert, Jose Luis	10	10	0	0	Soto, Derlis	5	2	3	1
Cohener, Osvaldo	2	1	1	1	Struway, Estanislao	12	12	0	3
Diaz, Ruben Ruiz	5	4	1	0	Suarez, Silvio	4	4	0	2
Enciso, Julio	15	14	1	4	Torres, Yegros	2	1	1	1
Esteche, Francisco	3	2	1	1	Villamayor, Juan	2	2	0	0

Group D Opponents Head-to-Head

12 June	Paraguay v Bulgaria	Montpellier	1.30 pm
19 June	Spain v Paraguay	Saint Etienne	8.00 pm
24 June	Nigeria v Paraguay	Toulouse	8.00 pm

Paraguay have never played Spain, Bulgaria or Nigeria in the World Cup.

World Cup Record

Year	Stage Reached	Year	Stage Reached
1930	First Round	1970	Did not qualify
1934	Did not enter	1974	Did not qualify
1938	Did not enter	1978	Did not qualify
1950	First Round	1982	Did not qualify
1954	Did not enter	1986	Second Round
1958	First Round	1990	Did not qualify
1962	Did not qualify	1994	Did not qualify
1966	Did not qualify		

Competition	P	W	D	L	F	A
World Cup Finals	11	3	4	4	16	25
World Cup Qualifying	66	29	14	23	89	71
Total	77	32	18	27	105	96

World Cup Notebook

- Paraguay last reached the World Cup finals in 1986, where they lost in the second round, 3-0 to England. Gary Lineker (two) and Peter Beardsley scored the goals.
- In the 1958 finals in Sweden, Paraguay suffered their biggest ever defeat in the finals when they lost 7-3 to France.

ROMANIA

Fédératia Roumaine de Football
Founded: 1908   **Affiliations:** UEFA – 1954 FIFA – 1930
Address: Bd. Poligrafiei 3 Sector 1, RO-71556 Bucuresti
Phone: +40 1/222 99 93   **Fax:** +40 1/223 23 60
National Stadium: Stadionul 23 August, Bucharest (65,000)
Colours: Yellow shirts, Yellow shorts, Yellow socks
Coach: Anghel Iordanescu
Key Players: Gheorghe Hagi, Viorel Moldovan

European First

Romania seemed to be on cruise control during their qualifying games, becoming the first UEFA team to secure their spot in the finals. Nine straight victories came within seven minutes of a 100% record but failed when Tony Cascarino equalised for the Republic of Ireland in the final group game.

Despite the record, the gloss is not so blinding when the opponents of Romania's qualifying group are analysed. Lithuania, Iceland, Macedonia, Liechtenstein and the current Republic side do not come out of the top drawer.

Six victories had seen Romania post a 20-0 goal tally. It was in their seventh game that keeper Bogdan Stelea conceded his first goals – two by Macedonia, but still finished on the winning side. Stelea conceded just two more goals in the group, by the end of which captain Gheorghe Hagi had established a national record of 32 goals for his country in 107 appearances.

Coach Anghel Iordanescu has come under criticism from several of his players and he responded by sidelining them or ignoring them altogether. And while many of Romania's players are erring on the wrong side of 30, they still have players capable of turning games when the mood takes them. Dan Petrescu, who has had such an impact at Chelsea, was the only player to feature in all ten of Romania's qualifying games, while Dorinel Munteanu pulls the strings along with Hagi – the 'Maradona of the Carpathians' as he has become known. Up front Gheorghe Popescu and Dinu Moldovan have found the score sheet with regularity.

Having reached the quarter finals in 1994, Romania will be hard pressed to match it again, but they may not be the soft touch many might predict.

UEFA Group 8 Results and Appearances

Date	Opponents	Ven	Result	Att	Scorers
31.08.96	Lithuania	H	3-0	10,500	Moldovan (21); Petrescu (65); Galca (77)
09.10.96	Iceland	A	4-0	43,750	Moldovan (22); Hagi (60); Popescu (75); Petrescu (89)
14.12.96	Macedonia	A	3-0	15,000	Popescu (37, 45, 90pen)
29.03.97	Leichtenstein	H	8-0	2,5000	Moldovan(10); Popescu (28, 30, 58, 82); Hagi (47); Petrescu (49); Craioveanu (71)
02.04.97	Lithuania	A	1-0	10,000	Moldovan (75)
30.04.97	Rep. Ireland	H	1-0	21,500	A.Ilie (32)
20.08.97	Macedonia	H	4-2	20,000	Moldovan (36pen, 62); Galca (42); Dumitrescu (65)
06.09.97	Leichtenstein	A	8-1		Moldovan (6); Dobos (36); Craioveanu (10, 32); Munteanu (44, 45, 69); Barbu (55).
10.09.97	Iceland	H	4-0	12,000	Hagi (8, 81pen); Petrescu (40); Galca (65)
11.10.97	Rep. Ireland	H	1-1	49,000	Hagi (53)

Scorers: 8 – Gh.Popescu; 7 – Moldovan; 5 – Hagi; 4 – Petrescu; 3 – Galca, Craioveanu, Munteanu; 1 – A. Ilie, Dumitrescu, Dobos, Barbu

Name	Tot	St	Sub	PS	Name	Tot	St	Sub	PS
Barbu, Constatin	2	0	2	0	Petrescu, Dan	10	10	0	2
Ciobotariu, Liviu	3	1	2	0	Popescu, Gabriel	4	0	4	0
Craioveanu, Gheorghe	6	3	3	3	Popescu, Gheorghe	8	8	0	1
Dobos, Anton	9	9	0	1	Potociano, Ioan Dan	1	0	1	0
Dumitrescu, Ilie	5	3	2	0	Prodan, Daniel	9	9	0	1
Filipescu, Iulian	6	3	3	0	Pruena, Florin	2	1	1	1
Galca, Constantin	9	9	0	2	Rotariu, Iosif	1	0	1	0
Gherasim, Daniel	1	0	1	0	Selymes, Tibor	9	8	1	1
Hagi, Gheorghe	6	6	0	3	Serban, Denis	2	2	0	0
Ilie, Adrian	8	7	1	4	Stefan, Liviu	1	0	1	0
Lacatus, Marius	1	0	1	0	Stelea, Bogdan	8	8	0	0
Lupescu, Ioan	2	2	0	1	Stinga, Ovidiu	2	0	2	0
Moldovan, Viorel	8	8	0	5	Stingaciu, Dumintru	1	1	0	1
Munteanu, Dorinel	8	8	0	1	Viorel, Ion	1	0	1	0
Panduru, Basarab	1	0	1	0	Vladoiu, Ion	4	3	1	2
Papura, Corneliu	1	1	0	0					

Group G Opponents Head-to-Head

15 June	Romania v Colombia	Lyon	4.30 pm
22 June	Romania v England	Toulouse	8.00 pm
26 June	Romania v Tunisia	Saint Denis	8.00 pm

Romania have come up against England in the finals once before, and twice in qualifying tournaments. The northern Mexican city of Guadalajara was the setting for the 1970 Group 3 encounter between the teams, which was rather bland and settled by a goal from Geoff Hurst 20 minutes from full-time.

The teams were pitted against each other in the qualifying stages for two successive World Cups, namely the lead-up to the 1982 and 1986 finals. Three of the games ended in draws (twice goalless and once 1-1) with the Romanians winning the very first encounter 2-1 in Bucharest.

Colombia, though, have provided the most recent opposition – the two teams meeting in Pasadena's Rose Bowl in 1994. In a fine contest the Romanians scored some terrific goals to win a memorable game 3-1.

Yr	Round	Opponents	Result	Scorers
1970	First Round	England	0-1	
1994	First Round	Romania	3-1	Raducioiu (2), Hagi

World Cup Record

Year	Stage Reached	Year	Stage Reached
1930	First Round	1970	First Round
1934	First Round	1974	Did not qualify
1938	First Round	1978	Did not qualify
1950	Did not enter	1982	Did not qualify
1954	Did not qualify	1986	Did not qualify
1958	Did not qualify	1990	Second Round
1962	Did not enter	1994	Quarter Final
1966	Did not qualify		

Competition	P	W	D	L	F	A
World Cup Finals	17	6	4	7	25	29
World Cup Qualifiers	74	42	15	17	148	70
Total	91	48	19	24	173	99

World Cup Notebook

- Romania came within seven minutes of having a perfect record in their qualifying group. Tony Cascarino's 83rd minute equaliser for the Republic of Ireland in Dublin put paid to what looked like being Romania's tenth successive win.
- Chelsea's Dan Petrescu was the only Romanian to feature in all ten qualifying games.

SAUDI ARABIA

Saudi Arabian Football Federation
Founded: 1959   **Affiliations:** AFC – 1972. FIFA – 1959
Address: Al Mather Quarter (Ol. Compl.), P.O. Box 5844, Ruyadh 11432
Phone: +966 1/482 2240   **Fax:** +966 1/482 1215
National Stadium: Alaz, Riyadh (30,000)
Colours: White shirts, Green shorts, White socks
Coach: To be appointed
Key Players: Mohammed Al Daeya, Sami Al Jaber

Spell Broken?

Despite an early exit from the Confederation Cup they hosted last December, Saudi Arabia have had one of the most successful spells of any Asian side. At the end of 1996 they won the Asian Cup for a record-tying third time and this came on the back of qualification for the 1996 Olympic Games football tournament and success in the 1994 Gulf Cup. The World Cup finals in 1994 was their first ever qualification and victories over Morocco and Belgium meant they became the most successful Asian side in the finals. Saudi this time go to the World Cup finals with a new coach in charge because Eguardo Vinganda's contract was not renewed despite him having masterminded that Asian Cup success.

Their route to the 1998 finals was almost as hectic as their previous schedules suggest – with no less than 14 games being needed to negotiate two round robin stages. The first of these saw five wins from six games with 18 goals scored and just one conceded. Progress to the second phase provided more testing opposition but the Saudis still managed to top the group and gain automatic qualification with four wins, two draws and two defeats from their eight group games.

Iran, who eventually qualified via a variety of play-off games, provided the most testing opposition, and after Saudi had put themselves in the group driving seat with a 1-0 win over them three games from home, a subsequent draw with China PR meant that Saudi had to avoid defeat in Qatar to ensure automatic qualification. The result was never really in doubt even though it needed a goal midway through the second half to ensure victory.

That goal was scored by Al Jaber, a 25-year-old striker who excels at running at defences with the ball at his feet. His four goals helped the Saudis, who perhaps show greater versatility in the goal scoring stakes than most. Thirteen different players made their mark along the way. Whether that will prove unlucky for Saudi Arabia or not remains to be seen.

AFC Results

Date	Opponents	Ven	Result	Att	Scorers
Round 1 – Group 1					
14.09.97	Ch. Taipei	†	2-0		Obied Al Dosary (34); Ibrahim Al Shahrani (37)
18.03.97	Malaysia	†	0-0		
20.03.97	Bangladesh	†	4-1		Khalid Al Muwalid (20); Khalid Al Temawi (27); Ibrahim Al Shahrani (65); Fahad Al Mehalel (73)
27.03.97	Bangladesh	*	3-0	20,000	Ibrahim Al Shahrani (2); Obeid Al Dosary (43); Abdullah Al Jamaan (79)
29.03.97	Malaysia	*	3-0	15,000	Khalid Al Muwalid (59, 85); Obied Al Shabrany (87)
31.03.97	Ch. Taipei	*	6-0	9,000	Sami Al Jaber (3, 16, 63); Khalid Al Muwalid (5); Abdul Aziz Al Dossary (30); Khamis Al Zahrani (46)

† Played in Kuala Lumpa
* Played in Jeddah

Date	Opponents	Ven	Result	Att	Scorers
Round 2 – Group A					
14.09.97	Kuwait	H	2-1	50,000	Fahad Mehalel (45); Youssef Al Thyniyan (54)
19.09.97	Iran	A	1-1	110,000	Ibrahim Al Shahrani (35)
03.10.97	China PR	A	0-1	65,000	
11.10.97	Qatar	H	1-0	25,000	Khalid Al Muwalid (66)
17.10.97	Kuwait	A	1-2	50,000	Khalid Musad (31)
24.10.97	Iran	H	1-0	60,000	Khalid Musad (89)
06.11.97	China PR	H	1-1	60,000	Khalid Musad (14)
12.11.97	Qatar	A	1-0	22,000	Sami Al Jaber (63)

Scorers: 5 – Khalid Al Muwalid; 4 – Ibrahim Al Shahrani, Sami Al Jaber; 3 – Khalid Musad; 2 – Fahad Mehalel, Obied Al Dossary; 1 – Abdul Aziz Al Dossary, Abdullah Al Jamaan, Khalid Al Temawi, Khamis Al Zahrani, Obied Al Shabrany, Youssef Al Thyniyan

Group C Opponents Head-to-Head

12 June	Saudi Arabia v Denmark	Lens	4.30 pm
18 June	France v Saudi Arabia	Saint Denis	8.00 pm
24 June	South Africa v Saudi Arabia	Bordeaux	3.00 pm

Saudi Arabia have never played any of their Group C opponents in the World Cup before.

AFC Appearances

Name	Tot	St	Sub	PS
Al Daeya, Mohammed	5	5	0	0
Al Dosary, Obeid	4	4	0	2
Al Dossary, Abdul Aziz	1	0	1	0
Al Dossary, Abdullah	2	1	1	1
Al Dossary, Ahmed	2	0	2	0
Al Dossary, Khamis	5	5	0	0
Al Harbi, Ibrahim	5	5	0	3
Al Jaber, Sami	3	0	3	0
Al Jahni, Mohammed	5	5	0	1
Al Janouby, Abdul	1	1	0	1
Al Khlaiwi, Mohammed	1	1	0	0
Al Muwalid, Khalid	4	4	0	1
Al Shabrany, Obied	1	1	0	0
Al Shahrani, Ibrahim	5	5	0	0
Al Temawi, Khalid	5	5	0	3
Al Zahrani, Khamis	1	0	1	0
Madani, Ahmed Jamil	3	3	0	0
Mehalel, Fahad	3	0	3	0
Sulaimani, Hussein	4	4	0	0
Zubromawi, Abdullah	5	5	0	0

Appearances for First Round games only but excluding final fixture against China Taipei.

World Cup Record

Year	Stage Reached		Year	Stage Reached
1930-74	Did not enter		1986	Did not qualify
1978	Did not qualify		1990	Did not qualify
1982	Did not qualify		1994	Second Round

Competition	P	W	D	L	F	A
World Cup Finals	4	2	0	2	5	6
World Cup Qualifiers	50	24	13	13	77	47
Total	54	26	13	15	82	53

World Cup Notebook

- Saudi Arabia qualified for their first World Cup finals in 1994 and a win against Belgium ensured them a place in the second round where they lost 2-1 to Sweden.

125

SCOTLAND

The Scottish Football Association
Founded: 1873
Affiliations: UEFA – 1954. FIFA – 1910-20, 1924-28, 1946
Address: 6 Park Gardens, Glasgow, G3 7YF
Phone: 0141 332 6372   **Fax:** 0141 332 7559
National Stadium: Hampden Park, Glasgow (38,113)
Colours: Dark Blue shirts, White shorts, Red with Dark Blue socks
Coach: Craig Brown   **Key Players:** Gary McAllister, Kevin Gallacher

Second Target

Could Scotland reach the second phase of a World Cup finals for the first time ever in France '98? There are many who believe they can although their Group A opponents may be stronger off paper then they might appear on it.

What paper does show though is just how strong the Scotland defence is: only three goals were conceded in their ten group games, which included eight clean sheets. Much of this is down to the fine form of veteran keeper Jim Leighton and the blond rock that is Blackburn's Colin Hendry.

Despite scoring 15 goals, it is in attack that Scotland have looked lightweight at times, and this may be their eventual undoing. The 'retirement' from international football of the controversial Duncan Ferguson has left Kevin Gallacher to shoulder most of the responsibility, which he has done in brilliant style, weighing in with six of the 15 goals. His partner, though, is often 35-year-old Ally McCoist, who cannot be considered a regular for his club side Rangers. Experience on the other hand often counts for more.

Coach Craig Brown does possess a settled side and, although only Tommy Boyd featured in all the qualifying games, the backbone of the team remained largely the same throughout their Group 4 games.

Scotland qualified for the finals by virtue of being the best runner-up in all the UEFA groups, Austria just nudging them out of top place. However, it did look as though Scotland would win the group outright. A goalless draw in Austria was followed by wins over Latvia and Sweden. Sandwiched between those two games, Scotland took the field in Tallinn to face Estonia but farcically, Scotland found themselves without any opposition because the Estonians refused to turn up after the FIFA observer ordered an earlier kick-off time because of fears over inadequate floodlights. Controversially, the game was ordered to be replayed in neutral Monaco where the Scots were held to a goalless draw.

Boyd scored his first international goal in the return game at Kilmarnock and a full house saw Kevin Gallacher notch the goals in the win over rivals Austria. Four days later, Austria were the visitors and, on a passionate night in front of 50,000 fans at Celtic Park, were defeated 2-0 thanks to a superb double by Kevin Gallacher. The only defeat of the campaign came in Sweden and effectively gave Austria the group championship despite a Scottish double over Belarus. A final 2-0 win over Latvia ensured the points and Scotland's position as best runner-up.

UEFA Group 4 Results and Appearances

Date	Opponents	Ven	Result	Att	Scorers
31.08.96	Austria	A	0-0	29,500	
05.10.96	Latvia	A	2-0	9,500	Collins (18); Jackson (75)
10.11.96	Sweden	H	1-0	46,738	McGinlay (8)
11.02.97	Estonia	*	0-0	4,000	
29.03.97	Estonia	H	2-0	17,996	Boyd (25); OG (53)
02.04.97	Austria	H	2-0	43,295	Gallacher (24, 77)
30.04.97	Sweden	A	1-2	40,000	Gallacher (83)
08.06.97	Belarus	A	1-0	12,000	G. McAllister (49 pen)
07.09.97	Belarus	H	4-1	20,160	Gallacher (5, 56); Hopkin (54, 87)
11.10.97	Lativia	H	2-0	47,613	Gallacher (43); Durie (80)

*Played in Monaco after Estonia failed to show-up for first game in Tallinn.
Scorers: 6 – Gallacher; 2 – Hopkin; 1 – Collins, Jackson, McGinlay, Boyd, Durie, G. McAllister, OG

Name	Tot	St	Sub	PS	Name	Tot	St	Sub	PS
Boyd, Tom	10	10	0	1	Jackson, Darren	6	6	0	5
Burley, Craig	8	8	0	1	Lambert, Paul	7	5	2	0
Calderwood, Colin	8	8	0	0	Leighton, John	7	7	0	0
Collins, John	8	8	0	0	McAllister, Brian	1	0	1	0
Dailly, Christian	3	3	0	0	McAllister, Gary	9	9	0	2
Dodds, Billy	3	0	3	0	McCall, Stuart	2	2	0	0
Donnelly, Simon	1	0	1	0	McCoist, Ally	4	1	3	1
Durie, Gordon	5	3	2	1	McGinlay, John	4	2	2	2
Ferguson, Duncan	2	2	0	0	McKinlay, Billy	3	1	2	0
Gallacher, Kevin	8	7	1	2	McKinlay, Tosh	8	7	1	3
Gemmill, Scot	3	1	2	0	McNamara, Jackie	3	2	1	1
Goram, Andy	3	3	0	0	McStay, Paul	3	2	1	1
Hendry, Colin	6	6	0	1	Spencer, John	3	2	1	1
Hopkin, David	2	1	1	1	Whyte, Derek	1	1	0	0

Group A Opponents Head-to-Head

10 June	Brazil v Scotland	Saint Denis	4.30 pm
16 June	Scotland v Norway	Bordeaux	4.30 pm
23 June	Scotland v Morocco	Saint Etienne	8.00 pm

The Scots have had three World Cup encounters with the Brazilians, all in the first-round group stages. Although the 1974 game in Frankfurt provided the most positive result, a 0-0 draw, it was the 1982 encounter that is often remembered the most, not least for a quite brilliant goal by David Narey in Seville that gave the Scots a brief lead before the Brazilians replied with four strikes of their own. In 1990, a goal eight minutes from time by Muller won the day after a blunder by Jim Leighton in the Scots goal.

The qualifying round for the 1990 tournament saw Scotland drawn in the same group as Norway with the Scots winning 2-1 in Oslo and drawing 1-1 in Glasgow.

Yr	Round	Opponents	Result	Scorers
1974	First Round	Brazil	0-0	
1982	First Round	Brazil	1-4	Narey
1990	First Round	Brazil	0-1	

World Cup Record

Year	Stage Reached	Year	Stage Reached
1930-38	Did not enter	1974	First Round
1950	Withdrew	1978	First Round
1954	First Round	1982	First Round
1958	First Round	1986	First Round
1962	Did not qualify	1990	First Round
1966	Did not qualify	1994	Did not qualify
1970	Did not qualify		

Competition	P	W	D	L	F	A
World Cup Finals	20	4	6	10	23	35
World Cup Qualifiers	79	44	15	20	140	88
Total	99	48	21	30	163	123

World Cup Notebook

- The Scots did not enter the first few World Cup competitions and, having qualified for their first finals in 1950, the Scottish FA refused to allow them to take part in the final stages.
- Despite a good qualification record, Scotland have never managed to progress beyond the first round of the World Cup finals.
- Scotland were involved in perhaps the most bizarre World Cup fixture ever during their qualification programme for France '98. After travelling to Tallinn for their group match against Estonia, the Scots made an official complaint about the inadequacy of the floodlights. The FIFA official on site agreed and the match was scheduled for a mid-afternoon kick-off. Estonia effectively refused to play the game at that time and failed to turn up. The Scots kicked off against no opponents and the referee then abandoned the match. After an appeal by the Estonians, the match was replayed in neutral Monaco and ended in a 0-0 draw.
- Despite being the two oldest international teams in the world, Scotland and England have never met in the World Cup finals. They have played twice in the qualifying competition with England winning 1-0 (1950) and 4-2 (1954).

SOUTH AFRICA

South African Football Association
Founded: 1892   **Affiliations:** CAF – 1957, 1992. FIFA – 1952-76, 1992
Address: First National Bank Stadium, PO 910. Johannesburg 2000
Phone: +27 11/494 3522/3446   **Fax:** +27 11/494 3013
National Stadium: Soccer City, Soweto (80,000)
Colours: Sky Blue shirts, White shorts, White socks
Coach: Phillipe Troussier
Key Players: Mark Fish, Phil Masinga, Lucas Radebe

New Pedigree

South Africa have little World Cup pedigree. Having been in sporting isolation for many years, they failed to come through the first qualifying stages for the 1994 World Cup – their first attempt at qualification. For 1998, though, six wins from eight games were enough to see them through in what was not an overly impressive run. Indeed, such was their slump in form that Clive Barker, their manager for three years, handed in his resignation before the end of 1997.

When Barker first took over there was only one overseas-based player in the squad. That has changed quite drastically now but there hasn't been a corresponding up-turn in performance.

South Africa began their route to the finals in June 1996 with an aggregate win over Malawi in the first round. In the round robin second round a win over Congo DR (formerly Zaire), thanks to a late Phil Masinga, goal got the group games off to a good start. But a goalless draw in Zambia was followed by a defeat in the Congo that left the group wide open. Three wins in their final three games turned things around, though, and Phil Masinga's early goal in front of 95,000 fans was enough for the final victory over Congo that ensured a place in the World Cup finals.

Despite being a relatively new country on the international stage the talent of many of their players has ensured contracts in top leagues all over the world. Former skipper Neil Tovey has already passed the 50-game mark for his country and in Sizwe Motaung they have an overlapping full back who is often the supplier for Phil Masinga, who scored winning goals in South Africa's run to the finals and first shot to fame playing for Leeds United before moving to Italy.

Lucas Radebe has taken over as captain, while central defender Mark Fish has attained cult status playing for Bolton Wanderers after a season in Italy with Lazio.

South Africa will not find their debut in the World Cup finals easy when they take on hosts France in Marseilles, but upsets can and do happen in the World Cup. If Bafana Bafana ('The Boys') can realise their true potential at last, you never know.

CAF Results and Appearances

Date	Opponents	Ven	Result	Att	Scorers
Round 1					
01.96.96	Malawi	A	1-0	60,000	Tinkler (21)
15.06.96	Malawi	H	3-0	42,000	Bartlett (4, 42); Fish (39)
	South Africa win 4-0 on aggregate.				
Round 2					
09.11.96	Congo DR *	H	1-0	65,000	Masinga (72)
11.01.97	Zambia	A	0-0	75,000	
06.04.97	Congo	A	0-2	38,000	
27.04.97	Congo DR *	A	2-1	7,000	Khumalo (21); Masinga (66)
08.06.97	Zambia	H	3-0	70,000	Mkhalele (9); Masinga (16); Williams (74)
17.08.97	Congo	H	1-0	95,000	Masinga (14)

* *Congo DR formally called Zaire*

Scorers: 4 – Masinga; 2 – Bartlett;
1 – Khumalo, Mkhalele, Williams, Tinkler, Fish

Name	Tot	St	Sub	PS	Name	Tot	St	Sub	PS
Arendse, Andri	8	8	0	0	Moeti, John	5	0	5	0
Augustine, Brendan	6	3	3	0	Motaung, Sizwe	8	8	0	0
Bartlett, Shaun	6	5	1	4	Moshoev, John	8	8	0	2
Buthelezi, Innocent	3	2	1	0	Ndlanya	1	0	1	0
Buthelezi, Linda	3	3	0	1	Ngobe, Dumisa	1	1	0	1
Fish, Mark	7	7	0	1	Nyathi, David	4	3	1	1
Khumalo, Doctor	6	6	0	2	Radebe, Lucas	8	8	0	0
Koumantarakis,					Sikhosana, Jerry	3	2	1	1
George	1	0	1	0	Tinkler, Eric	8	8	0	1
Lane, Gavin	1	0	1	0	Tovey, Neil	7	7	0	0
Masinga, Phil	6	6	0	3	Tshisevhe	1	1	0	1
Mkhalele, Helman	5	2	3	2	Williams	2	0	2	0

Group C Opponents Head-to-Head

12 June	France v South Africa	Marseilles	8.00 pm
18 June	South Africa v Denmark	Toulouse	4.30 pm
24 June	South Africa v Saudi Arabia	Bordeaux	3.00 pm

South Africa have not played France, Denmark or Saudi Arabia at any stage of the World Cup.

World Cup Record

Competition	P	W	D	L	F	A
World Cup Finals	0	0	0	0	0	0
World Cup Qualifiers	12	8	2	2	13	7
Total	12	8	2	2	13	7

World Cup Notebook

- South Africa are relatively new to the international scene following 30 years of exile enforced by the old apartheid regime.
- South Africa's first post-apartheid international was in 1992 against Cameroon.
- Clive Barker resigned as manager of South Africa just six months prior to the finals starting. Having taken Bafana Bafana to the finals, a string of bad results prompted him to hand in his resignation.

SOUTH KOREA

Korea Football Association
Founded: 1928   **Affiliations:** CAF – 1954. FIFA – 1948
Address: 110-39, Kyeonji-Dong, Chongro-Ku, Seoul
Phone: +82 2/733 6764   **Fax:** +82 2/735 2755
National Stadium: Olympic Stadium, Seoul (100,000)
Colours: Red shirts, Black shorts, Red socks
Coach: Cha Bum Kun
Key Players: Choi Young-Su, Hong Myung-bo, Ko Jong-so

More Surprises

'Tall and powerful with no little skill' sums up the industrious South Korean
side – perhaps contrary to what you might expect. The Republic side are the
most successful ever to come out of Asia and will be seeking to reach the
competition's final phase for the first time in their fourth consecutive try.

Coach Cha Bum Kun has taken his side to France via 12 qualifying games
and he has the experience of playing there himself in the days when he was
captain of the side in what was their second finals in 1986.

The first-round stage proved simple enough with Hong Kong and Thailand
providing only token opposition. Matters got tougher in the second round in a
group that included Japan, but the Koreans still managed to gain automatic
qualification with three games still to play. The basis of their continued
progress came off the back of four straight wins including a 2-1 victory in
Japan. Japan gained some revenge by beating the Koreans 2-0 on their home
soil but qualification had already been achieved by that point.

The goals of Choi Yong-soo have proved vital for Korea in their march to
the World Cup finals and he remains the top name in their football. However,
it is a 19-year-old midfield player who might well hold the key to their
chances of moving out of the round robin stage. Ko Jong-so is generally
regarded as their greatest talent but, having undergone extensive knee surgery
in July 1997, his chances of making the Koreans' final squad hang in the
balance.

AFC Results

Date	Opponents	Ven	Result	Att	Scorers
Round 1 – Group 6					
23.02.97	Hong Kong	A	2-0	16,960	Seo Jung-won (69); Choi Moon-sik (75)
02.03.97	Thailand	A	3-1	25,000	Roh Sang-rae (19); Ha Seok-ju (75); Kim Bong-so (86)
28.05.97	Hong Kong	H	4-0	25,000	Yoo Sang-chul (25pen); Choi Yong-su (40, 70); Park Kun-ha (85)
01.06.97	Thailand	H	0-0	25,000	
Round 2 – Group B					
06.09.97	Kazakhstan	H	3-0		Choi Yong-su (24, 76); Ha Seok-ju (68)
12.09.97	Uzbekistan	H	2-1		Choi Yong-su (15); Lee Song-yoon (87)
28.09.97	Japan	A	2-1	60,000	Lee Min-sung (86); Seo Jong-won (83)
04.10.97	UAE	H	3-0	55,000	Ha Seok-ju (7); Yoo Sang-chul (72); Lee Sang-yoon (84)
11.10.97	Kazakhstan	A	1-1	4,000	Choi Yong-su (4)
18.10.97	Uzbekistan	A	5-1	30,000	Choi Yong-su (19); OG (24); Yoo Sang-chul (38); Ko Jung-woon (58); Kim Do-hoon (70)
01.11.97	Japan	H	0-2	80,000	
09.11.97	UAE	A	3-1		Lee Sang-yoon (11); Kim Do-hoon (42, 67)

Scorers: 7 – Choi Yong-su; 3 – Ha Seok-ju, Kim Do-hoon, Lee Sang-yoon, Yoo Sang-chul; 2 – Seo Jong-won; 1 – Choi Moon-sik , Kim Bong-so, Ko Jung-woon, Lee Min-sung, Park Kun-ha, Roh Sang-rae, OG

Group E Opponents Head-to-Head

14 June	South Korea v Mexico	Lyon	4.30 pm
20 June	Holland v South Korea	Marseilles	8.00 pm
25 June	Belgium v South Korea	Paris	3.00 pm

South Korea have met only Belgium in their previous visits to the World Cup finals. Their only pairing came in 1990 when the Europeans ran out 2-0 winners in Italy.

Yr	Round	Opponents	Result	Scorers
1990	First Round	Belgium	0-2	

133

AFC Appearances

Name	Tot	St	Sub	PS
An Jung-hwan	2	0	2	0
Choi Moon-sik	4	0	4	0
Choi Sung-yong	5	3	2	0
Choi Yong-su	9	9	0	4
Choi Young-il	11	11	0	0
Ha Seok-ju	9	8	1	0
Hong Myung-bo	8	8	0	2
Jang Dae-il	4	3	1	0
Jang Htung-seok	3	2	1	1
Jung Jae-kwon	2	2	0	2
Kim Bong-so	2	2	0	0
Kim Byung-ji	7	7	0	0
Kim Dae-evi	2	0	2	0
Kim Do-hoon	7	4	3	3
Kim Do-keun	2	0	2	0
Kim Gi-dong	3	1	2	0
Kim Hyun-soo	1	1	0	1
Kim Sang-hoon	3	2	1	0
Kim Tae-young	5	5	0	1
Ko Jong-su	4	4	0	1
Ko Jung-woon	6	4	2	3
Lee Ki-hyung	10	10	0	2
Lee Min-sung	8	8	0	0
Lee Sang-yoon	8	7	1	4
Lee Sang-hun	2	1	1	0
Park Kun-ha	8	5	3	3
Park Tae-ha	1	0	1	0
Roh Sang-rae	4	2	2	2
Seo Dong-mung	3	3	0	0
Seo Jung-won	11	9	2	4
Yoo Sang-chul	11	10	1	1
Yoon Jong-hwan	1	1	0	1
Young Hoo-seo	1	0	1	0

World Cup Record

Year	Stage Reached
1930-50	Did not enter
1954	First Round
1958	Did not enter
1962	Did not qualify
1966	Did not enter
1970	Did not qualify
1974	Did not qualify
1978	Did not qualify
1982	Did not qualify
1986	First Round
1990	First Round
1994	First Round

Competition	P	W	D	L	F	A
World Cup Finals	10	0	2	8	9	34
World Cup Qualifying	77	48	20	9	158	50
Total	87	48	22	17	167	84

World Cup Notebook

- South Korea have qualified for five finals and 1998 marks their fourth successive appearance in the final stages. However, they have never progressed beyond the first round.
- South Korea have never won a game in the finals, but have managed two draws.
- South Korea will co-host the 2002 World Cup finals with Japan.

SPAIN

Real Federación Espaniõla de Fútbol
Founded: 1913 **Affiliations:** UEFA – 1954. FIFA – 1904
Address: Alberto Bosch 13, Apartado Postal 347, E-28014 Madrid
Phone: +34 1/420 13 62 **Fax:** +34 1/420 20 94
Colours: Red shirts, Blue shorts, Blue with Red and Yellow trim socks
Coach: Javier Clemente
Key Players: Luis Enrique Martinez, Gonzalez Raul, Josep Guardiola

Fine Form

If football tradition has a say in the World Cup finals, then Spain will flatter
to deceive and spin out of the competition by the quarter final stage. So often
the Spanish national team have promised so much, only to falter before they
start. They come into the World Cup finals on a fine run of form, which they
will need to maintain if they are to negotiate a sticky looking Group D which
includes Bulgaria, Nigeria and Paraguay – all potential Spanish banana skins.

Unbeaten for over three seasons, Spain were undefeated in UEFA Group 6
and recorded eight wins from their ten games against stiff opposition. A 6-2
win in mid North Sea saw a comfortable three points secured from the Faroe
Islands' whipping boys. But a draw in the Czech Republic and significant
home wins over Slovakia and the ever improving Yugoslavia put them in firm
control. Back-to-back wins over Malta marked three successive clean sheets
and Hierro's penalty looked to have secured a win in Yugoslavia until the
home side equalised in similar fashion minutes from time. Hierro was again
the penalty striker in a win over the Czech Republic before a win in the
penultimate game against Slovakia all but mathematically secured Javier
Clemente's team a place in the finals.

Coach Clemente has often shunned the big-name flair players that might
have made a difference in the past, but whereas goals were hard to come by in
Euro '96, that has not been the case in recent times with Alfonso, Luis
Enrique and the cool-headed Fernando Hierro finding the onion bag with
regularity. But it is perhaps an unknown – Real Madrid's Raul – who could
unlock the door and let Spain into the party. Only 20 and with only one goal
in the qualifiers, he is regarded as being potentially the best forward Spain
has ever had.

The weak link may be in defence, though, and in particular between the
sticks where Zubizarreta has re-established himself in Clemente's favour and
was an ever present in qualifying.

UEFA Group 6 Results and Appearances

Date	Opponents	Ven	Result	Att	Scorers
04.09.96	Faroe Islands	A	6-2	4,000	Luis Enrique (37); OG (70); Alfonso (63, 84, 87); Hierro (85)
09.10.96	Czech Rep.	A	0-0	19,223	
13.11.96	Slovakia	H	4-1	35,000	Pizzi (32); Amor (46); Luis Enrique (56); Hierro (61)
14.12.96	Yugoslavia	H	2-0	49,000	Guardiola (19pen); Raul (38)
18.12.96	Malta	A	3-0	6,000	Guerrero (9, 26, 33)
12.02.97	Malta	H	4-0		Guardiola (25); Alfonso (40, 46), Pizzi (90)
30.04.97	Yugoslavia	A	1-1	53,000	Hierro (19pen)
08.06.97	Czech Rep.	H	1-0	25,000	Hierro (40pen)
24.09.97	Slovakia	A	2-1	13,667	Kiko (47), Amor (76)
11.10.97	Faroe Islands	H	3-1	25,000	Luis Enrique (19, 84); Oli (85)

Scorers: 5 – Alfonso; 4 – Luis Enrique, Hierro; 3 – Guerrero; 2 – Amor, Guardiola, Pizzi; 1 – Kiko, Oli, Raul, OG

Sent Off: Amor v Malta (away 86 min)

Name	Tot	St	Sub	PS		Name	Tot	St	Sub	PS
Abelardo Fernandez	8	7	1	0		Lopez, Juan Manuel	1	0	1	0
Aguilera, Carlos	2	1	1	0		Luis Enrique Martinez	9	8	1	0
Alfonso Perez	7	6	1	4		Manjarin, Javier	4	2	2	1
Alkorta, Rafael	7	7	0	1		Nadal, Miguel Angel	8	8	0	0
Amavisca, Jose Emilio	2	1	1	1		'Oli' Oliviro Alvarez	4	2	2	0
Amor, Guillermo	8	3	5	2		Pizzi, Juan Antonio	5	4	1	2
Aranzabal, Agustin	3	3	0	1		Raul, Gonzalez	9	9	0	3
Belsue, Alberto	3	3	0	1		Rios, Roberto	8	4	4	1
Ferrer, Albert	3	2	1	1		Santi	1	1	0	0
Guardiola, Josep	9	6	3	2		Sergi Barjuan	7	7	0	0
Guerrero, Julen	6	3	3	2		Urzaiz, Ismael	2	0	2	0
Hierro, Fernando Ruiz	8	8	0	3		Zubizarreta, Andoni	10	10	0	0
'Kiko' (F. Navaez)	6	5	1	4						

Group D Opponents Head-to-Head

13 June	Spain v Nigeria	Nantes	1.30 pm
19 June	Spain v Paraguay	Saint Etienne	8.00 pm
24 June	Spain v Bulgaria	Lens	8.00 pm

Spain have not played any of their Group D opponents in the World Cup.

World Cup Record

Year	Stage Reached	Year	Stage Reached
1930	Did not enter	1970	Did not qualify
1934	Quarter Final	1974	Did not qualify
1938	Did not enter	1978	First Round
1950	Second Round	1982	Second Round
1954	Did not qualify	1986	Quarter Final
1958	Did not qualify	1990	Second Round
1962	First Round	1994	Quarter Final
1966	First Round		

Competition	P	W	D	L	F	A
World Cup Finals	37	15	9	13	53	44
World Cup Qualifiers	69	44	14	11	152	56
Total	106	59	23	24	205	100

World Cup Notebook

- Veteran goalkeeper Andoni Zubizarreta was the only Spanish player to play in all ten of their qualifying games.
- Spain have never progressed beyond the quarter final stage of the World Cup finals.
- Spain did make a memorable mark in their first fixture in the World Cup finals when they beat Brazil 3-1 in Italy in 1934.
- Spain's biggest win in the World Cup also came in 1934 when they beat Iberian rivals Portugal 9-0 in the qualifying competition!

TUNISIA

Fédération Tunisienne De Football
Founded: 1956   **Affiliations:** CAF – 1960. FIFA – 1960
Address: 16, Rue de la Ligue Arabe, El Menzah VI, Tunis 1004
Phone: +216 1/23 33 03   **Fax:** +216 1/76 79 29
National Stadium: El Menzah, Tunis (50,000)
Colours: Red shirts, White shorts, Red socks
Coach: Henryk Kasperczak
Key Players: Adel Sellimi, Skander Souayah

Home from Home

Tunisia have qualified for only their second World Cup finals and it is somewhat ironic that the man who led them to it, coach Henrky Kasperczak, was part of the team that ended their interests in the competition in 1978. Kasperczak played his part in the Polish side that beat the north Africans 1-0 in Argentina.

The early signs have been good. Tunisia remained undefeated in qualifying and their arrival in the World Cup finals comes on the back of two successive appearances in the African Nations Cup finals.

Tunisia will start their World Cup final schedule against England in Marseilles and the Velodrome is a venue known to them, having played the second leg of their first round tie with Rwanda there. Some 6,000 Tunisians made the trip for that game and there will be more than double that in France supporting them in the summer. In the second round of six games, Tunisia won the first four and a goalless draw in Cairo against Egypt secured their place which was cemented with a final win over Namibia. In those eight games just two goals were conceded by a well-organised defence.

As well as a familiarity with the Marseilles stadíum, many of their players are earning a living in the French league, including top scorer Adel Sellimi, who normally features strongly on the left side of midfield for both country and Nantes. Despite being just 24, he may well reach the 70 cap mark during the finals. Skander Souayah is perhaps the most skilful of the bunch but has often been criticised for his poor work rate within the team.

CAF Group 2 Results and Appearances

Date	Opponents	Ven	Result	Att	Scorers
1st Round					
02.06.96	Rwanda	A	3-1	8,000	Sellimi (43pen, 46); Slimane (60)
16.06.96	Rwanda	H	2-0	6,000	Ben Rekhissa (17); Sellimi (47 pen)
	Played in Marseille				
2nd Round – Group 2					
10.11.96	Liberia	A	1-0	25,000	Jelassi (87)
12.01.97	Egypt	H	1-0	35,000	Beya (10)
06.04.97	Namibia	A	2-1	7,200	Herichi (15); Badra (68)
27.04.97	Liberia	H	2-0	40,000	Sellimi (11); Badra (75)
08.06.97	Egypt	A	0-0	46,000	
17.08.97	Namibia	H	4-0	35,000	Beya (19, 57); Soueyah (31); Liman (72)

Scorers: 4 – Sellimi; 3 – Beya; 2 – Badra; 1 – Slimane, Ben Rekhissa, Jelassi, Herichi, Soueyah, Liman.

Name	Tot	St	Sub	PS	Name	Tot	St	Sub	PS
Badra, Khaled	6	5	1	0	Herichi, Taoufik	2	2	0	0
Ben Rekhissa, Hedi	2	2	0	0	Jaidi, Radhi	2	2	0	0
Ben Younes, Imed	1	0	1	0	Jelassi, Riadh	5	3	2	1
Benslimane, Mehdi	2	2	0	2	Liman, Jameleddine	5	3	2	3
Beya, Zoubeir	7	7	0	4	Mkacher, Mohamed	2	0	2	0
Bokri, Marouane	2	0	2	0	Nouira, Hakim	3	2	1	1
Bouazizi, Riadh	6	5	1	1	Sdiri, Maher	1	0	1	0
Bouimnijel, Ali	2	2	0	1	Sellimi, Adel	6	6	0	1
Boukadida, Mornir	5	5	0	0	Slimane, Mehdi	5	3	2	3
Chihi, Sirajeddine	4	3	1	0	Souayah, Skander	6	6	0	3
Chouchane, Ferid	5	5	0	1	Thabet, Trake	5	5	0	0
El Ouaer, Chokri	3	3	0	0	Trabelsi, Sami	6	6	0	0
Fekih, Soufiane	7	4	3	0	Zdiri, Maher	1	0	1	0
Ghodhbame, Kaies	4	4	0	1	Zitouni, Baubaker	4	3	1	0
Hanini, Lascaad	1	0	1	0					

Group G Opponents Head-to-Head

15 June	England v Tunisia	Marseilles	1.30 pm
22 June	Colombia v Tunisia	Montpellier	4.30 pm
26 June	Romania v Tunisia	Saint Denis	8.00 pm

Tunisia have not faced any of their Group G opponents in the World Cup before.

World Cup Record

Year	Stage Reached		Year	Stage Reached
1930-58	Did not enter		1978	First Round
1962	Did not qualify		1982	Did not qualify
1966	Did not enter		1986	Did not qualify
1970	Did not qualify		1990	Did not qualify
1974	Did not qualify		1994	Did not qualify

Competition	P	W	D	L	F	A
World Cup Finals	3	1	1	1	3	2
World Cup Qualifiers	56	26	15	15	80	47
Total	59	27	16	16	83	49

World Cup Notebook

- Tunisia will face England in Marseilles in their opening game of the World Cup. They have already played a World Cup game here when they beat Rwanda 2-0 in the first round of the CAF qualifying tournament.
- Tunisia won their first ever match in the finals of the World Cup when they beat Mexico 3-1 in Argentina.
- Tunisia conceded just two goals in their qualifying competition and only Egypt succeeded in taking a point off them in a 0-0 draw.

USA

US Soccer
Founded: 1913   **Affiliations:** Concacaf – 1961. FIFA – 1913
Address: US Soccer House, 1801-1811 S. Prairie Ave, Chicago, IL 60616
Phone: +1 312/808 1300   **Fax:** +1 312/808 1301
National Stadium: Rose Bowl, Passadena (104,000)
Colours: White shirts, White shorts, White socks
Coach: Steve Sampson
Key Players: Jeff Agoos, Tab Ramos, Alexi Lalas

Fitness Doubts

In the 1994 finals on home turf, the USA beat Colombia 2-1 and held Brazil for much of their game only to lose by a single goal. In their qualifying games for this year's finals, they twice held another regular finalist, Mexico, to goalless draws. The States may not be the walk over that their group opponents may think.

Having played 16 games to come through two CONCACAF groups, the Americans lost just two games and were undefeated at home. Interestingly, both away defeats came against Costa Rica in the States' two phases of qualification.

In the first phase, four wins and a draw made the defeat against Costa Rica irrelevant as they put paid to Guatemala and Trinidad & Tobago to move into the final round of the CONCACAF group. USA finished second behind Mexico and along with Jamaica formed the three qualifiers. In addition to the draws with Mexico, Jamaica also provided draws and it was on the strength of two wins over Canada and a win against El Salvador and Costa Rica that the USA could switch their attentions to France.

For many, their clash with Iran may be the highlight of the group. Emotions will no doubt be high in the Iranian camp and coach Steve Sampson may need all his man-management skills to ensure that football remains the number one thought.

There remain doubts over the fitness of the USA's most talented and influential player, Tab Ramos, and the condition of his left knee may be a decisive factor in how well the States fair. They have experience, though, especially between the goal posts, where Kasey Keller and Brad Friedel are Premiership quality. Scoring goals may be their most difficult task, with no one player able to find the net with any degree of regularity. Frustrate and then break may be the USA game plan.

CONCACAF Results and Appearances

Date	Opponents	Ven	Result	Att	Scorers
Group 1					
03.11.96	Guatemala	H	2-0	30,082	Wynalda (55); McBride (89)
10.11.96	Trinadad & T.	H	2-0	19,312	Dooley (52); Wynalda (85)
24.11.96	Trinadad & T.	A	1-0	8,000	Moore (34)
01.12.96	Costa Rica	A	1-2	30,000	Jones (90)
14.12.96	Costa Rica	H	2-1	40,527	McBride (17); Lassiter (90)
21.12.96	Guatemala	A	2-2	7,106	Preki (7); Hedjuk (49)
Final Round					
02.03.97	Jamaica	A	0-0	35,246	
16.03.97	Canada	H	3-0	28,896	Wynalda (8pen); Pope (14); Stewart (89)
23.03.97	Costa Rica	A	2-3	23,000	Wynalda (24); Lassiter (68)
20.04.97	Mexico	H	2-2	54,407	Pope (35); (OG 74)
29.06.97	El Salvador	A	1-1	35,000	Lassiter (51)
07.09.97	Costa Rica	H	1-0	27,396	Ramos (79)
03.10.97	Jamaica	H	1-1	51,000	Wynalda (49pen)
02.11.97	Mexico	A	0-0	105,000	
09.11.97	Canada	A	3-0	8,420	Reyna (5); Wegerle (81, 89)
16.11.97	El Salvador	H	4-2	53,193	McBride (22, 28); Henderson (49), Preki (82)

Scorers: 4 – McBride, Wynalda; 3 – Lassiter; 2 – Pope, Preki, Wegerle; 1 – Dooley, Moore, Jones, Hedjuk, Stewart, Ramos, Reyna, Henderson, OG

Sent Off: Agoos v Mexico (away 32 min)

Name	Tot	St	Sub	PS	Name	Tot	St	Sub	PS
Agoos, Jeff	14	13	1	0	McBride, Brian	6	4	2	2
Balboa, Marcelo	7	7	0	0	Moore, Joe-Max	8	6	2	2
Burns, Michael	11	4	7	0	Pope, Eddie	13	13	0	3
Caligiuri, Paul	3	2	1	0	Radosavijic, Precki	7	4	3	2
Dooley, Thomas	12	12	0	3	Ramos, Tab	5	5	0	1
Friedel, Brad	7	7	0	1	Reyna, Claudio	15	14	1	6
Harkes, John	12	12	0	1	Sanneh	1	1	0	0
Hedjuk, Frankie	1	1	0	0	Sommer, Jurgen	1	0	1	0
Henderson, Chris	2	1	1	1	Sorber, Mike	7	4	3	1
Jones, Cobi	13	9	4	3	Stewart, Ernie	12	11	1	1
Keller, Kasey	9	9	0	0	Vanner	1	0	1	0
Kirovski, Jovan	3	2	1	1	Vasquez, Martin	3	2	1	1
Kreis, Jason	1	1	0	0	Vermes, Peter	2	1	1	0
Lalas, Alexi	12	12	0	1	Wagner, David	4	3	1	2
Lassiter, Roy	5	2	3	1	Wegerle, Roy	3	3	0	2
Maisonneuve, Chris	1	0	1	0	Wynalda, Eric	11	11	0	4
Mason, Michael	3	0	3	0					

Group F Opponents Head-to-Head

15 June	Germany v USA	Paris	8.00 pm
21 June	USA v Iran	Lyon	8.00 pm
25 June	USA v Yugoslavia	Nantes	8.00 pm

The USA have not played Germany, Iran or Yugoslavia at any stage of the World Cup before.

World Cup Record

Year	Stage Reached	Year	Stage Reached
1930	Semi Final	1970	Did not qualify
1934	First Round	1974	Did not qualify
1938	Did not qualify	1978	Did not qualify
1950	First Round	1982	Did not qualify
1954	Did not qualify	1986	Did not qualify
1958	Did not qualify	1990	First Round
1962	Did not qualify	1994	Second Round
1966	Did not qualify		

Competition	P	W	D	L	F	A
World Cup Finals	14	4	1	9	17	33
World Cup Qualifiers	67	26	18	23	100	108
Total	81	30	19	32	117	141

World Cup Notebook

- The USA were involved in what is still regarded as the greatest upset ever in World Cup football when they beat England 1-0 in the 1950 Brazil finals in Belo Horizonte. The goal was scored by Larry Gaetjens, a native of Haiti.
- The USA recorded another famous victory, over England, in a pre-World Cup tournament, 2-0.
- It is often forgotten that the USA reached the semi-finals of the World Cup in 1930. Their team, consisting mainly of ex-pat Englishmen and Scotsmen, lost 6-1 to Argentina.

YUGOSLAVIA

Fédération Yougoslave de Football
Founded: 1919   **Affiliations:** UEFA – 1954. FIFA – 1919
Address: 35 Terazije, PO Box 263, YU-11000 Beograd.
Phone: +381 11/32 33 447   **Fax:** +381 11/32 33 433
National Stadium: Red Star Stadium (97,422)
Colours: Blue shirts, White shirts, Red socks
Coach: Slobodan Santrac
Key Players: Predrag Mijatovic, Dejan Savicevic, Dragan Stojkovic

Goal Mania

Seventeen goals in their first three games in UEFA Group 8 was what might
have been expected given that Yugoslavia's opening fixture list read Faroe
Islands (home and away) and Malta (home). What could not have been
predicted was the emphatic nature of their play-off victory over Hungary,
whom they beat 12-1 on aggregate, which rather made the footballing world
sit up and take note.

It was Spain that took the automatic qualifying place out of their group, by
virtue of the fact that they recorded a two-goal win in Spain, but it is a look
down the results list that shows where the emphasis lay – goals. Yugoslavia
would seem to have a forward line second to none with Predrag Mijatovic
(Real Madrid), Dejan Savicevic (Milan) and Savo Milosevic (Aston Villa)
notching 31 goals between them, with Mijatovic's 14 strikes making him the
top scorer in UEFA qualifying games.

Yugoslavia have had to regroup. The civil war in their country left them
out in the wilderness until FIFA sanctioned their return from isolation in
1994, and of course they have lost the talented input of players from Croatia
and Bosnia.

Consistency in team selection has no doubt helped coach Slobodan Santrac
get the most from his team with the likes of Djorovic, Djukic, Jokanovic,
Jugovic, Mihajlovic, Mijatovic, Savicevic and Stojkovic being almost ever
present.

Despite the cavalier nature of their attack, it should not go unnoticed that
Yugoslavia possess a pretty mean rear guard with only eight goals being
conceded and only Spain managing more than one against them.

What is significant, though, is that the majority of the Yugoslav squad ply
their trade in greener pastures, so while the national side may lack fixtures in
recent years, the players are hardened to football at the highest European
level. They could be the surprise team of the tournament.

UEFA Group 6 Results and Appearances

Date	Opponents	Ven	Result	Att	Scorers
24.04.96	Faroe Islands	H	3-1	25,000	Savicevic (3, 30); Milosevic (38)
02.06.96	Malta	H	6-0	20,000	Milosevic (2, 68); Mijatovic (39); Stojkovic (46); Savicevic (70pen, 73)
06.10.96	Faroe Islands	A	8-1	1,017	Milosevic (7, 36, 45); Jokanovic (10, 57); Mijatovic (30); Jugovic (68); Stojkovic (90)
10.11.96	Czech Rep.	H	1-0	50,000	Mijatovic (18)
14.12.96	Spain	A	0-2	49,000	
02.04.97	Czech Rep.	A	2-1	19,137	Mijatovic (28); Milosevic (90)
30.04.97	Spain	H	1-1	53,000	Mijatovic (87pen)
08.06.97	Slovakia	H	2-0	40,000	Savicevic (17); Mijatovic (75)
10.09.97	Slovakia	A	1-1	22,500	Mihajolovic (80)
11.10.97	Malta	A	5-0	3,000	Milosevic (8); Mihajolovic (24); Savicevic (44); Mijatovic (55); Jugovic (76)

Play-Off

29.10.97	Hungary	A	7-1	13,175	Brnovic (2); Djukic (6); Savicevic (12); Milosevic (63); Mijatovic (27, 42, 51).
15.11.97	Hungary	H	5-0	60,000	Milosevic (17); Mijatovic (44, 45pen, 71, 88)

Scorers: 14 – Mijatovic; 10 – Milosevic; 7 – Savicevic; 2 – Jokanovic, Jugovic, Mihajolovic, Stojkovic; 1 – Brnovic, Djukic

Sent Off: Savelijic v Spain (away 86 min)

Name	Tot	St	Sub	PS	Name	Tot	St	Sub	PS
Brnovic, Branko	8	6	2	0	Kralji, Ivica	6	6	0	1
Ciric, Dragan	1	0	1	0	Lekovic, Dragoje	2	1	1	1
Curcic, Sasa	2	1	1	1	Mihajolovic, Sinisa	11	11	0	3
Dadj, Albert	7	3	4	2	Mijatovic, Predrag	11	11	0	1
Djorovic, Goran	10	9	1	1	Milosevic, Savo	9	6	3	6
Djukic, Miroslav	11	11	0	0	Mirkovic, Zoran	8	7	1	0
Drobnjak, Anton	1	0	1	0	Pantic, Milinko	2	0	2	1
Drulovic, Lubinko	6	1	5	0	Petrovic, Zeljko	3	1	2	0
Govedariva, Dejan	4	2	2	0	Saveljic, Nisa	3	2	1	0
Jokanovic, Siavisa	11	11	0	1	Savicevic, Dejan	11	11	0	5
Jugovic, Vladimir	10	10	0	1	Stojkovic, Dragan	12	12	0	2
Kocic, Aleksandar	6	5	1	0	Vidakovic, Risto	5	5	0	4
Kovacevic, Darko	1	0	1	0	Zivkovic, Bratislav	1	0	1	0

Group F Opponents Head-to-Head

14 June	Yugoslavia v Iran	Saint Etienne	4.30 pm
21 June	Germany v Yugoslavia	Lens	1.30 pm
25 June	USA v Yugoslavia	Nantes	8.00 pm

Iran and The United States provide new opposition for Yugoslavia in the World Cup, but Germany are old adversaries, although they have only ever met in the final stages. Four of their five meetings have come at the quarter-final stage and Germany have won four of their encounters. The only Yugoslavian success came in Chile in 1962 – their third successive meeting – when Radakovic scored the winner four minutes from time. The only other goal scored by Yugoslavia came from the boot of Jozic in the 4-1 defeat in Italia 1990.

Yr	Round	Opponents	Result	Scorers
1954	Quarter Final	West Germany	0-2	
1958	Quarter Final	West Germany	0-1	
1962	Quarter Final	West Germany	1-0	Radakovic
1974	Quarter Final	West Germany	0-2	
1990	First Round	West Germany	1-4	Jozic

World Cup Record

Year	Stage Reached		Year	Stage Reached
1930	Semi Final		1970	Did not qualify
1934	Did not qualify		1974	Second Round
1938	Did not qualify		1978	Did not qualify
1950	First Round		1982	First Round
1954	Quarter Final		1986	Did not qualify
1958	Quarter Final		1990	Quarter Final
1962	Semi Final (4th Place)		1994	Did not enter
1966	Did not qualify			

Competition	P	W	D	L	F	A
World Cup Finals	33	14	7	12	55	42
World Cup Qualifiers	79	47	18	14	172	77
Total	112	61	25	26	227	119

World Cup Notebook

- Predrag Mijatovic was the top scorer in the UEFA section of the World Cup qualifying groups with 14 goals from 12 games. He was third top scorer overall.
- Dragan Stojkovic was the only Yugoslav player to feature in all 12 of the team's qualifying games.

THE WORLD CUP FINALS

1930 – Uruguay

The first World Cup was won by the first hosts – Uruguay – but it was far from the sort of competition we have today, in that it was not truly representative of the world. In fact, just 13 countries entered the competition, and as such there was no pre-qualifying competition. Indeed just two months prior to the opening game not one European country had entered. None of the Home Countries were eligible to play as they had withdrawn from FIFA two years earlier, in 1928. By the time the competition kicked off, Europe had stumped up entries in the form of Belgium, France and Romania, although they participated reluctantly.

The 13 teams were drawn into four groups with the winners of each group progressing to the semi finals. Of the four seeded countries only Brazil, who were defeated 2-1 by Yugoslavia, failed to advance to the next stage. The semi finals were one-sided affairs, with Argentina and Uruguay running up identical 6-1 scorelines to drill the USA and Yugoslavia respectively out of the competition.

The final, played between arch rivals Argentina and Uruguay, was amazingly played in reasonably good spirit. Uncontroversial and entertaining, Uruguay came back from behind to win 4-2.

Pool 1			Pool 3		
France	Mexico	4-1	Romania	Peru	3-1
Argentina	France	1-0	Uruguay	Peru	1-0
Chile	Mexico	3-0	Uruguay	Romania	4-0
Chile	France	1-0	**Pool 4**		
Argentina	Mexico	6-3	USA	Belgium	3-0
Argentina	Chile	3-1	USA	Paraguay	3-0
Pool 2			Paraguay	Belgium	1-0
Yugoslavia	Brazil	2-1	**Semi Finals**		
Yugoslavia	Bolivia	4-0	Argentina	USA	6-1
Brazil	Bolivia	4-0	Uruguay	Yugoslavia	6-1

The Final – 30 July 1930   *Centenario, Montevideo*   *93,000*

Uruguay   **4**   **Argentina**   **2**

Dorado (12), Cea (58),   Peucelle (20), Stabile (37)
Iriarte (68), Castro (89)

Uruguay: Ballesteros, Nasazzi, Mascheroni, Andrade J., Fernandez, Gestido, Dorado, Scarone, Castro, Cea, Iriarte
Argentina: Botasso, Della Torre, Paternoster, Evaristo J., Monti, Suarez, Peucelle, Varallo, Stabile, Ferreira, Evaristo M.

Italy acted as hosts in 1934 and once again home advantage proved decisive. If the 1930 competition was devoid of European teams then it was the South American teams who were missing from the first European event. The most notable absentees were holders Uruguay. Despite being hosts, Italy had to go through the first qualifying tournament held prior to the tournament proper. Crazily, Mexico and USA were made to travel to Italy in March 1934 to play a final eliminator game, which the USA won 4-2.

Group games were dispensed with, which meant that eight of the sixteen finalists played just one match. The second round was composed entirely of European teams and the most notable game was Italy's single-goal defeat of Spain in a replay; the initial encounter was so brutal the replay saw both sides field several reserves!

The Italians overcame the much fancied Austrians in the semis whilst the Czechoslovakian team were much too strong for the Germans.

Despite featuring the hosts, the final was far from sold out but, the Italians rallied through to come from behind to beat Czechoslovakia 2-1.

Round 1			**Round 2**		
Italy	USA	7-1	Germany	Sweden	2-1
Czechoslovakia	Romania	2-1	Austria	Hungary	2-1
Germany	Belgium	5-2	Italy	Spain	†1-1
Austria	France	†3-2	Italy	Spain	r1-0
Spain	Brazil	3-1	Czechoslovakia	Switzerland	3-2
Switzerland	Holland	3-2			
Sweden	Argentina	3-2	**Semi Finals**		
Hungary	Egypt	4-2	Czechoslovakia	Germany	3-1
			Italy	Austria	1-0
	† after extra time				
	r replay		**3rd Place**		
			Germany	Austria	3-2

The Final – 10 June 1934		*PNF, Rome*		*55,000*
Italy	**2**	**Czechoslovakia**		**1**

Orsi (81), Schiavio (95)   Puc (71)

Italy: Combi, Monzeglio, Allemandi, Ferraris IV, Monti, Bertoloni, Guaita, Meazza, Schiavio, Ferrari, Orsi

Czechoslovakia: Planicka, Zenisek, Ctyroky, Kostalek, Cambal, Krcil, Junek, Svoboda, Sobotka, Nejedly, Puc

Italy became the first nation to retain the World Cup when they won the 1938 competition in France. With World War II looming over the horizon, the competition lacked many leading countries.

Brazil were the only representatives from South America, while Civil War plagued Spain, and the strong Austrians had seen their country swallowed by the Germans. FIFA offered England Austria's place but the invitation was declined.

The Hungarians and Brazilians provided the bulk of Italy's opposition in a competition that was made up of more minnows than giants. Cuba got their comeuppance in the quarter finals when they were thrashed 8-0 by Sweden. The Scandinavians themselves came unstuck against Hungary in the semi finals and found themselves in the final facing Italy, who had dispensed with the Brazilians by the odd goal in three. The final in Paris was won 4-2 by the Italians with a brace of goals apiece from Colaussi and Piola.

Round 1			Round 2		
Switzerland	Germany	†1-1	Sweden	Cuba	8-0
Switzerland	Germany	r4-2	Hungary	Switzerland	2-0
Cuba	Romania	†3-3	Italy	France	3-1
Cuba	Romania	r2-1	Brazil	Czechoslovakia	†1-1
Hungary	Dutch East Indies	6-0	Brazil	Czechoslovakia	r2-1
France	Belgium	3-1	**Semi Finals**		
Czechoslovakia	Holland	†3-0	Italy	Brazil	2-1
Brazil	Poland	†6-5	Hungary	Sweden	5-1
Italy	Norway	†2-1	**3rd Place**		
			Brazil	Sweden	4-2

The Final – 19 June 1938　　　　　*Colombes, Paris*　　　　　*55,000*
Italy　　　　　　　　　　　**4**　**Hungary**　　　　　　　　**2**
Colaussi (5, 35), Piola (16, 82)　　　Titkos (7), Sarosi (70)
Italy: Olivieri, Foni, Rava, Serantoni, Andreolo, Locatelli, Biavati, Meazza, Piola, Ferrari, Colaussi
Hungary: Szabo, Polgar, Biro, Szalay, Szucs, Lazar, Sas, Vincze, Sarosi, Szengeller, Titkos

1950 – Brazil

With the war over and the competition returning to South America, Uruguay entered the fray for the second time and once again ran out World Cup winners in Brazil.

Again the non-participation of the majority of European countries hampered the competition's credibility. Although the Home Countries had rejoined FIFA and were eligible, Scotland declined their finals place as they had only finished second to England in the qualifying group. France, Portugal, Czechoslovakia, Hungary and then Argentina withdrew, leaving just 13 finalists.

The tournament organisation was a shambles. The opening round robin consisted of four groups formed of anywhere between four and two teams, with the winners of each group progressing to a final round-robin group with the ultimate winner of that being crowned World Cup winners. This was the only time in the history of the competition that there would not be a final. That said, the final match of the group was contested between the only two countries capable of winning the competition.

Brazil played all but one of their games in Rio, whilst the other entrants were forced to travel huge distances between matches. The competition marked possibly

England's most embarrassing defeat at the hands of the USA in Belo Horizonte. Having already disposed of Chile 2-0, England lost their final game to Spain and were eliminated. The defending champions, Italy, were eliminated, but they had lost several of their top players in a plane crash the previous year.

The 'final' round consisted of six matches. Brazil dominated their opposition while Uruguay struggled past theirs. The two met in the final group match with the 'home' side needing just a draw to win the competition. A world-record crowd of 199,854 packed the newly built Maracana stadium in Rio and saw Brazil take the lead early in the second half. But Uruguay came back with two second-half goals to win the competition.

Pool 1			Final Pool		
Brazil	Mexico	4-0	Uruguay	Spain	2-2
Brazil	Switzerland	2-2	Brazil	Sweden	7-1
Brazil	Yugoslavia	2-0	Uruguay	Sweden	3-2
Yugoslavia	Switzerland	3-0	Brazil	Spain	6-1
Yugoslavia	Mexico	4-1	Sweden	Spain	3-1
Switzerland	Mexico	2-1	Uruguay	Brazil	2-1

Pool 2									
Spain	USA	3-1	**Final Table**	P	W	D	L	F	A	Pt
England	Chile	2-0	Uruguay	3	2	1	0	7	5	5
USA	England	1-0	Brazil	3	2	0	1	14	4	4
Spain	Chile	2-0	Sweden	3	1	0	2	6	11	2
Spain	England	1-0	Spain	3	0	1	2	4	11	1
Chile	USA	5-2								
Sweden	Italy	3-2								
Sweden	Paraguay	2-2								
Italy	Paraguay	2-0								
Uruguay	Bolivia	8-0								

1954 – Switzerland

The 1954 competition in Switzerland could be truly regarded as the first representative World Cup, with participants from Asia and Central America in the form of South Korea and Mexico. In addition defending champions Uruguay took part in Europe for the first time.

The 16 entrants were divided into four groups with the top two sides from each group proceeding to the quarter finals. Despite the round-robin nature it was decided that there would be no drawn group games! In the event of games being level after 90 minutes, extra time was played and a replay staged if required. The Hungarian genius Puskas was making his mark on the competition and was cynically dealt with by the Germans.

The surprise of the competition was the elimination of the Italians by the Swiss, 4-1, in the group play-off. The quarter finals saw the staging of the infamous 'Battle of Berne' when Brazil lost an ill-tempered match against Hungary 4-2. It spilled over into a mass brawl in the changing rooms long after the game had finished.

In the semi finals, Germany walked over the Austrians 6-1, while Hungary and Uruguay produced a highly entertaining game which the Europeans won 4-2.

The Hungarians, undefeated in 33 matches, were favourites. Two goals to the good, after eight minutes it looked all over, but the Germans clawed it back and won the game in the final minutes.

Pool 1			**Pool 4**		
Yugoslavia	France	1-0	England	Belgium	4-4
Brazil	Mexico	5-0	England	Switzerland	2-0
France	Mexico	3-2	Switzerland	Italy	2-1
Brazil	Yugoslavia	†1-1	Italy	Belgium	4-1
Pool 2			Switzerland	Italy	play off 4-1
Hungary	South Korea	9-0			
Germany	Turkey	4-1	**Quarter Finals**		
Hungary	Germany	8-3	Germany	Yugoslavia	2-0
Turkey	South Korea	7-0	Hungary	Brazil	4-2
Germany	Turkey	play off 7-2	Austria	Switzerland	7-5
Pool 3			Uruguay	England	4-2
Austria	Scotland	1-0	**Semi Finals**		
Uruguay	Czechoslovakia	2-0	Germany	Austria	6-1
Austria	Czechoslovakia	5-0	Hungary	Uruguay	†4-2
Uruguay	Scotland	7-0	**Third Place**		
			Austria	Uruguay	3-1

The Final – 4 July 1954		*Wankdorf, Berne*		*60,000*
West Germany	**3**	**Hungary**		**2**

Morlock (11), Rahn (16, 83) Puskas (6), Czibor (8)

West Germany: Turek, Posipal, Liebrich, Kohlmeyer, Eckel, Mai, Rahn, Morlock, Walter O., Walter F., Schafer

Hungary: Grosics, Buzanszky, Lorant, Lantos, Bozsik, Zakarias, Czibor, Kocsis, Hidegkuti, Puskas, Toth

1958 – Sweden

Sweden was the setting for the 1958 tournament which heralded the arrival of the brilliant Brazilians. Previous winners Uruguay and Italy were absent, the latter having been eliminated by Northern Ireland. The success of the Irish meant that all four Home Countries qualified for the first and, so far, only time.

England, with a side still depleted by the Munich air crash, went out in the first round play-offs but fared better than Scotland who failed to negotiate the group stages. Northern Ireland and Wales, however, made the quarter final stage, only to fall to France and Brazil respectively. Their two victors were paired in the semi finals with the superior skill of the Brazilians seeing them through against a French side that played a man short for much of the game. In the other game, the Swedes captured their national limelight by coming from behind to beat the Germans 3-1.

A goal in the fourth minute filled the Swedish team with confidence, but a Pele-inspired Brazil had turned the deficit around by the interval and cruised to a 5-2 victory in the second half, helped by a sensational goal from their number 10.

Pool 1				Pool 4		
West Germany	Argentina	3-1		England	Russia	2-2
Ireland	Czechoslovakia	1-0		Brazil	Austria	3-0
West Germany	Czechoslovakia	2-2		England	Brazil	0-0
Argentina	Ireland	3-1		Russia	Austria	2-0
West Germany	Ireland	2-2		Brazil	Russia	2-0
Czechoslovakia	Argentina	6-1		England	Austria	2-2
Pool 2				Russia	England	p/o1-0
France	Paraguay	7-3				
Yugoslavia	Scotland	1-1		**Quarter Finals**		
Paraguay	Scotland	3-2		France	Ireland	4-0
Yugoslavia	France	3-2		West Germany	Yugoslavia	1-0
France	Scotland	2-1		Sweden	Russia	2-0
Yugoslavia	Paraguay	3-3		Brazil	Wales	1-0
Pool 3				**Semi Finals**		
Sweden	Mexico	3-0		Brazil	France	5-2
Hungary	Wales	1-1		Sweden	West Germany	3-1
Wales	Mexico	1-1				
Sweden	Hungary	2-1		**Third Place**		
Sweden	Wales	0-0		France	West Germany	6-3
Hungary	Mexico	4-0				
Wales	Hungary	p/o2-1		p/o=play off game.		

The Final – 29 June 1958		*Rasunda, Stockholm*		*49,000*
Brazil	**5**	**Sweden**	**2**	

Vava (10, 32), Pele (56, 89), Zagalo (68) — Liedholm (4), Simonsson (80)

Brazil: Gilmar, Djalma Santos, Bellini, Orlando Pecanha, Nilton Santos, Zito, Didi, Garrincha, Vava, Pele, Zagalo

Sweden: Svensson, Bergmark, Gustavsson, Axbom, Borjesson, Parling, Hamrin, Gren G., Simonsson, Liedholm, Skoglund

1962 – Chile

Brazil retained the Jules Rimet trophy in Chile at the end of a tournament that took place soon after the country had been rocked by earthquakes. The fragile nature of the country's economy at the time didn't help matches, and many of the games were played in front of sparse crowds.

The event will be forever synonymous with the famous 'Battle of Santiago'. The game between Chile and Italy was played against a backdrop of ill-feeling that spilled onto the pitch – many of the off-the-ball incidents going unnoticed or unpunished by the match officials. Italy's Ferrini was sent off after only seven minutes and they were reduced to nine men just after the interval when Mario David was sent off for kicking a Chilean in the throat! The match remained goalless until the final stages when two goals in the 74th and 86th minutes settled the tie.

The other group games were largely uninspiring, with the top two teams in the four groups of four moving into the quarter finals. England qualified second in their group behind Hungary and their reward was a quarter final tie with the Brazilians.

Two goals midway through the second half settled the contest in favour of the South Americans. For the third consecutive tournament the West Germans met Yugoslavia in the quarter finals but, unlike the previous meetings, it was the Slavs who won this time around.

Hosts Chile and Czechoslovakia came through their games, but it was the latter who fared better in the semi finals, beating Yugoslavia with two late goals. Chile, who went 3-0 down to Brazil, battled back to 3-2 but battled too hard in the final stages and were reduced to nine men, before the Brazilians added a fourth goal. The final looked predictable and went with Brazil 3-1, despite the fact that the Czechs took the lead.

Group 1			**Group 4**		
Uruguay	Colombia	2-1	Argentina	Bulgaria	1-0
Russia	Yugoslavia	2-0	Hungary	England	2-1
Yugoslavia	Uruguay	3-1	England	Argentina	3-1
Russia	Colombia	4-4	Hungary	Bulgaria	6-1
Russia	Uruguay	2-1	Argentina	Hungary	0-0
Yugoslavia	Colombia	5-0	England	Bulgaria	0-0

Group 2			**Quarter Final**		
Chile	Switzerland	3-1	Yugoslavia	West Germany	1-0
West Germany	Italy	0-0	Brazil	England	3-1
Chile	Italy	2-0	Chile	Russia	2-1
West Germany	Switzerland	2-1	Czechoslovakia	Hungary	1-0
West Germany	Chile	2-0			
Italy	Switzerland	3-0	**Semi Final**		
			Brazil	Chile	4-2
Group 3			Czechoslovakia	Yugoslavia	3-1
Brazil	Mexico	2-0			
Czechoslovakia	Spain	1-0	**Third Place**		
Brazil	Czechoslovakia	0-0	Chile	Yugoslavia	1-0
Spain	Mexico	1-0			
Brazil	Spain	2-1			
Mexico	Czechoslovakia	3-1			

The Final – 17 June 1962	Estadio Nacional, Santiago		68,000
Brazil	**3**	**Czechoslovakia**	**1**
Amarildo (18), Zito (69),		Masopust (16)	
Vava (77)			

Brazil: Gilmar, Djalma Santos, Mauro R. Oliveira, Zozimo, Nilton Santos, Zito, Didi, Garrincha, Vava, Amarildo, Zagalo

Czechoslovakia: Schrojf, Tichy, Pluskal, Popluhar, Novak, Kvasnak, Masopust, Pospichal, Scherer, Kadraba, Jelinek

1966 – England

With England acting as hosts it was disappointing that none of the other Home Countries made it through the qualifying rounds to the finals. Overall, England's victory apart, the tournament was drab from the footballing point of view and

153

littered with ill-tempered matches that often ended in kicking contests. Pele was literally kicked out of the tournament by the opposition and England manager Alf Ramsey was not shy in labelling the Argentinean team as 'animals'. 1966 was also notable for being the last finals in which substitutes were not allowed.

The tone of the competition was perhaps set by the opening game – with England held in a dour goalless draw by the cynical Uruguayans. But two goal wins over Mexico and France saw England through the first round. In the other groups Brazil suffered their first World Cup defeat, 3-1 to Hungary, since 1954 and then lost again to Portugal by the same score and were out. Germany advanced from Group Two along with the Argentinians, who were reprimanded by FIFA for their foul play. Group Four provided the glamour as the North Koreans beat Italy.

FIFA's warning to Argentina went unheeded and their quarter final game with England was a disgraceful affair which resulted in Rattin being sent off. The game was won with a header by Geoff Hurst near the end. England Manager Ramsey was so incensed by their tactics he raced on the pitch at the end of the game and stopped the England players exchanging shirts with the Argentinians.

West Germany beat Uruguay and the Soviet Union defeated the Hungarians in the other games. The North Koreans continued to astound and at Everton raced into a 3-0 lead after only 20 minutes. Their opponents Portugal kept their heads though and, inspired by Eusebio, rallied back to a 5-3 win.

West Germany won a violent semi final, beating the nine-man Soviet Union 2-1 with the winner by Franz Beckenbauer. In a totally different contest, two Bobby Charlton screamers earned England a 2-1 win in their semi at Wembley. The final will always be remembered for Geoff Hurst's hat-trick and his shot that cannoned off the underside of the bar and down. Was it over the line? The Russian linesman said yes and England ran out 4-2 winners in extra time.

Group 1			**Group 4**		
England	Uruguay	0-0	Russia	North Korea	3-0
France	Mexico	1-1	Italy	Chile	2-0
Uruguay	France	2-1	Chile	North Korea	1-1
England	Mexico	2-0	Russia	Italy	1-0
Uruguay	Mexico	0-0	North Korea	Italy	1-0
England	France	2-0	Russia	Chile	2-1
Group 2			**Quarter Finals**		
West Germany	Switzerland	5-0	England	Argentina	1-0
Argentina	Spain	2-1	West Germany	Uruguay	4-0
Spain	Switzerland	2-1	Portugal	North Korea	5-3
Argentina	West Germany	0-0	Russia	Hungary	2-1
Argentina	Switzerland	2-0	**Semi Finals**		
West Germany	Spain	2-1	West Germany	Russia	2-1
Group 3			England	Portugal	2-1
Brazil	Bulgaria	2-0	**Third Place**		
Portugal	Hungary	3-1	Portugal	Russia	2-1
Hungary	Brazil	3-1			
Portugal	Bulgaria	3-0			
Portugal	Brazil	3-1			
Hungary	Bulgaria	3-1			

The Final – 30 July 1966   *Wembley, London*   96,000
England   **4** **West Germany**   **2**
Hurst (19, 100, 119), Peters (77)   Haller (13), Weber (89)
England: Banks, Cohen, Charlton J, Moore, Wilson, Stiles, Charlton B, Ball, Hunt, Hurst, Peters
West Germany: Tilkowski, Hottges, Schulz, Weber, Schnellinger, Haller, Beckenbauer, Seeler, Held, Overath, Emmerich

1970 – Mexico

The 1970 competition had originally been awarded to Argentina but, with internal political strife escalating, FIFA switched the tournament to Mexico at the eleventh hour. The qualifying tournament had seen the provision of an African and Asian group for the first time and thus promoted increased entries from these regions. Elsewhere El Salvador had declared war on Honduras as a result of a fracas during their qualification match.

The round-robin stage of the finals was pretty dull and the highlight of the series came when El Salvador played Mexico. With the game goalless, El Salvador were awarded a free kick. However, one of the Mexican players, Perez, kicked the ball up field and Valdiva scored. Amazingly, the Egyptian referee, Hussain Kandil, let the goal stand. To avoid continued controversy he blew for half-time and in the second half the El Salvadorians conceded three more goals to lose 4-0. The pick of the games, though, was the one group game between Brazil and England. Regarded as one of the great games of all time, Jairzinho scored the only goal of the game that will always be remembered for Gordon Banks' save from Pele's header.

In the quarter finals Brazil and Italy won at a canter and Uruguay went through in extra time. The final match brought England and West Germany together for a repeat of the previous World Cup final. England went 2-0 up and, with the game seemingly won, Sir Alf Ramsey replaced the influential Bobby Charlton and Martin Peters. The game turned and the Germans pulled back to win in extra time. In the semi finals Brazil came from behind to see off Uruguay while Italy and West Germany played out an extra-time thriller which the Italians won 4-3.

Italy and Brazil had both won the trophy twice before and Jules Rimet had decreed that any team to win the World Cup final three times could keep the trophy for all time. The final saw the Italians largely outplayed and Brazil ran out deserved winners. It was Pele's last World Cup match and a fitting end that he should score one of his country's four goals.

Group 1			Group 2		
Mexico	Russia	0-0	Uruguay	Israel	2-0
Belgium	El Salvador	3-0	Sweden	Italy	1-0
Russia	Belgium	4-1	Uruguay	Italy	0-0
Mexico	El Salvador	4-0	Sweden	Israel	1-1
Russia	El Salvador	2-0	Sweden	Uruguay	1-0
Mexico	Belgium	1-0	Italy	Israel	0-0

Group 3			Morocco	Bulgaria	1-1
England	Romania	1-0	**Quarter Finals**		
Brazil	Czechoslovakia	4-1	West Germany	England	3-2
Romania	Czechoslovakia	2-1	Brazil	Peru	4-2
Brazil	Romania	3-2	Italy	Mexico	4-1
England	Czechoslovakia	1-0	Uruguay	Russia	1-0
Group 4			**Semi Finals**		
Peru	Bulgaria	3-2	Italy	West Germany	4-3
West Germany	Morocco	2-1	Brazil	Uruguay	3-1
Peru	Morocco	3-0			
West Germany	Bulgaria	5-2	**Third Place**		
West Germany	Peru	3-1	West Germany	Uruguay	1-0

The Final – 21 June 1970	*Azteca, Mexico City*	*107,000*
Brazil	**4**	**Italy**	**1**

Pele (18), Gerson (66),   Boninsegna (37)
Jairzinho (71), Carlos Alberto (86)

Brazil: Felix, Carlos Alberto, Brito, Piazza, Everaldo, Clodoaldo, Gerson, Jairzinho, Tostao, Pele, Rivelino

Italy: Albertosi, Burgnich, Cera, Rosato, Facchetti, Bertini (Juliano), Mazzola, De Sisti, Domenghini, Boninsegna (Rivera), Riva

1974 – West Germany

The 1974 tournament will be remembered for the fantastic Dutch team who played their free-flowing brand of 'total football', but eventually failed to secure the ultimate prize when they went down to the hosts, West Germany, in the final.

The format of the finals took on a new look with FIFA deciding to extend the round-robin group format beyond the first round to the second round, with the winners of the second-round groups contesting the final. The first-round group saw Zaire and Australia representing Asia and Oceania in the finals for the first time. England were absent, having been ousted by the Poles.

Scotland did qualify but didn't make the second round and became the first team to exit the World Cup finals without losing a game. The first round also saw the first ever meeting between East and West Germany, which the East won with a goal eight minutes from time. The second round consisted of two groups of four teams. In Group A the Dutch had a 100% record and didn't concede a goal. In Group B it was West Germany who started to find their form and also produced three straight victories.

The final between Holland and West Germany had an explosive start, with English referee Jack Taylor awarding a penalty to the Oranje when the brilliant Johan Cruyff was felled inside the first minute. Neeskens scored from the spot. Despite Dutch domination, the Germans found an equaliser from the spot before the prolific Gerd Muller netted what proved to be the winner shortly after the interval.

Group 1		
West Germany	Chile	1-0
East Germany	Australia	2-0
East Germany	Chile	1-1
East Germany	West Germany	1-0
Chile	Australia	0-0
West Germany	Australia	3-0

Group 2		
Brazil	Yugoslavia	0-0
Scotland	Zaire	2-0
Brazil	Scotland	0-0
Yugoslavia	Zaire	9-0
Scotland	Yugoslavia	1-1
Brazil	Zaire	3-0

Group 3		
Holland	Uruguay	2-0
Sweden	Bulgaria	0-0
Holland	Sweden	0-0
Bulgaria	Uruguay	1-1
Holland	Bulgaria	4-1
Sweden	Uruguay	3-0

Group 4		
Italy	Haiti	3-1
Poland	Argentina	3-2
Italy	Argentina	1-1
Poland	Haiti	7-0
Argentina	Haiti	4-1
Poland	Italy	2-1

Group A		
Brazil	East Germany	1-0
Holland	Argentina	4-0
Holland	East Germany	2-0
Brazil	Argentina	2-1
Holland	Brazil	2-0
Argentina	East Germany	1-1

Group B		
Poland	Sweden	1-0
West Germany	Yugoslavia	2-0
Poland	Yugoslavia	2-1
West Germany	Sweden	4-2
Sweden	Yugoslavia	2-1
West Germany	Poland	1-0

Third Place		
Poland	Brazil	1-0

The Final – 7 July 1974   *Olympiastadion, Munich*   77,000

West Germany	**2**	**Holland**	**1**

Breitner (25 pen), Muller (43)   Neeskens (1 pen)

West Germany: Maier, Vogts, Schwarzenbeck, Beckenbauer, Breitner, Bonhof, Hoeness, Overath, Grabowski, Muller, Holzenbein

Holland: Jongbloed, Suurbier, Rijsbergen (De Jong), Haan, Krol, Jansen, Neeskens, Van Hanegem, Rep, Cruyff, Rensenbrink (Van de Kerkhof)

1978 – Argentina

The format for the 1978 competition was the same as for the 1974 one, but the award of the finals to Argentina was surrounded by controversy, not least because the military coup in the country in 1976 had been followed by human-rights violations. However, it went ahead in newly built stadiums and overall was a great success, ending as it did in a wave of national hysteria as the hosts finished victorious.

Only Scotland of the Home Countries qualified, and the tournament marked the first appearances of Tunisia and Iran. In the first round of group games Argentina seemed to be aided by some curious refereeing decisions, while the Brazilians in Group 3 seemed to be playing under a cloud of discontent, but still made progress.

The Scots had travelled to South America with their manager Ally MacLeod somewhat over-confident and suffered when they found themselves humiliated 3-1 by Peru and then held 1-1 by Iran. Some pride was salvaged with a win over the Dutch but it was too late.

In the second round Poland found themselves in a group with the South Americans, while the other group was composed totally of European teams. The Dutch had started to find their form of four years previous and they beat Italy in their final group game 2-1, to pip the Azzuri for a place in the final itself. In the other group Argentina went into their final game against Peru needing a four goal win to make the final. They won 6-0 as Peru seemingly capitulated and the rumours of foul play have continued ever since. In the final the hosts used gamesmanship to its bitter end and, with the run of the ball, and the referee, in their favour, ran out 3-1 winners after extra time.

Group 1					
Argentina	Hungary	2-1			
Italy	France	2-1			
Argentina	France	2-1			
Italy	Hungary	3-1			
Italy	Argentina	1-0			
France	Hungary	3-1			

Group 2		
West Germany	Poland	0-0
Tunisia	Mexico	3-1
Poland	Tunisia	1-0
West Germany	Mexico	6-0
Poland	Mexico	3-1
West Germany	Tunisia	0-0

Group 3		
Austria	Spain	2-1
Sweden	Brazil	1-1
Austria	Sweden	1-0
Brazil	Spain	0-0
Spain	Sweden	1-0
Brazil	Austria	1-0

Group 4		
Peru	Scotland	3-1
Holland	Iran	3-0
Scotland	Iran	1-1

Holland	Peru	0-0
Peru	Iran	4-1
Scotland	Holland	3-2

Group A		
Italy	West Germany	0-0
Holland	Austria	5-1
Italy	Austria	1-0
Austria	West Germany	3-2
Holland	Italy	2-1
Holland	West Germany	2-2

Group B		
Argentina	Poland	2-0
Brazil	Peru	3-0
Argentina	Brazil	0-0
Poland	Peru	1-0
Brazil	Poland	3-1
Argentina	Peru	6-0

Third Place		
Brazil	Italy	2-1

The Final – 25 June 1978   Monumental, Buenos Aires   77,000

Argentina   **3**   **Holland**   **1**

Kempes (37, 104), Bertoni (114)   Nanninga (81)

Argentina: Fillol, Olguin, Galvan, Passarella, Tarantini, Ardiles (Larrosa), Gallego, Kempes, Bertoni, Luque, Ortiz (Houseman)

Holland: Jongbloed, Krol, Poortvliet, Brandts, Jansen (Suurbier), Van de Kerkhof W., Neeskens, Haan, Rep (Nanninga), Rensenbrink, Van de Kerkhof R.

1982 – Spain

The 1982 tournament saw the number of finalists increased from 16 to 24, not least to accommodate extra teams from Africa and Asia. To facilitate this the teams were divided into six groups of four with the top two from each group progressing to the second round where the teams were split into four groups of three! Missing from the finals were the Dutch, who had been possibly the best team never to win the World Cup. England, Scotland and Northern Ireland all qualified.

The first round produced some interesting results. West Germany were felled by Algeria while Italy and Czechoslovakia were held to draws by Cameroon and Kuwait. However, the minnows didn't have it all their own way – El Salvador were slaughtered 10-1 by Hungary! Northern Ireland enjoyed their best tournament, qualifying for the second phase having beaten Spain 1-0.

The winners of each of the second phase round-robin games progressed to the semi finals. France and Poland cruised through their games to the final four where they were joined by Germany at the expense of England. Brazil, who had defeated holders Argentina 3-1, looked certain to make their fourth qualifier, but in the group decider a hat-trick by Paolo Rossi saw the Azzuri through. Rossi had just returned to the national team having served a two- year ban following a bribery scandal!

Rossi scored twice more in the semis to ease Italy past Poland into the final. The other semi was a classic which saw Germany come back from 3-1 to the talented French to win a penalty shoot-out 5-4. In the final, the Italians continued their fine form and, despite recording the first ever penalty miss in the final, Rossi again proved the difference by opening the scoring and helping his team to a 3-1 victory.

Group 1				**Group 5**		
Italy	Poland	0-0		Spain	Honduras	1-1
Cameroon	Peru	0-0		Yugoslavia	N. Ireland	0-0
Italy	Peru	1-1		Spain	Yugoslavia	2-1
Cameroon	Poland	0-0		Honduras	N. Ireland	1-1
Poland	Peru	5-1		Honduras	Yugoslavia	0-1
Italy	Cameroon	1-1		Spain	N. Ireland	0-1
Group 2				**Group 6**		
Algeria	West Germany	2-1		Brazil	Russia	2-1
Austria	Chile	1-0		Scotland	New Zealand	5-2
West Germany	Chile	4-1		Brazil	Scotland	4-1
Algeria	Austria	0-2		Russia	New Zealand	3-0
Algeria	Chile	3-2		Scotland	Russia	2-2
West Germany	Austria	1-0		Brazil	New Zealand	4-0
Group 3				**Group A**		
Argentina	Belgium	0-1		Poland	Belgium	3-0
Hungary	El Salvador	10-1		Belgium	Russia	0-1
Argentina	Hungary	4-1		Russia	Poland	0-0
Belgium	El Salvador	1-0				
Belgium	Hungary	1-1		**Group B**		
Argentina	El Salvador	2-0		West Germany	England	0-0
				West Germany	Spain	2-1
Group 4				Spain	England	0-0
England	France	3-1				
Czechoslovakia	Kuwait	1-1		**Group C**		
England	Czechoslovakia	2-0		Italy	Argentina	2-1
France	Kuwait	4-1		Brazil	Argentina	3-1
France	Czechoslovakia	1-1		Italy	Brazil	3-2
England	Kuwait	1-0				

Group D

France	Austria	1-0
Austria	N. Ireland	2-2
France	N. Ireland	4-1

Semi Final

Italy	Poland	2-0
West Germany	France	3-3

West Germany win 5-4 on penalties

Third Place

Poland	France	3-2

The Final – 11 July 1982   *Bernabeu, Madrid*   *90,000*

Italy	**3**	**West Germany**	**1**

Rossi (56), Tardelli (69),   Breitner (82)
Altobelli (80)

Italy: Zoff, Cabrini, Scirea, Gentile, Collavati, Oriali, Bergomi, Tardelli, Conti, Rossi, Graziani (Altobelli) (Causio)

West Germany: Schumacher, Kaltz, Stielike, Forster K-H, Forster B, Breitner, Briegel, Dremmler (Hrubesch), Rummenigge (Muller), Littbarski, Fischer

1986 – Mexico

For the second time in 16 years Mexico were awarded the finals, although only after FIFA's original choice, Colombia, had failed to come up with the necessary financial guarantees. Mexico was not a popular choice, not least because of the intense heat.

The competition format remained the same – with 24 teams but with the two qualifiers from each group going into a straight knock-out competition. The qualifiers for the finals included England, Scotland and Northern Ireland. England started poorly and after a draw with Morocco needed a Gary Lineker hat-trick to beat Poland to ensure progression to the next stage – as runners-up to the surprise group winners Morocco, who went through undefeated!

In the second round England disposed of Paraguay comfortably and Brazil had an equally easy passage past Poland. It took all the German resilience to overcome Morocco, thanks to a goal from Matthaus. The potentially explosive encounter between Argentina and Uruguay never developed, with Argentina winning by the only goal.

Three of the four quarter finals were decided on penalties. France beat Brazil in a thriller, Germany squeezed past Mexico, and Belgium overcame Spain. The other game between Argentina and England needed divine intervention, with Maradona's hand of God nudging the South Americans to a 2-0 victory. Maradona repeated his two-goal strike in the semi final with Belgium, and Germany once again broke the French hearts in the other game.

The World Cup trophy looked to be heading back to Argentina, who took a two goal lead early in the second half. The Germans fought back and equalised with nine minutes of play remaining. But as the Germans pressed for a dramatic winner Argentina broke and won the game with six minutes remaining.

Round 1

Group A

Italy	Bulgaria	1-1
Argentina	South Korea	3-1
Italy	Argentina	1-1
Bulgaria	South Korea	1-1
Italy	South Korea	3-2
Argentina	Bulgaria	2-0

Group B

Mexico	Belgium	2-1
Paraguay	Iraq	1-0
Mexico	Paraguay	1-1
Belgium	Iraq	2-1
Mexico	Iraq	1-0
Belgium	Paraguay	2-2

Group C

France	Canada	1-0
USSR	Hungary	6-0
France	USSR	1-1
Hungary	Canada	2-0
France	Hungary	3-0
USSR	Canada	2-0

Group D

Spain	Brazil	0-1
Algeria	N. Ireland	1-1
N. Ireland	Spain	1-2
Brazil	Algeria	1-0
Algeria	Spain	0-3
N. Ireland	Brazil	0-3

Group E

Denmark	Scotland	1-0
West Germany	Uruguay	1-1
West Germany	Scotland	2-1
Denmark	Uruguay	6-1
Scotland	Uruguay	0-0
Denmark	West Germany	2-0

Group F

Portugal	England	1-0
Morocco	Poland	0-0
Poland	Portugal	1-0
Morocco	England	0-0
Morocco	Portugal	3-1
England	Poland	3-0

Round 2

Belgium	USSR	4-3
Mexico	Bulgaria	2-0
Brazil	Poland	4-0
Argentina	Uruguay	1-0
France	Italy	2-0
West Germany	Morocco	1-0
England	Paraguay	3-0
Denmark	Spain	1-5

Quarter Finals

France	Brazil	1-1
France win 4-3 on penalties		
Mexico	West Germany	0-0
West Germany win 4-1 on penalties		
Argentina	England	2-1
Belgium	Spain	1-1
Belgium win 5-4 on penalties		

Semi Final

Argentina	Belgium	2-0
West Germany	France	2-0

Third Place

France	Belgium	4-2

The Final – 29 July 1986   *Azteca, Mexico City*   114,000

Argentina 3 **West Germany** 2

Brown (22), Valdano (56),   Rummenigge (73), Voller (82)
Burruchaga (84)

Argentina: Pumpido, Cuciuffo, Brown, Ruggeri, Olarticoechea, Batista, Giusti, Enrique, Burruchaga (Trobbiani), Maradona, Valdano
West Germany: Schumacher, Jakobs, Forster K-H, Briegel, Brehme, Eder, Berthold, Matthaus, Magath (Hoeness), Rummenigge, Allofs (Voller)

The Republic of Ireland qualified for the finals for the first time ever and were joined in Italy by England and Scotland. Another qualifier was the USA, who earned their place by default after Mexico were expelled for fielding over-age players in other competitions.

The sparks started to fly at the off when defending champions Argentina were sensationally beaten by Cameroon. It was a small set back from the South Americans though, who progressed from their group and ultimately went all the way to the final itself.

Scotland again pressed their self-destruct button when they lost to Costa Rica and ultimately lost their place in the next round. The Republic earned a draw with England, who had been paired in the same group, and progressed to the second round without having won a game.

In the second round Cameroon again came good at the expense of Colombia. One moment of magic from Maradona gave the Argentine a win over Brazil, while the Republic beat Romania on penalties and a last-minute extra-time winner gave England superiority against Belgium.

Italy proved a bridge too far for the Irish, who had their opportunities in the first of the quarter finals. Argentina struggled past Yugoslavia and a penalty saw Germany past Czechoslovakia. England and Cameroon provided the best entertainment. Despite going in front, the Africans' self-discipline let them down and England squeezed through thanks to two penalties.

Both semi final games were settled by penalty shoot-outs after finishing 1-1. West Germany again got the better of England and Argentina disposed of Italy. The final between West Germany and Argentina was awful and was won by a penalty five minutes from time.

Round 1			Brazil	Costa Rica	1-0
Group A			Scotland	Sweden	2-1
Italy	Austria	1-0	Brazil	Scotland	1-0
Czechoslovakia	USA	5-1	Costa Rica	Sweden	2-1
Italy	USA	1-0			
Austria	Czechoslovakia	0-1	**Group D**		
Italy	Czechoslovakia	2-0	Colombia	UAE	2-0
Austria	USA	2-1	West Germany	Yugoslavia	4-1
			Yugoslavia	Colombia	1-0
Group B			West Germany	UAE	5-1
Argentina	Cameroon	0-1	West Germany	Colombia	1-1
Romania	USSR	2-0	Yugoslavia	UAE	4-1
Argentina	USSR	2-0			
Cameroon	Romania	2-1	**Group E**		
Argentina	Romania	1-1	Belgium	South Korea	2-0
USSR	Cameroon	4-0	Spain	Uruguay	0-0
			Spain	South Korea	3-1
Group C			Belgium	Uruguay	3-1
Brazil	Sweden	2-1	Spain	Belgium	2-1
Costa Rica	Scotland	1-0	Uruguay	South Korea	1-0

Group F			**Quarter Finals**		
England	Ireland	1-1	Italy	Ireland	1-0
Holland	Egypt	1-1	West Germany	Czechoslovakia	1-0
England	Holland	0-0	England	Cameroon	3-2
Egypt	Ireland	0-0	Argentina	Yugoslavia	0-0
England	Egypt	1-0	*Argentina win 3-2 on penalties*		
Ireland	Holland	1-1	**Semi Finals**		
Round 2			Argentina	Italy	1-1
Cameroon	Colombia	2-1	*Argentina win 4-3 on penalties*		
Czechoslovakia	Costa Rica	4-1	West Germany	England	1-1
Argentina	Brazil	1-0	*West Germany win 4-3 on penalties*		
West Germany	Holland	2-1			
Ireland	Romania	0-0	**Third Place**		
Ireland win 5-4 on penalties			Italy	England	2-1
Italy	Uruguay	2-0			
Yugoslavia	Spain	2-1			
England	Belgium	1-0			

The Final – 8 July 1990		*Olimpic, Rome*		*73,000*
West Germany	**1**	**Argentina**		**0**

Brehme (85)

West Germany: Illgner, Berthold, Kohler, Augenthaler, Buchwald, Brehme, Hassler, Matthaus, Littbarski, Voller, Klinsmann
Argentina: Goycochea, Ruggeri, Simon, Serrizuela, Sensini, Basualdo, Burruchaga, Trogilo, Lorenzo, Maradona, Dezotti

1994 – USA

Despite there being no structured professional football in the USA, FIFA awarded the States the 1994 competition, which proved to be a huge success. The tournament was devoid of any Home Countries but the British Isles were represented by the Republic of Ireland, whose manager Jack Charlton courted the wrath of FIFA for openly criticising them for not allowing players to drink water during games played in intense heat.

With 16 of the 24 finalists qualifying for the second phase, there was little room for any shocks in the first phase of competition. Cameroon failed to show the spark of 1990 but 42-year-old Roger Milla became the oldest man to play and score in the finals. The biggest story was Maradona's failure to pass a post-match drug test – he was sent packing by FIFA.

The two most exciting games in the second round were Germany's 3-2 win over Belgium and Nigeria's stubborn resistance to Italy. The Azzuri won in extra time but only after they had found an equaliser moments before the end of normal time. Brazil scraped past the hosts by a single goal, while Romania beat the Maradonaless Argentina.

Seven of the eight quarter finalists hailed from Europe. The eighth country, Brazil, beat Holland 3-2 in an entertaining game, but the upset came with the Bulgarians ousting the Germans. Italy progressed at the expense of Spain, and

Sweden won the penalty shoot-out with Romania. In the semi finals Italy were too strong for Bulgaria in the heat of New York while a Romario goal ten minutes from time put Brazil into the final at the expense of Sweden.

The final was again a non-event and in the Californian heat went the full distance without score. Roberto Baggio missed the vital penalty in the shoot-out and Brazil won the trophy for the fourth time.

Round 1		
Group A		
USA	Switzerland	1-1
Colombia	Romania	1-3
Romania	Switzerland	1-4
USA	Colombia	2-1
USA	Romania	0-1
Switzerland	Colombia	0-2
Group B		
Cameroon	Sweden	2-2
Brazil	Russia	2-0
Brazil	Cameroon	3-0
Russia	Sweden	1-3
Brazil	Sweden	1-1
Cameroon	Russia	1-6
Group C		
Germany	Bolivia	1-0
Spain	South Korea	2-2
Germany	Spain	1-1
Bolivia	South Korea	3-2
Bolivia	Spain	1-3
Group D		
Argentina	Greece	4-0
Nigeria	Bulgaria	3-0
Argentina	Nigeria	2-1
Bulgaria	Greece	4-0
Argentina	Bulgaria	0-2
Nigeria	Greece	2-0
Group E		
Italy	Rep. Ireland	0-1
Norway	Mexico	1-0
Italy	Norway	1-0

Rep. Ireland	Mexico	1-2
Norway	Rep. Ireland	0-0
Italy	Mexico	1-1
Group F		
Belgium	Morocco	1-0
Saudi Arabia	Holland	1-2
Belgium	Holland	1-0
Morocco	Saudi Arabia	1-2
Belgium	Saudi Arabia	0-1
Holland	Morocco	2-1
Round 2		
Germany	Belgium	3-2
Spain	Switzerland	3-0
Saudi Arabia	Sweden	1-3
Argentina	Romania	2-3
Holland	Rep. Ireland	2-0
Brazil	USA	1-0
Italy	Nigeria	2-1
Bulgaria	Mexico	†1-1
Bulgaria win 3-1 on penalties		
Quarter Finals		
Italy	Spain	2-1
Brazil	Holland	3-2
Bulgaria	Germany	2-1
Romania	Sweden	†2-2
Sweden win 5-4 on penalties		
Semi Finals		
Italy	Bulgaria	2-1
Brazil	Sweden	1-0
Third Place		
Sweden	Bulgaria	4-0

The Final – 17 July	*Rose Bowl, Pasadena*	*94,194*
Brazil	0	**Italy**	0

Brazil win 3-2 on penalties after extra time

Brazil: Taffarel, Jorginho (Cafu 21), Aldair, Marcio Santos, Branco, Mauro Silva, Dunga, Zinho (Cafu 109), Mazinho, Bebeto, Romario.
Italy: Pagliuca, Benarrivo, Baresi, Maldini, Mussi (Apolloni 34), D. Baggio (Evani 101), Albertini, Berti, Donadoni, R.Baggio, Massaro

GOLDEN BOOT WINNERS

Year	Winner	County	Goals
1930	Guillermo Stabile	Argentina	8
1934	Oldrich Nejeldy	Czechoslovakia	5
1938	Leonidas da Silva	Brazil	8
1950	Ademir Menezes	Brazil	9
1954	Sandor Kocsis	Hungary	11
1958	Just Fontaine	France	13
1962	Florin Albert	Hungary	4
	Garrincha	Brazil	4
	Valentin Ivanov	USSR	4
	Drazen Jerkovic	Yugoslavia	4
	Leonel Sanchez	Chile	4
	Vava	Brazil	4
1966	Eusebio	Portugal	9
1970	Gerd Muller	West Germany	10
1974	Grzegorz Lato	Poland	7
1978	Mario Kempes	Argentina	6
1982	Paolo Rossi	Italy	6
1986	Gary Lineker	England	6
1990	Toto Schillaci	Italy	6
1994	Oleg Salenko	Russia	6
	Hristo Stoichkov	Bulgaria	6

HOW THEY QUALIFIED

Introduction

The following pages contain details of all 634 games in the qualifying competition. Results are arranged by each region's governing body. The qualifiers for France '98 by region are:

AFC   Iran, Japan, Saudi Arabia, South Korea.

CAF   Cameroon, Morocco, Nigeria, South Africa, Tunisia.

CONCACAF   Jamaica, Mexico, USA.

CONMEBOL Argentina, Brazil (holders), Chile, Colombia, Paraguay.

OFC   –

UEFA   Austria, Belgium, Bulgaria, Croatia, Denmark, England, France (hosts), Germany, Holland, Italy, Norway, Romania, Scotland, Spain, Yugoslavia.

AFC

Qualification Rules

The 36 participating teams all entered at the first-round stage. The teams were divided into ten groups (six groups of four teams and four groups of three teams). Each group decided on the system of play. Most groups decided on a tournament system with qualifying games played over a few days at a single venue; a few played on a normal round-robin home and away basis. This produced ten group winners who progressed to the second round of competition. These teams were divided into two leagues of five teams. Each league then played against each other once at a neutral venue. The two group winners qualified for the World Cup finals. The runner-up in each group then played off with the winner occupying the final automatic qualification place in the World Cup finals. The losing team then played the winner of OFC on a home and away basis with the aggregate winner progressing to the World Cup finals.

First Round

Group 1

Saudi Arabia

16.03.97*	Chinese Taipei v Saudi Arabia	0-2
16.03.97*	Malaysia v Bangladesh	2-0
18.03.97*	Malaysia v Saudi Arabia	0-0
18.03.97*	Bangladesh v Chinese Taipei	1-3
20.03.97*	Bangladesh v Saudi Arabia	1-4
20.03.97*	Malaysia v Chinese Taipei	2-0
27.03.97†	Chinese Taipei v Malaysia	0-0
27.03.97†	Saudi Arabia v Bangladesh	3-0
29.03.97†	Chinese Taipei v Bangladesh	1-2
29.03.97†	Saudi Arabia v Malaysia	3-0
31.03.97†	Bangladesh v Malaysia	0-1
31.03.97†	Saudi Arabia v Chinese Taipei	6-0

*Played in Malaysia. †Played in Jeddah.

Final Table	P	W	D	L	F	A	Pts
Saudi Arabia	6	5	1	0	18	1	16
Malaysia	6	3	2	1	5	3	11
Chinese Taipei	6	1	1	4	4	13	4
Bangladesh	6	1	0	5	4	14	3

Group 2   Iran

02.06.97* Syria v Kyrgyzstan	abandoned
02.06.97* Maldives v Iran	0-17
04.06.97* Syria v Maldives	12-0
04.06.97* Kyrgyzstan v Iran	0-7
06.06.97* Syria v Iran	0-1
06.06.97* Kyrgyzstan v Maldives	3-0
09.06.97† Iran v Kyrgyzstan	3-1
09.06.97† Maldives v Syria	0-12
11.06.97† Iran v Maldives	9-0
11.06.97† Kyrgyzstan v Syria	2-1
13.06.97† Iran v Syria	2-2
13.06.97† Maldives v Kyrgyzstan	0-6

Final Table

	P	W	D	L	F	A	Pts
Iran	6	5	1	0	39	3	16
Kyrgyzstan	5	3	0	2	12	11	9
Syria	5	2	1	2	27	5	7
Maldives	6	0	0	5	0	59	0

*Played in Damascus. †Played in Tehran.

Group 3   United Arab Emirates

08.04.97* Jordan v UAE	0-0
11.04.97* Bahrain v UAE	1-2
14.04.97* Bahrain v Jordan	1-0
19.04.97† Jordan v Bahrain	4-1
22.04.97† UAE v Bahrain	3-0
26.04.97† UAE v Jordan	2-0

*Played in Manama. †Played in Sharjah.

Final Table

	P	W	D	L	F	A	Pts
UAE	4	3	1	0	7	1	10
Jordan	4	1	1	2	4	4	4
Bahrain	4	1	0	3	3	9	3

Group 4   Japan

23.03.97* Nepal v Macao	1-1
23.03.97* Oman v Japan	0-1
25.03.97* Macao v Japan	0-1
25.03.97* Oman v Nepal	1-0
27.03.97* Nepal v Japan	0-6
27.03.97* Oman v Macao	4-0
22.06.97† Japan v Macao	10-0
22.06.97† Nepal v Oman	0-6
25.06.97† Japan v Nepal	3-0
25.06.97† Macao v Oman	0-2
28.06.97† Japan v Oman	1-1
28.06.97† Macao v Nepal	2-1

*Played in Muscat. †Played in Tokyo.

Final Table

	P	W	D	L	F	A	Pts
Japan	6	5	1	0	31	6	16
Oman	6	4	1	1	14	2	13
Macao	6	1	1	4	3	28	4
Nepal	6	0	1	5	2	19	1

Final Table	P	W	D	L	F	A	*Pts*
South Korea	4	3	1	0	9	1	10
Thailand	4	1	1	2	5	6	4
Hong Kong	4	1	0	3	3	10	3

Group 7   Kuwait

13.04.97	Lebanon v Singapore	1-1
26.04.97	Singapore v Kuwait	0-1
08.05.97	Kuwait v Lebanon	2-0
24.05.97	Singapore v Lebanon	1-2
05.06.97	Kuwait v Singapore	4-0
22.06.97	Lebanon v Kuwait	1-3

Final Table	P	W	D	L	F	A	*Pts*
Kuwait	4	4	0	0	10	1	12
Lebanon	4	1	1	2	4	7	4
Singapore	4	0	1	3	2	8	1

Group 8   China Peoples Republic

04.05.97	Tajikistan v Vietnam SR	4-0
04.05.97	Turkmenistan v China PR	1-4
11.05.97	Tajikistan v China PR	0-1
11.05.97	Turkmenistan v Vietnam SR	2-1
25.05.97	Vietnam SR v China PR	1-3
25.05.97	Turkmenistan v Tajikistan	1-2
01.06.97	China PR v Turkmenistan	1-0

Group 5   Uzbekistan

06.04.97	Indonesia v Cambodia	8-0
13.04.97	Indonesia v Yemen	0-0
20.04.97	Cambodia v Yemen	0-1
27.04.97	Cambodia v Indonesia	1-1
09.05.97	Yemen v Uzbekistan	0-1
16.05.97	Yemen v Cambodia	7-0
25.05.97	Uzbekistan v Cambodia	6-0
01.06.97	Indonesia v Uzbekistan	1-1
13.06.97	Yemen v Indonesia	1-1
20.06.97	Uzbekistan v Indonesia	3-0
29.06.97	Cambodia v Uzbekistan	1-4
13.07.97	Uzbekistan v Yemen	not played

Final Table	P	W	D	L	F	A	*Pts*
Uzbekistan	5	4	1	0	15	2	13
Yemen	5	2	2	1	9	4	8
Indonesia	6	1	4	1	11	6	7
Cambodia	6	0	1	5	2	27	1

Group 6   South Korea

23.02.97	Hong Kong v South Korea	0-2
02.03.97	Thailand v South Korea	1-3
09.03.97	Thailand v Hong Kong	2-0
30.03.97	Hong Kong v Thailand	3-2
28.05.97	South Korea v Hong Kong	4-0

01.06.97 Vietnam SR v Tajikistan ... 0-4
08.06.97 China PR v Tajikistan ... 0-0
08.06.97 Vietnam SR v Turkmenistan ... 0-4
22.06.97 China PR v Vietnam SR ... 4-0
22.06.97 Tajikistan v Turkmenistan ... 5-0

Final Table

	P	W	D	L	F	A	Pts
China PR	6	5	1	0	13	2	16
Tajikistan	6	4	1	1	15	4	13
Turkmenistan	6	2	0	4	8	13	6
Vietnam SR	6	0	0	6	2	21	0

Group 9   Kazakhstan

11.05.97 Kazakhstan v Pakistan ... 3-0
23.05.97 Pakistan v Iraq ... 2-6
06.06.97 Iraq v Kazakhstan ... 1-2
11.06.97 Pakistan v Kazakhstan ... 0-7
20.06.97 Iraq v Pakistan ... 6-1
29.06.97 Kazakhstan v Iraq ... 3-1

Final Table

	P	W	D	L	F	A	Pts
Kazakhstan	4	4	0	0	15	2	12
Iraq	4	2	0	2	14	8	6
Pakistan	4	0	0	4	3	22	0

Group 10   Qatar

20.09.96 Qatar v Sri Lanka ... 3-0
21.09.96 India v Philippines ... 2-0

23.09.96 Qatar v Philippines ... 5-0
24.09.96 Sri Lanka v India ... 1-1
26.09.96 Philippines v Sri Lanka ... 0-3
27.09.96 Qatar v India ... 6-0
All matches played in Doha, Qatar.

Final Table

	P	W	D	L	F	A	Pts
Qatar	3	3	0	0	14	0	9
Sri Lanka	3	1	1	1	4	4	4
India	3	1	1	1	3	7	4
Philippines	3	0	0	3	0	10	0

Second Round

Group A   Saudi Arabia

13.09.97 China PR v Iran ... 2-4
14.09.97 Saudi Arabia v Kuwait ... 2-1
19.09.97 Iran v Saudi Arabia ... 1-1
19.09.97 Qatar v Kuwait ... 0-2
26.09.97 Kuwait v Iran ... 1-1
26.09.97 Qatar v China PR ... 1-1
03.10.97 China PR v Saudi Arabia ... 1-0
03.10.97 Iran v Qatar ... 3-0
10.10.97 Kuwait v China PR ... 1-2
11.10.97 Saudi Arabia v Qatar ... 1-0
17.10.97 Iran v China PR ... 4-1
17.10.97 Kuwait v Saudi Arabia ... 2-1

24.10.97	Kuwait v Qatar	0-1
24.10.97	Saudi Arabia v Iran	1-0
31.10.97	China PR v Qatar	2-3
31.10.97	Iran v Kuwait	0-0
06.11.97	Saudi Arabia v China PR	1-1
07.11.97	Qatar v Iran	2-0
12.11.97	China PR v Kuwait	1-0
12.11.97	Qatar v Saudi Arabia	0-1

Final Table

	P	W	D	L	F	A	Pts
Saudi Arabia	8	4	2	2	8	6	14
Iran	8	3	3	2	13	8	12
China PR	8	3	2	3	11	14	11
Qatar	8	3	1	4	7	10	10
Kuwait	8	2	2	4	7	8	8

Iran enter play-offs with Japan from Group B.

11.10.97	Uzbekistan v Japan	1-1
11.10.97	Kazakhstan v South Korea	1-1
18.10.97	Uzbekistan v South Korea	1-5
18.10.97	Kazakhstan v UAE	3-0
25.10.97	Uzbekistan v Kazakhstan	4-0
26.10.97	Japan v UAE	1-1
01.11.97	South Korea v Japan	0-2
02.11.97	UAE v Uzbekistan	0-0
08.11.97	Japan v Kazakhstan	5-1
09.11.97	UAE v South Korea	1-3

Final Table

	P	W	D	L	F	A	Pts
South Korea	8	6	1	1	19	7	19
Japan	8	3	4	1	17	9	13
UAE	8	2	3	3	9	12	9
Uzbekistan	8	1	3	4	13	18	6
Kazakhstan	8	1	3	4	7	19	6

Final Play-Off

Group A and Group B elimination match.

16.11.97	Japan v Iran (aet in Malaysia)	3-2

Japan qualify for World Cup finals.

Group B   South Korea

06.09.97	South Korea v Kazakhstan	3-0
07.09.97	Japan v Uzbekistan	6-3
12.09.97	Korea Rep. v Uzbekistan	2-1
12.09.97	UAE v Kazakhstan	4-0
19.09.97	UAE v Japan	0-0
20.09.97	Kazakhstan v Uzbekistan	1-1
27.09.97	Uzbekistan v UAE	2-3
28.09.97	Japan v South Korea	1-2
04.10.97	South Korea v UAE	3-0
04.10.97	Kazakhstan v Japan	1-1

CAF

Qualification Rules

Four teams were exempt from playing in the first round: Cameroon, Nigeria, Morocco and Egypt. All other teams were then drawn in a straightforward home and away match basis. The aggregate winners of each tie progressed to the second round where they joined the remaining CAF teams to form five groups of four. Each team played on a round-robin basis with the group winner progressing to the World Cup finals.

First Round

31.05.96	Mauritania v Burkina Faso	0-0
16.06.96	Burkina Faso v Mauritania	2-0

Burkina Faso win 2-0 on aggregate.

01.06.96	Namibia v Mozambique.............	2-0
16.06.96	Mozambique v Namibia	1-1

Namibia win 3-1 on aggregate.

01.06.96	Malawi v South Africa	0-1
15.06.96	South Africa v Malawi	3-0

South Africa win 4-0 on aggregate.

01.06.96	Uganda v Angola	0-2
16.06.96	Angola v Uganda	3-1

Angola win 5-1 on aggregate.

01.06.96	Guinea-Bissau v Guinea	3-2
16.06.96	Guinea v Guinea-Bissau	3-1

Guinea win 5-4 on aggregate.

01.06.96	Gambia v Liberia	2-1
23.06.96	Liberia v Gambia *	4-0

Liberia win 5-2 on aggregate.

* *Match played in Accra, Ghana, because of the war situation in Liberia.*

02.06.96	Swaziland v Gabon	0-1
16.06.96	Gabon v Swaziland	2-0

Gabon win 3-0 on aggregate.

02.06.96	Burundi v Sierra Leone	1-0
15.06.96	Sierra Leone v Burundi	0-1

Burundi win 2-0 on aggregate. †

02.06.96	Madagascar v Zimbabwe	1-2
16.06.96	Zimbabwe v Madagascar	2-2

Zimbabwe win 4-3 on aggregate.

02.06.96	Congo v Ivory Coast................	2-0
16.06.96	Ivory Coast v Congo	1-1

Congo win 3-1 on aggregate.

02.06.96	Mauritius v Zaire	1-5
16.06.96	Zaire v Mauritius	2-0

Zaire win 7-1 on aggregate.

| 02.06.96 | Rwanda v Tunisia | ... | 1-3 |
| 16.06.96 | Tunisia v Rwanda | ... | 2-0 |

Tunisia win 5-1 on aggregate.

| 02.06.96 | Kenya v Algeria | ... | 3-1 |
| 14.06.96 | Algeria v Kenya | ... | 1-0 |

Kenya win 3-2 on aggregate.

| 02.06.96 | Togo v Senegal | ... | 2-1 |
| 15.06.96 | Senegal v Togo | ... | 1-1 |

Tongo win 3-2 on aggregate.

| 02.06.96 | Sudan v Zambia | ... | 2-0 |
| 16.06.96 | Zambia v Sudan | ... | 3-0 |

Zambia win 3-2 on aggregate.

| 08.06.96 | Tanzania v Ghana | ... | 0-0 |
| 17.06.96 | Ghana v Tanzania | ... | 2-1 |

Ghana win 2-1 on aggregate.

† *Burundi subsequently withdrew from competition so Sierra Leone were reinstated in their place*

Second Round

Group 1   Nigeria

09.11.96	Nigeria v Burkina Faso	...	2-0
10.11.96	Guinea v Kenya	...	3-1
12.01.97	Kenya v Nigeria	...	1-1
12.01.97	Burkina Faso v Guinea	...	0-2
05.04.97	Nigeria v Guinea	...	2-1

06.04.97	Kenya v Burkina Faso	...	4-3
27.04.97	Kenya v Guinea	...	1-0
27.04.97	Burkina Faso v Nigeria	...	1-2
07.06.97	Nigeria v Kenya	...	3-0
08.06.97	Guinea v Burkina Faso	...	3-1
16.08.97	Burkina Faso v Kenya	...	2-4
17.08.97	Guinea v Nigeria	...	1-0

Final Table	P	W	D	L	F	A	Pts
Nigeria	6	4	1	1	10	4	13
Guinea	6	4	0	2	10	5	12
Kenya	6	3	1	2	11	12	10
Burkina Faso	6	0	0	6	7	17	0

Group 2   Tunisia

08.11.96	Egypt v Namibia	...	7-1
10.11.96	Liberia v Tunisia	...	0-1
11.01.97	Namibia v Liberia	...	0-0
12.01.97	Tunisia v Egypt	...	1-0
06.04.97	Liberia v Egypt	...	1-0
06.04.97	Namibia v Tunisia	...	1-2
26.04.97	Namibia v Egypt	...	2-3
27.04.97	Tunisia v Liberia	...	2-0
08.06.97	Liberia v Namibia	...	1-2
08.06.97	Egypt v Tunisia	...	0-0
17.08.97	Tunisia v Namibia	...	4-0
17.08.97	Egypt v Liberia	...	5-0

Final Table	P	W	D	L	F	A	Pts
Tunisia	6	5	1	0	10	1	16
Egypt	6	3	1	2	15	5	10
Liberia	6	1	1	4	2	10	4
Namibia	6	1	1	4	6	17	4

Group 3 — South Africa

09.11.96	South Africa v Zaire	1-0
10.11.96	Congo v Zambia	1-0
11.01.97	Zambia v South Africa	0-0
12.01.97	Zaire v Congo	1-1
06.04.97	Congo v South Africa	2-0
09.04.97	Zaire v Zambia	2-2
27.04.97	Zaire v South Africa	1-2
27.04.97	Zambia v Congo	3-0
08.06.97	Congo v Congo DR (Zaire)	1-0
08.06.97	South Africa v Zambia	3-0
16.08.97	Zambia v Congo DR (Zaire)	2-0
16.08.97	South Africa v Congo	1-0

Final Table	P	W	D	L	F	A	Pts
South Africa	6	4	2	0	7	3	13
Congo	6	3	1	2	5	5	10
Zambia	6	2	2	2	7	6	8
Congo DR *	6	0	2	4	4	9	2

Congo DR formerly Zaire.

Group 4 — Cameroon

10.11.96	Angola v Zimbabwe	2-1
10.11.96	Togo v Cameroon	2-4
12.01.97	Cameroon v Angola	0-0
12.01.97	Zimbabwe v Togo	3-0
06.04.97	Angola v Togo	3-1
06.04.97	Cameroon v Zimbabwe	1-0
27.04.97	Cameroon v Togo	2-0
27.04.97	Zimbabwe v Angola	0-0
08.06.97	Angola v Cameroon	1-1
08.06.97	Togo v Zimbabwe	2-1
17.08.97	Togo v Angola	1-1
17.08.97	Zimbabwe v Cameroon	1-2

Final Table	P	W	D	L	F	A	Pts
Cameroon	6	4	2	0	10	4	14
Angola	6	2	4	0	7	4	10
Zimbabwe	6	1	1	4	6	7	4
Togo	6	1	1	4	6	14	4

Group 5 — Morocco

09.11.96	Morocco v Sierra Leone	4-0
10.11.96	Gabon v Ghana	1-1
11.01.97	Sierra Leone v Gabon	1-0
12.01.97	Ghana v Morocco	2-2
05.04.97	Sierra Leone v Ghana	1-1
06.04.97	Gabon v Morocco	0-4

26.04.97	Sierra Leone v Morocco	0-1
27.04.97	Ghana v Gabon	3-0
07.06.97	Morocco v Ghana	1-0
08.06.97	Gabon v Sierra Leone	postponed
17.08.97	Morocco v Gabon	2-0
17.08.97	Ghana v Sierra Leone	0-2

Final Table	P	W	D	L	F	A	Pts
Morocco	6	5	1	0	14	4	16
Sierra Leone	5	2	1	2	6	7	7
Ghana	6	1	3	2	7	7	6
Gabon	5	0	1	4	1	11	1

CONMEBOL

Qualification Rules

The nine participating teams will play a qualifying tournament in which each team plays 16 matches, for a total of 72 matches. The top four teams qualify – plus Brazil as defending world champions.

24.04.96	Argentina v Bolivia	3-1
24.04.96	Colombia v Paraguay	1-0
24.04.96	Ecuador v Peru	4-1
24.04.96	Venezuela v Uruguay	0-2
02.06.96	Ecuador v Argentina	2-0
02.06.96	Peru v Colombia	1-1
02.06.96	Uruguay v Paraguay	0-2
02.06.96	Venezuela v Chile	1-1
07.07.96	Bolivia v Venezuela	6-1
07.07.96	Chile v Ecuador	4-1

Final Table

	P	W	D	L	F	A	Pts
Argentina	16	8	6	2	23	13	30
Paraguay	16	9	2	5	21	14	29
Colombia	16	8	4	4	23	15	28
Chile	16	7	4	5	32	18	25
Peru	16	7	4	5	19	20	25
Ecuador	16	6	3	7	22	21	21
Uruguay	16	6	3	7	18	21	21
Bolivia	16	4	5	7	18	21	17
Venezuela	16	0	3	13	8	41	3

07.07.96	Colombia v Uruguay	3-1
07.07.96	Peru v Argentina	0-0
01.09.96	Argentina v Paraguay	1-1
01.09.96	Bolivia v Peru	0-0
01.09.96	Colombia v Chile	4-1
01.09.96	Ecuador v Venezuela	1-0
08.10.96	Uruguay v Bolivia	1-0
09.10.96	Ecuador v Colombia	0-1
09.10.96	Paraguay v Chile	2-1
09.10.96	Venezuela v Argentina	2-5
10.11.96	Bolivia v Colombia	2-2
10.11.96	Paraguay v Ecuador	1-0
10.11.96	Peru v Venezuela	4-1
12.11.96	Chile v Uruguay	1-0
15.12.96	Argentina v Chile	1-1
15.12.96	Bolivia v Paraguay	0-0
15.12.96	Uruguay v Peru	2-0
15.12.96	Venezuela v Colombia	0-2
12.01.97	Bolivia v Ecuador	2-0
12.01.97	Peru v Chile	2-1
12.01.97	Uruguay v Argentina	0-0
12.01.97	Venezuela v Paraguay	0-2
12.02.97	Bolivia v Chile	1-1
12.02.97	Colombia v Argentina	0-1
12.02.97	Ecuador v Uruguay	4-0
12.02.97	Paraguay v Peru	2-1
02.04.97	Bolivia v Argentina	2-1
02.04.97	Paraguay v Colombia	2-1
02.04.97	Peru v Ecuador	1-1
02.04.97	Uruguay v Venezuela	3-1
29.04.97	Chile v Venezuela	6-0
30.04.97	Argentina v Ecuador	2-1
30.04.97	Colombia v Peru	0-1
30.04.97	Paraguay v Uruguay	3-1
08.06.97	Ecuador v Chile	1-1
08.06.97	Uruguay v Colombia	1-1
08.06.97	Venezuela v Bolivia	1-1
08.06.97	Argentina v Peru	2-0
05.07.97	Chile v Colombia	4-1
06.07.97	Paraguay v Argentina	1-2
06.07.97	Peru v Bolivia	2-1
06.07.97	Venezuela v Ecuador	1-1
20.07.97	Argentina v Venezuela	2-0
20.07.97	Bolivia v Uruguay	1-0
20.07.97	Chile v Paraguay	2-1
20.07.97	Colombia v Ecuador	1-0
20.08.97	Colombia v Bolivia	3-0
20.08.97	Ecuador v Paraguay	2-1
20.08.97	Uruguay v Chile	1-0
20.08.97	Venezuela v Peru	0-3
10.09.97	Chile v Argentina	1-2
10.09.97	Colombia v Venezuela	1-0
10.09.97	Paraguay v Bolivia	2-1
10.09.97	Peru v Uruguay	2-1

12.10.97	Ecuador v Bolivia	......	1-0
12.10.97	Paraguay v Venezuela	......	1-0
12.10.97	Argentina v Uruguay	......	0-0
12.10.97	Chile v Peru	......	4-0

16.11.97	Argentina v Colombia	......	1-1
16.11.97	Chile v Bolivia	......	3-0
16.11.97	Peru v Paraguay	......	1-0
16.11.97	Uruguay v Ecuador	......	5-3

CONCACAF

Qualification Rules

There was a preliminary competition involving teams in a Caribbean Zone and a Central American Zone. The Caribbean Zone played two rounds of matches, each round consisting of home and away matches with the aggregate winners moving on to the next round where additional seeded teams enter the competition. The three teams remaining at the end of the third round qualified for the semi final round. The Central American Zone was a single round which provided two teams for the semi final round.

The five qualifying teams were joined by seven exempt teams to participate in the semi final round. This consisted of three groups of four teams playing on a round-robin basis. The top two teams from each group qualified for the final round. The final round, between the six remaining teams, was played on a round-robin basis with the top three teams qualifying for the World Cup finals.

Caribbean Zone – First Round

| 24.03.96 | Dominican R. v Aruba | ...... | 3-2 |
| 31.03.96 | Aruba v Dominican R. | ...... | 1-3 |

Dominican Republic win 6-3 on aggregate.

| 29.03.96 | Guyana v Grenada | ...... | 1-2 |
| 07.04.96 | Grenada v Guyana | ...... | 6-0 |

Grenada win 8-1 on aggregate.

Bahamas v St. Kitts & Nevis

The Bahamas withdraw from the 1998 World Cup preliminary competition. St. Kitts & Nevis advance to Second Round.

| 10.03.96 | Dominica v Antigua | ...... | 3-3 |
| 31.03.96 | Antigua v Dominica | ...... | 1-3 |

Dominica win 6-4 on aggregate.

Caribbean – Second Round

| 31.03.96 | Surinam v Jamaica | 0-1 |
| 21.04.96 | Jamaica v Surinam | 1-0 |

Jamaica win 2-0 on aggregate.

| 04.05.96 | Puerto Rico v St. Vincent | 1-2 |
| 12.05.96 | St. Vincent v Puerto Rico | 7-0 |

St. Vincent & G. win 9-1 on aggregate.

| 05.05.96 | St. Kitts v St. Lucia | 5-1 |
| 19.05.96 | St. Lucia v St. Kitts | 0-1 |

St. Kitts & Nevis win 6-1 on aggregate.

| 12.05.96 | Cayman v Cuba | 0-1 |
| 14.05.96 | Cuba v Cayman | 5-0 |

Cuba win 6-0 on aggregate.

| 12.05.96 | Haiti v Grenada | 6-1 |
| 18.05.96 | Grenada v Haiti | 0-1 |

Haiti win 7-1 on aggregate.

| 14.05.96 | Dominica v Barbados | 0-1 |
| 19.05.96 | Barbados v Dominica | 1-0 |

Barbados win 2-0 on aggregate.

| 04.05.96 | Dominican R. v Neth. Antilles... | 2-1 |
| 11.05.96 | Neth. Antilles v Dominican R. | 0-0 |

Dominican Republic win 2-1 on aggregate.

Bermuda v Trinidad & Tobago
Bermuda withdraw.
Trinidad & Tobago advance to Third Round.

Caribbean – Third Round

| 10.06.96 | Cuba v Haiti | 6-1 |
| 30.06.96 | Haiti v Cuba | 1-1 |

Cuba win 7-2 on aggregate.

| 23.06.96 | St. Kitts v St. Vincent | 2-2 |
| 30.06.96 | St. Vincent v St. Kitts/ | 0-0 |

2-2 on aggregate.
St. Vincent & G. win on away goals rule.

| 23.06.96 | Barbados v Jamaica | 0-1 |
| 30.06.96 | Jamaica v Barbados | 2-0 |

Jamaica win 3-0 on aggregate.

| 15.06.96 | Dominican R. v Trinidad & T. | 1-4 |
| 23.06.96 | Trinidad & T. v Dominican R. | 8-0 |

Trinidad & Tobago win 12-1 on aggregate.

C.America Zone – First Round

| 05.05.96 | Nicaragua v Guatemala | 0-1 |
| 10.05.96 | Guatemala v Nicaragua | 2-1 |

Guatemala win 3-1 on aggregate.

| 02.06.96 | Belize v Panama | 1-2 |
| 09.06.96 | Panama v Belize | 4-1 |

Panama win 6-2 on aggregate.

Semi Final Round

Group 1   United States & Costa Rica

01.09.96	Trinidad & T. v Costa Rica... 0-1
06.10.96	Trinidad & T. v Guatemala... 1-1
03.11.96	USA v Guatemala 2-0
10.11.96	USA v Trinidad & T. 2-0
17.11.96	Costa Rica v Guatemala 3-0
24.11.96	Trinidad & T. v USA 0-1
24.11.96	Guatemala v Costa Rica 1-0
01.12.96	Costa Rica v USA 2-1
08.12.96	Guatemala v Trinidad & T. 2-1
14.12.96	USA v Costa Rica 2-1
21.12.96	Costa Rica v Trinidad & T. 2-1
21.12.96	Guatemala v USA 2-2

Final Table

	P	W	D	L	F	A	Pts
United States	6	4	1	1	10	5	13
Costa Rica	6	4	0	2	9	6	12
Guatemala	6	2	2	2	6	9	8
Trinidad & T.	6	0	1	5	3	9	1

Group 2   Canada & El Salvador

30.08.96	Canada v Panama... 3-1
08.09.96	Cuba v El Salvador 0-5
22.09.96	Cuba v Panama 3-1
06.10.96	Panama v El Salvador 1-1
10.10.96	Canada v Cuba 2-0
13.10.96	Cuba v Canada 0-2
27.10.96	Panama v Canada 0-0
03.11.96	Canada v El Salvador 1-0
10.11.96	El Salvador v Panama 3-2
01.12.96	El Salvador v Cuba 3-0
15.12.96	Panama v Cuba 3-1
15.12.96	El Salvador v Canada 0-2

Final Table

	P	W	D	L	F	A	Pts
Canada	6	5	1	0	10	1	16
El Salvador	6	3	1	2	12	6	10
Panama	6	1	2	3	8	11	5
Cuba	6	1	0	5	4	16	3

Group 3   Jamaica & Mexico

15.09.96	Jamaica v Honduras... 3-0
15.09.96	St. Vincent & G. v Mexico... 0-3
21.09.96	Honduras v Mexico 2-1
23.09.96	St. Vincent & G. v Jamaica.. 1-2
13.10.96	St. Vincent & G. v Honduras 1-4
16.10.96	Mexico v Jamaica 2-1
27.10.96	Honduras v Jamaica 0-0
30.10.96	Mexico v St. Vincent & G. 5-1
06.11.96	Mexico v Honduras 3-1
10.11.96	Jamaica v St. Vincent & G. 5-0

17.11.96 Honduras v St. Vincent & G. 11-3
17.11.96 Jamaica v Mexico 1-0

Final Table

	P	W	D	L	F	A	Pts
Jamaica	6	4	1	1	12	3	13
Mexico	6	4	0	2	14	6	12
Honduras	6	3	1	2	18	6	11
St. Vincent & G.	6	0	0	6	6	30	0

Final Round

Mexico, USA, Jamaica

02.03.97	Jamaica v USA	0-0
02.03.97	Mexico v Canada	4-0
16.03.97	Costa Rica v Mexico	0-0
16.03.97	USA v Canada	3-0
23.03.97	Costa Rica v USA	3-2
06.04.97	Canada v El Salvador	0-0
13.04.97	Mexico v Jamaica	6-0
20.04.97	USA v Mexico	2-2
27.04.97	Canada v Jamaica	0-0
04.05.97	El Salvador v Costa Rica	2-1
11.05.97	Costa Rica v Jamaica	3-1
18.05.97	Jamaica v El Salvador	1-0
01.06.97	Canada v Costa Rica	1-0
08.06.97	El Salvador v Mexico	0-1
29.06.97	El Salvador v USA	1-1
10.08.97	Costa Rica v El Salvador	0-0
07.09.97	USA v Costa Rica	1-0
07.09.97	Jamaica v Canada	1-0
14.09.97	Jamaica v Costa Rica	1-0
14.09.97	El Salvador v Canada	4-1
03.10.97	USA v Jamaica	1-1
05.10.97	Mexico v El Salvador	5-0
12.10.97	Canada v Mexico	2-2
02.11.97	Mexico v USA	0-0
09.11.97	Mexico v Costa Rica	3-3
09.11.97	Canada v USA	0-3
09.11.97	El Salvador v Jamaica	2-2
16.11.97	Jamaica v Mexico	0-0
16.11.97	Costa Rica v Canada	3-1
16.11.97	USA v El Salvador	4-2

Final Table

	P	W	D	L	F	A	Pts
Mexico	10	4	6	0	23	7	18
USA	10	4	5	1	17	9	17
Jamaica	10	3	5	2	7	12	14
Costa Rica	10	3	3	4	13	12	12
El Salvador	10	2	4	4	11	16	10
Canada	10	1	3	6	5	20	6

OFC

Qualification Rules

The first round consisted of two geographical groups. The winner of the Melanesian group qualified for the second round. In addition, the winner of a match between the winner of the Polynesian group and the runner-up of the Melanesian group also qualified for the second round. The three qualifiers moved to the second round where they were joined by three other teams to form two groups of three teams. These played on a round-robin basis. The winner of each group play-off qualified for a play-off with a qualifier from the AFC. The winner of the OFC v AFC encounter qualified for the World Cup finals.

181

Melanesian Group

Papua New Guinea		
16.09.96	Papua NG v Solomon Is. ……………	1-1
18.09.96	Solomon Is. v Vanuatu ……………	1-1
20.09.96	Papua NG v Vanuatu ……………	2-1

Games played in Lae, PNG.

Final Table

	P	W	D	L	F	A	Pts
Papua NG	2	1	1	0	3	2	4
Solomon Islands	2	0	2	0	2	2	2
Vanuatu	2	0	1	1	2	3	1

Polynesian Group

Tonga		
11.11.96	Tonga v Cook Is. ……… ……	2-0
13.11.96	Western Samoa v Cook Is. …… …	2-1
15.11.96	Tonga v Western Samoa …… ……	1-0

Games played in Tonga.

Final Table

	P	W	D	L	F	A	Pts
Tonga	2	2	0	0	3	0	6
Western Samoa	2	1	0	1	2	2	3
Cook Islands	2	0	0	2	1	4	0

First Round Playoff

Winner Polynesia v Runner-up Melanesia		
15.02.97	Tonga v Solomon Islands ……………	0-4
01.03.97	Solomon Islands v Tonga ……………	9-0

Solomon Islands win 13-0 on aggregate.

Group 1

		Australia
11.06.97	Australia v Solomon Islands	13-0
13.06.97	Australia v Tahiti	5-0
15.06.97	Solomon Islands v Tahiti	4-1
17.06.97	Solomon Islands v Australia	2-6
19.06.97	Tahiti v Australia	0-2
21.06.97	Tahiti v Solomon Islands	1-1

Games played in Sydney, Australia.

Final Table	P	W	D	L	F	A	Pts
Australia	4	4	0	0	26	2	12
Solomon Islands	4	1	1	2	7	21	4
Tahiti	4	0	1	3	2	12	1

Group 2

		New Zealand
31.05.97	Papua NG v New Zealand	1-0
07.06.97	Fiji v New Zealand	0-1
11.06.97	New Zealand v Papua NG	7-0
15.06.97	Fiji v Papua NG	3-1
18.06.97	New Zealand v Fiji	5-0
21.06.97	Papua NG v Fiji	0-1

Final Table	P	W	D	L	F	A	Pts
New Zealand	4	3	0	1	13	1	9
Fiji	4	2	0	2	4	7	6
Papua NG	4	1	0	3	2	11	3

28.06.97	New Zealand v Australia	0-3
05.07.97	Australia v New Zealand	2-0

Australia win 5-0 on aggregate.

AFC-OFC

OFC Winner v Group loser elimination matches

22.11.97	Iran v Australia	1-1
29.11.97	Australia v Iran	2-2

3-3 on aggregate. Iran qualify on away goals rule.

Qualification Rules

The 38 teams were drawn into nine groups. Each team played one another on a home and away basis and the nine group winners and best runner-up qualified directly for the World Cup finals. The eight remaining group runners-up were then drawn in four matches with the winners across two legs advancing to the World Cup finals.

To determine the best runner-up in the nine groups (which was Scotland) only the matches played against the teams coming top, third and fourth in each group were taken into account.

Group Round

Group 1

		Denmark
24.04.96	Greece v Slovenia	2-0
01.09.96	Greece v Bosnia-H.	3-0
01.09.96	Slovenia v Denmark	0-2
09.10.96	Denmark v Greece	2-1
08.10.96	Bosnia-H. v Croatia	1-4

10.11.96	Slovenia v Bosnia-H.	1-2
10.11.96	Croatia v Greece	1-1
29.03.97	Croatia v Denmark	1-1
02.04.97	Croatia v Slovenia	3-3
02.04.97	Bosnia-H. v Greece	0-1
30.04.97	Denmark v Slovenia	4-0
30.04.97	Greece v Croatia	0-1
08.06.97	Denmark v Bosnia-H.	2-0
20.08.97	Bosnia-H. v Denmark	3-0
06.09.97	Croatia v Bosnia-H.	3-2
06.09.97	Slovenia v Greece	0-3
10.09.97	Denmark v Croatia	3-1
10.09.97	Bosnia-H. v Slovenia	1-0
11.10.97	Greece v Denmark	0-0
11.10.97	Slovenia v Croatia	1-3

Final Table	P	W	D	L	F	A	Pts
Denmark	8	5	2	1	14	6	17
Croatia	8	4	3	1	17	12	15
Greece	8	4	2	2	11	4	14
Bosnia-Herz.	8	3	0	5	9	14	9
Slovenia	8	0	1	7	5	20	1

Group 2 — England

01.09.96	Moldova v England	0-3
05.10.96	Moldova v Italy	1-3
09.10.96	England v Poland	2-1
09.10.96	Italy v Georgia	1-0
09.11.96	Georgia v England	0-2
10.11.96	Poland v Moldova	2-1
12.02.97	England v Italy	0-1
29.03.97	Italy v Moldova	3-0
02.04.97	Poland v Italy	0-0
30.04.97	England v Georgia	2-0
30.04.97	Italy v Poland	3-0
31.05.97	Poland v England	0-2
07.06.97	Georgia v Moldova	2-0
14.06.97	Poland v Georgia	4-1
10.09.97	England v Moldova	4-0
10.09.97	Georgia v Italy	0-0
24.09.97	Moldova v Georgia	0-1
07.10.97	Moldova v Poland	0-3
11.10.97	Italy v England	0-0
11.10.97	Georgia v Poland	3-0

Final Table	P	W	D	L	F	A	Pts
England	8	6	1	1	15	2	19
Italy	8	5	3	0	11	1	18
Poland	8	3	1	4	10	12	10
Georgia	8	3	1	4	7	9	10
Moldova	8	0	0	8	2	21	0

Group 3 — Norway

02.06.96	Norway v Azerbaijan	5-0
31.08.96	Azerbaijan v Switzerland	1-0
01.09.96	Hungary v Finland	1-0
06.10.96	Finland v Switzerland	2-3
09.10.96	Norway v Hungary	3-0
10.11.96	Switzerland v Norway	0-1
10.11.96	Azerbaijan v Hungary	0-3
02.04.97	Azerbaijan v Finland	1-2
30.04.97	Norway v Finland	1-1
30.04.97	Switzerland v Hungary	1-0
08.06.97	Finland v Azerbaijan.	3-0
08.06.97	Hungary v Norway	1-1
20.08.97	Hungary v Switzerland	1-1
20.08.97	Finland v Norway	0-4
06.09.97	Switzerland v Finland	1-2
06.09.97	Azerbaijan v Norway	0-1
10.09.97	Hungary v Azerbaijan	3-1
10.09.97	Norway v Switzerland	5-0
11.10.97	Finland v Hungary	1-1
11.10.97	Switzerland v Azerbaijan	5-0

Final Table	P	W	D	L	F	A	Pts
Norway	8	6	2	0	21	2	20
Hungary	8	3	3	2	10	8	12
Finland	8	3	2	3	11	12	11
Switzerland	8	3	1	4	11	12	10
Azerbaijan	8	1	0	7	3	22	3

Group 4 — Austria & Scotland

Date	Fixture	Score
01.06.96	Sweden v Belarus	5-1
31.08.96	Austria v Scotland	0-0
31.08.96	Belarus v Estonia	1-0
01.09.96	Latvia v Sweden	1-2
05.10.96	Estonia v Belarus	1-0
05.10.96	Latvia v Scotland	0-2
09.10.96	Sweden v Austria	0-1
09.10.96	Belarus v Latvia	1-1
09.11.96	Austria v Latvia	2-1
10.11.96	Estonia v Scotland	0-0
11.02.97	Scotland v Sweden	1-0
29.03.97	Scotland v Estonia	2-0
02.04.97	Scotland v Austria	2-0
30.04.97	Austria v Estonia	2-0
30.04.97	Sweden v Scotland	2-1
18.05.97	Latvia v Belarus	2-0
08.06.97	Estonia v Latvia	1-3
08.06.97	Estonia v Sweden	2-3
08.06.97	Latvia v Austria	1-3
20.08.97	Belarus v Scotland	0-1
20.08.97	Estonia v Austria	0-3
06.09.97	Belarus v Sweden	1-2
06.09.97	Austria v Sweden	1-0
07.09.97	Latvia v Estonia	1-0
07.09.97	Scotland v Belarus	4-1
10.09.97	Sweden v Latvia	1-0
10.09.97	Belarus v Austria	0-1
11.10.97	Austria v Belarus	4-0
11.10.97	Scotland v Latvia	2-0
11.10.97	Sweden v Estonia	1-0

Final Table

	P	W	D	L	F	A	Pts
Austria	10	8	1	1	17	4	25
Scotland	10	7	2	1	15	3	23
Sweden	10	7	0	3	16	9	21
Latvia	10	3	1	6	10	14	10
Estonia	10	1	1	8	4	16	4
Belarus	10	1	1	8	5	21	4

Group 5 — Bulgaria

Date	Fixture	Score
01.09.96	Israel v Bulgaria	2-1
01.09.96	Russia v Cyprus	4-0
08.10.96	Luxembourg v Bulgaria	1-2
09.10.96	Israel v Russia	1-1
10.11.96	Cyprus v Israel	2-0
10.11.96	Luxembourg v Russia	0-4
14.12.96	Cyprus v Bulgaria	1-3
15.12.96	Israel v Luxembourg	1-0
29.03.97	Cyprus v Russia	1-1
31.03.97	Luxembourg v Israel	0-3
02.04.97	Bulgaria v Cyprus	4-1
30.04.97	Israel v Cyprus	2-0
30.04.97	Russia v Luxembourg	3-0
08.06.97	Bulgaria v Luxembourg	4-0

08.06.97 Russia v Israel 2-0
20.08.97 Bulgaria v Israel 1-0
07.09.97 Luxembourg v Cyprus 1-3
10.09.97 Bulgaria v Russia 1-0
11.10.97 Cyprus v Luxembourg 2-0
11.10.97 Russia v Bulgaria 4-2

Final Table	P	W	D	L	F	A	Pts
Bulgaria	8	6	0	2	18	9	18
Russia	8	5	2	1	19	5	17
Israel	8	4	1	3	9	7	13
Cyprus	8	3	1	4	10	17	10
Luxembourg	8	0	0	8	2	22	0

Group 6   Spain

24.04.96 Yugoslavia v Faroe Is. ... 3-1
02.06.96 Yugoslavia v Malta 6-0
31.08.96 Faroe Is. v Slovakia 1-2
04.09.96 Faroe Is. v Spain 2-6
18.09.96 Czech Rep. v Malta 6-0
22.09.96 Slovakia v Malta 6-0
06.10.96 Faroe Is. v Yugoslavia ... 1-8
09.10.96 Czech Rep. v Spain 0-0
23.10.96 Slovakia v Faroe Is. 3-0
10.11.96 Yugoslavia v Czech Rep. .. 1-0
13.11.96 Spain v Slovakia 4-1
14.12.96 Spain v Yugoslavia 2-0

18.12.96 Malta v Spain 0-3
12.02.97 Spain v Malta 4-0
31.03.97 Malta v Slovakia 0-2
02.04.97 Czech Rep. v Yugoslavia .. 1-2
30.04.97 Malta v Faroe Is. 1-2
30.04.97 Yugoslavia v Spain 1-1
08.06.97 Spain v Czech Rep. 1-0
08.06.97 Yugoslavia v Slovakia 2-0
08.06.97 Faroe Is. v Malta 2-1
20.08.97 Czech Rep. v Faroe Is. ... 2-0
24.08.97 Slovakia v Czech Rep. 2-1
06.09.97 Faroe Is. v Czech Rep. ... 0-2
10.09.97 Slovakia v Yugoslavia 1-1
24.09.97 Malta v Czech Rep. 0-1
24.09.97 Slovakia v Spain 1-2
11.10.97 Malta v Yugoslavia 0-5
11.10.97 Spain v Faroe Is. 3-1
11.10.97 Czech Rep. v Slovakia 3-0

Final Table	P	W	D	L	F	A	Pts
Spain	10	8	2	0	26	6	26
Yugoslavia	10	7	2	1	29	7	23
Czech Republic	10	5	1	4	16	6	16
Slovakia	10	5	1	4	18	14	16
Faroe Islands	10	2	0	8	10	31	6
Malta	10	0	0	10	2	37	0

Group 7 — Holland

Date	Match	Score
02.06.96	San Marino v Wales	0-5
31.08.96	Belgium v Turkey	2-1
31.08.96	Wales v San Marino	6-0
05.10.96	Wales v Holland	1-3
09.10.96	San Marino v Belgium	0-3
09.11.96	Holland v Wales	7-1
10.11.96	Turkey v San Marino	7-0
14.12.96	Belgium v Holland	0-3
14.12.96	Wales v Turkey	0-0
29.03.97	Wales v Belgium	1-2
29.03.97	Holland v San Marino	4-0
02.04.97	Turkey v Holland	1-0
30.04.97	Turkey v Belgium	1-3
30.04.97	San Marino v Holland	0-6
07.06.97	Belgium v San Marino	6-0
20.08.97	Turkey v Wales	6-4
06.09.97	Holland v Belgium	3-1
10.09.97	San Marino v Turkey	0-5
11.10.97	Belgium v Wales	3-2
11.10.97	Holland v Turkey	0-0

Final Table

	P	W	D	L	F	A	Pts
Holland	8	6	1	1	26	4	19
Belgium	8	6	0	2	20	11	18
Turkey	8	4	2	2	21	9	14
Wales	8	2	1	5	20	21	7
San Marino	8	0	0	8	0	42	0

Group 8 — Romania

Date	Match	Score
24.04.96	Macedonia v Liechtenstein	3-0
01.06.96	Iceland v Macedonia	1-1
31.08.96	Liechtenstein v Rep. Ireland	0-5
31.08.96	Romania v Lithuania	3-0
05.10.96	Lithuania v Iceland	2-0
09.10.96	Iceland v Romania	0-4
09.10.96	Rep. Ireland v Macedonia	3-0
09.11.96	Lithuania v Liechtenstein	2-1
09.11.96	Liechtenstein v Macedonia	1-11
10.11.96	Rep. Ireland v Iceland	0-0
14.12.96	Macedonia v Romania	0-3
29.03.97	Romania v Liechtenstein	8-0
02.04.97	Lithuania v Romania	0-1
02.04.97	Macedonia v Rep. Ireland	3-2
30.04.97	Liechtenstein v Lithuania	0-2
30.04.97	Romania v Rep. Ireland	1-0
21.05.97	Rep. Ireland v Liechtenstein	5-0
07.06.97	Macedonia v Iceland	1-0
11.06.97	Iceland v Lithuania	0-0
20.08.97	Liechtenstein v Iceland	0-4
20.08.97	Rep. Ireland v Lithuania	0-0
20.08.97	Romania v Macedonia	4-2

06.09.97	Iceland v Rep. Ireland	...	2-4
06.09.97	Liechtenstein v Romania	...	1-8
06.09.97	Lithuania v Macedonia	...	2-0
10.09.97	Romania v Iceland	...	4-0
10.09.97	Lithuania v Rep. Ireland	...	1-2
11.10.97	Iceland v Liechtenstein	...	4-0
11.10.97	Rep. Ireland v Romania	...	1-1
11.10.97	Macedonia v Lithuania	...	1-2

Final Table

	P	W	D	L	F	A	Pts
Romania	10	9	1	0	37	4	28
Rep. Ireland	10	5	3	2	22	8	18
Lithuania	10	5	2	3	11	8	17
FYR Macedonia	10	4	1	5	22	18	13
Iceland	10	2	3	5	11	16	9
Liechtenstein	10	0	0	10	3	51	0

Group 9   Germany

31.08.96	N. Ireland v Ukraine	...	0-1
31.08.96	Armenia v Portugal	...	0-0
05.10.96	N. Ireland v Armenia	...	1-1
05.10.96	Ukraine v Portugal	...	2-1
09.10.96	Albania v Portugal	...	0-3
09.10.96	Armenia v Germany	...	1-5
09.11.96	Albania v Armenia	...	1-1
09.11.96	Germany v N. Ireland	...	1-1
09.11.96	Portugal v Ukraine	...	1-0
14.12.96	N. Ireland v Albania	...	2-0
14.12.96	Portugal v Germany	...	0-0
29.03.97	Albania v Ukraine	...	0-1
29.03.97	N. Ireland v Portugal	...	0-0
02.04.97	Ukraine v N. Ireland	...	2-1
30.04.97	Germany v Albania	...	2-0
30.04.97	Armenia v N. Ireland	...	0-0
07.05.97	Ukraine v Armenia	...	1-1
07.06.97	Portugal v Albania	...	2-0
07.06.97	Ukraine v Germany	...	0-0
20.08.97	N. Ireland v Germany	...	1-3
20.08.97	Portugal v Armenia	...	3-1
20.08.97	Ukraine v Albania	...	1-1
06.09.97	Germany v Portugal	...	1-1
06.09.97	Armenia v Albania	...	3-0
10.09.97	Albania v N. Ireland	...	4-0
10.09.97	Germany v Armenia	...	4-0
11.10.97	Germany v Albania	...	4-3
11.10.97	Portugal v N. Ireland	...	1-0
11.10.97	Armenia v Ukraine	...	0-2

Final Table

	P	W	D	L	F	A	Pts
Germany	10	6	4	0	23	9	22
Ukraine	10	6	2	2	10	6	20
Portugal	10	5	4	1	12	4	19
Armenia	10	1	5	4	8	17	8
Northern Ireland	10	1	4	5	6	10	7
Albania	10	1	1	8	7	20	4

Play-off Round

Play-offs for the eight remaining runners-up

29.10.97	Russia v Italy	1-1
15.11.97	Italy v Russia	1-0
	Italy win 2-1 on aggregate.	
29.10.97	Hungary v Yugoslavia	1-7
15.11.97	Yugoslavia v Hungary	5-0
	Yugoslavia win 12-1 on aggregate.	
29.10.97	Rep. Ireland v Belgium	1-1
15.11.97	Belgium v Rep. Ireland	2-1
	Belgium win 3-2 on aggregate.	
29.10.97	Croatia v Ukraine	2-0
15.11.97	Ukraine v Croatia	1-1
	Croatia win 3-1 on aggregate.	

DAY-BY-DAY FIXTURES

GROUP GAMES – 10th June to 26th June – all times BST

Wednesday, June 10th

Saint Denis	4.30	Group A 2 - 1 Brazil v Scotland	BBC	4.30 pm
Montpellier	8.00	Group A 2 - 2 Morocco v Norway	ITV	8.00 p

Thursday, June 11th

Bordeaux	4.30	Group B 2 - 2 Italy v Chile	ITV	4.30 p
Toulouse	8.00	Group B 1 - 1 Cameroon v Austria	BBC	8.00 p

Friday, June 12th

Montpellier	1.30	Group D 0 - 0 Paraguay v Bulgaria	ITV
Lens	4.30	Group C 0 - 1 Saudi Arabia v Denmark	BBC
Marseille	8.00	Group C 3 - 0 France v South Africa	ITV

Saturday, June 13th

Nantes	1.30	Group D 2 - 3 Spain v Nigeria	BBC
Lyon	4.30	Group E 1 - 3 South Korea v Mexico	ITV
Saint Denis	8.00	Group E 0 - 0 Holland v Belgium	BBC

Sunday, June 14th

Toulouse	1.30	Group H 1 - 0 Argentina v Japan	ITV
Saint Etienne	4.30	Group F 1 - 0 Yugoslavia v Iran	BBC
Lens	8.00	Group H 1 - 3 Jamaica v Croatia	ITV

Monday, June 15th

Marseille	1.30	Group G 2 - 0 England v Tunisia	BBC
Lyon	4.30	Group G 1 - 0 Romania v Colombia	ITV
Paris	8.00	Group F 2 - 0 Germany v USA	BBC

Tuesday, June 16th

Bordeaux	4.30	Group A 1 - 1 Scotland v Norway	ITV
Nantes	8.00	Group A 3 - 0 Brazil v Morocco	ITV

Wednesday, June 17th

Saint Etienne	4.30	Group B 1 - 1 Chile v Austria	BBC
Montpellier	8.00	Group B 3 - 0 Italy v Cameroon	ITV

Thursday, June 18th

| Toulouse | 4.30 | Group C 1-1 South Africa v Denmark ITV |
| Saint Denis | 8.00 | Group C 4-0 France v Saudi Arabia BBC |

Friday, June 19th

| Paris | 4.30 | Group D 1-0 Nigeria v Bulgaria ITV |
| Saint Etienne | 8.00 | Group D 0-0 Spain v Paraguay BBC |

Saturday, June 20th

Nantes	1.30	Group H 0-1 Japan v Croatia ITV
Bordeaux	4.30	Group E 2-2 Belgium v Mexico BBC
Marseille	8.00	Group E 5-0 Holland v South Korea ITV

Sunday, June 21st

Lens	1.30	Group F 2-2 Germany v Yugoslavia BBC
Paris	4.30	Group H 5-0 Argentina v Jamaica ITV
Lyon	8.00	Group F 0-2 USA v Iran BBC

Monday, June 22nd

| Montpellier | 4.30 | Group G 1-0 Colombia v Tunisia BBC |
| Toulouse | 8.00 | Group G 2-1 Romania v England ITV |

Tuesday, June 23rd

Nantes	3.00	Group B 1-1 Chile v Cameroon ITV
Saint Denis	3.00	Group B 2-1 Italy v Austria ITV
Saint Etienne	8.00	Group A 0-3 Scotland v Morocco BBC
Marseille	8.00	Group A 1-2 Brazil v Norway BBC

Wednesday, June 24th

Lyon	3.00	Group C 2-1 France v Denmark BBC
Bordeaux	3.00	Group C 2-2 South Africa v Saudi Arabia BBC
Lens	8.00	Group D 6-1 Spain v Bulgaria ITV
Toulouse	8.00	Group D 1-3 Nigeria v Paraguay ITV

Thursday, June 25th

Paris	3.00	Group E 1-1 Belgium v South Korea BBC
Saint Etienne	3.00	Group E 2-2 Holland v Mexico BBC
Montpellier	8.00	Group F 2-0 Germany v Iran ITV
Nantes	8.00	Group F 0-1 USA v Yugoslavia ITV

Friday, June 26th

Bordeaux	3.00	Group H 1-0 Argentina v Croatia ITV
Lyon	3.00	Group H 1-2 Japan v Jamaica ITV
Lens	8.00	Group G 0-2 Colombia v England BBC
Saint Denis	8.00	Group G 1-1 Romania v Tunisia BBC

191

SECOND ROUND
Saturday, June 27th

Marseille	3.30	Game 2	1st Group B v 2nd Group A
Paris	8.00	Game 1	1st Group A v 2nd Group B

ITALY..1 — NORWAY..0

Sunday, June 28th

Lens	3.30	Game 3	1st Group C v 2nd Group D
Saint Denis	8.00	Game 4	1st Group D v 2nd Group C

BRAZIL..4   CHILE..1
FRANCE..1 PARAGUAY..0 Golden Goal

Monday, June 29th

Montpellier	3.30	Game 6	1st Group F v 2nd Group E
Toulouse	8.00	Game 5	1st Group E v 2nd Group F

GERMANY..2 MEXICO..1
NIGERIA..1 DENMARK..4

Tuesday, June 30th

Bordeaux	3.30	Game 7	1st Group G v 2nd Group H
Saint Etienne	8.00	Game 8	1st Group H v 2nd Group G

YUGOSLAVIA..1 HOLLAND..2
ROMANIA...0 CROATIA..1

QUARTER FINALS
Friday, July 3

Saint Denis	3.30	Game B	Game 2 winner v Game 3 winner
Nantes	8.00	Game A	Game 1 winner v Game 4 winner

ENGLAND..2 ARGENTINA..2
(LOST 3-4 PEN)
ITALY..0 FRANCE..0

Saturday, July 4

Marseille	3.30	Game C	Game 5 winner v Game 8 winner
Lyon	8.00	Game D	Game 6 winner v Game 7 winner

BRAZIL..3 DENMARK..2
ARGENTINA..1 HOLLAND..2
GERMANY...0 CROATIA..3

SEMI FINALS
Tuesday, July 7

Marseille	8.00	Game A winner v Game C winner
Saint Denis	8.00	Game B winner v Game D winner

BRAZIL... HOLLAND...
FRANCE... CROATIA...

3RD PLACE PLAY-OFF
Saturday, July 11

Paris	8.00	Semi-Final losers

WORLD CUP FINAL
Sunday, July 12

Saint Denis	8.00	Semi-Final winners